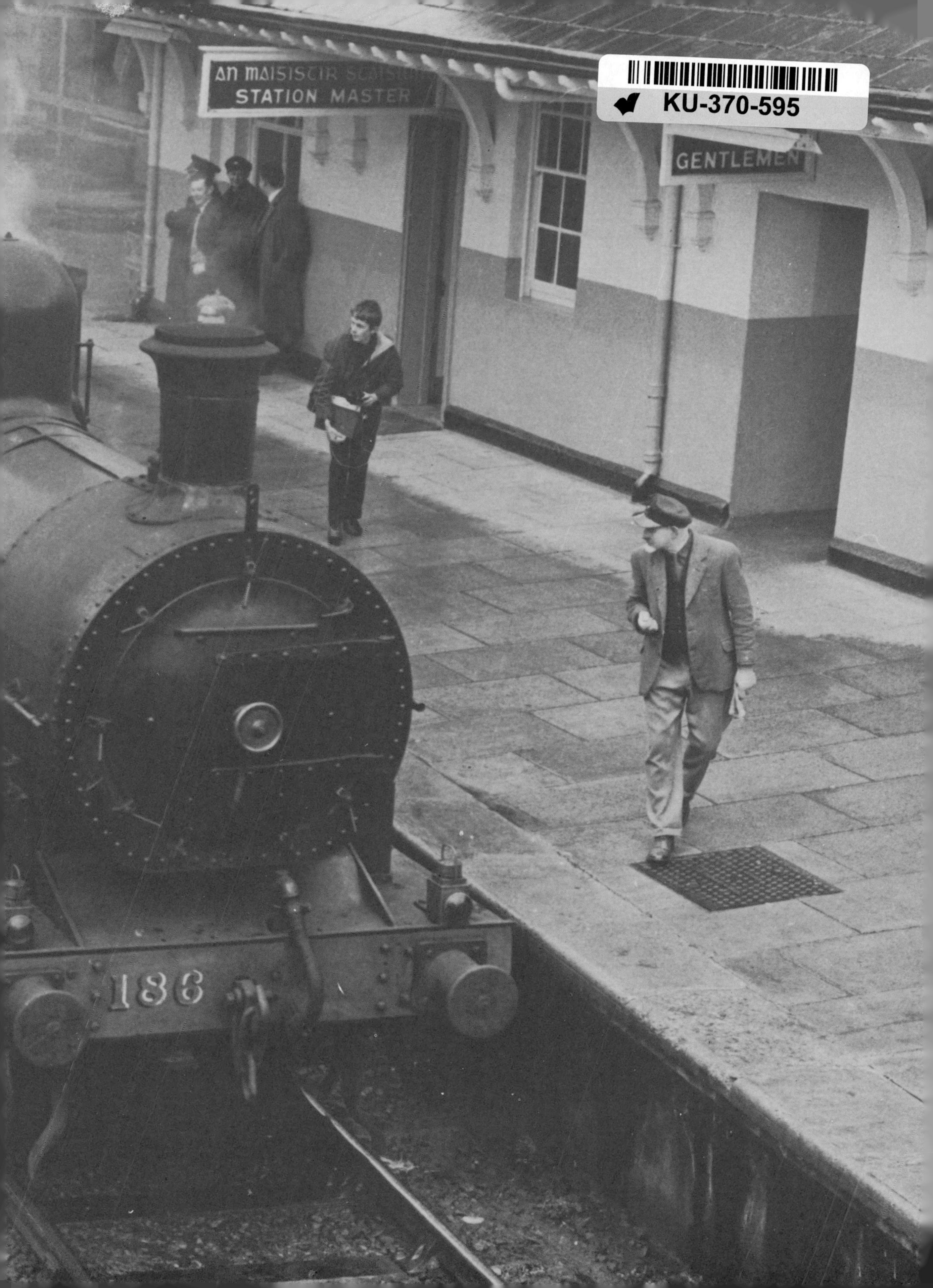
STATION MASTER
GENTLEMEN
186

To:- Roy
From:- Anne & Jessie
With Love.

ONE HUNDRED AND FIFTY YEARS OF
IRISH RAILWAYS

ONE HUNDRED AND FIFTY YEARS OF IRISH RAILWAYS

FERGUS MULLIGAN

APPLETREE
PRESS

First published and printed by
The Appletree Press Ltd
7 James Street South
Belfast BT2 8DL
1983

10   9   8   7   6   5   4   3   2   1

British Library Cataloguing in Publication Data
Mulligan, Fergus
    One hundred and fifty years of Irish railways.
    1. Railroads—Ireland—History
    I. Title
    385'.09415   HE1783.I73

    ISBN 0–86281–117–1

Cover photograph: Rail-viaduct, Ballydehob, Co. Cork (Lawrence Collection, National Library of Ireland).

Contents

Abbreviations

A&EJR	Athenry & Ennis Junction Railway	D&DR	Dublin & Drogheda Railway
BBC&PJR	Ballymena, Ballymoney, Coleraine & Portrush Junction Railway	D&ER	Dundalk & Enniskillen Railway
B&BR	Belfast & Ballymena Railway	D&KR	Dublin & Kingstown Railway
B&CDR	Belfast & County Down Railway	D&MR	Dublin & Meath Railway
BCR	Belfast Central Railway	DN&GR	Dundalk Newry & Greenore Railway
BC&RBR	Ballymena, Cushendall & Red Bay Railway	DRRRRRR	Dublin, Rathmines, Rathgar, Roundtown, Rathfarnham & Rathcoole Railway
BH&BR	Belfast Holywood & Bangor Railway		
B&I	British & Irish Line (shipping)	D&SER	Dublin & South Eastern Railway
B&NCR	Belfast & Northern Counties Railway	DUTC	Dublin United Transport Company
BPW	Board of Public Works	D&WR	Dublin & Wicklow Railway
BR	Ballycastle Railway	DW&WR	Dublin Wicklow & Wexford Railway
BR	British Rail	F&RR&HC	Fishguard & Rosslare Railways & Harbours Company
BTC	British Transport Commission		
CB&PR	Cork Blackrock & Passage Railway	FVR	Finn Valley Railway
C&BR	Cork & Bandon Railway	GCIR	Great Central Ireland Railway
CB&SCR	Cork Bandon & South Coast Railway	GNRB	Great Northern Railway Board
CDR	County Donegal Railway	GNR(I)	Great Northern Railway (Ireland)
CDRJC	County Donegal Railways Joint Committee	GSR	Great Southern Railways
CIE	Córas Iompair Éireann	GS&WR	Great Southern & Western Railway
C&LR	Cavan & Leitrim Railway		
C&MDR	Cork & Macroom Direct Railway	GWR	Great Western Railway
C&MLR	Cork & Muskerry Light Railway	IGWR	Irish Great Western Railway
CVR	Clogher Valley Railway	INWR	Irish North Western Railway
C&YR	Cork & Youghal Railway		
D&BJR	Dublin & Belfast Junction Railway	IRRS	Irish Railway Record Society
DD&NR	Downpatrick, Dundrum & Newcastle Railway	L&BR	Listowel & Ballybunion Railway

L & ER	Londonderry & Enniskillen Railway	RPSI	Railway Preservation Society of Ireland
L & LSR	Londonderry & Lough Swilly Railway	SL & NCR	Sligo Leitrim & Northern Counties Railway
L & MR	Liverpool & Manchester Railway	S & LR	Strabane & Letterkenny Railway
LMS	London Midland & Scottish Railway	T & DR	Tralee & Dingle Railway
		T & FR	Tralee & Fenit Railway
LNER	London North Eastern Railway	U & CLR	Ulster & Connaught Light Railway
LNWR	London North Western Railway	UR	Ulster Railway
		UTA	Ulster Transport Authority
MGWR	Midland Great Western Railway	W & CIR	Waterford & Central Ireland Railway
MR	Midland Railway		
NCC	Northern Counties Committee	WDR	West Donegal Railway
		W & LR	Waterford & Limerick Railway
NIR	Northern Ireland Railways		
NIRTB	Northern Ireland Road Transport Board	WL & WR	Waterford Limerick & Western Railway
N & KR	Navan & Kingscourt Railway	W & TR	Waterford & Tramore Railway
OIE	Óstlanna Iompair Éireann	WWW & DR	Waterford, Wicklow, Wexford & Dublin Railway
P & PBR	Parsonstown & Portumna Bridge Railway		

CIE train of new rolling stock

Foreword

THE 150th anniversary of Ireland's first railway, the Dublin & Kingstown, seems a good time to write a general account of railways in Ireland. In this book I have tried to place the emphasis on people rather than machines, the men and women involved, rather than the more technical aspects of rail operations. An abundance of the latter often makes such books dry and indigestible to all but the most committed enthusiast.

From the time I was a child and watched the little trains of the Cavan & Leitrim as they rattled through Ballinamore (sometimes without waiting for the gates to open) I have been fascinated by trains. Paul Theroux says that he never sees a train going somewhere but he wishes he was on it. I share his sentiment fully.

Travelling by train is a civilised way of getting around. It is not like flying, where you are strapped in like a child or a lunatic, served plastic food and more drink than you need or want to arrive at your destination tired and irritable, twelve hours before your body does. Nor is it like driving, where you face the hazards of juggernauts, traffic jams, bad roads and Morris Minor drivers. On any decent train you can have a bite to eat or a drink at your leisure, go for a stroll, read, do the crossword or just snooze.

Today the Irish rail network is much smaller than it was at its peak in the 1920s but it is unlikely to contract any further. CIE and NIR operate excellent services under difficult conditions. NIR had its crisis a number of years ago, but whether the railways in the Republic stay under the control of one national transport organisation remains to be seen. Whatever the future holds it has at last dawned on successive Irish governments that running a railway which needs an annual subsidy is not a matter of shame. It is the same all over the world. Of course, that is not say changes are not needed in some areas.

This book is divided into the major groupings of lines before the 1925 and subsequent amalgamations, with one chapter for each major company and the independent standard and narrow gauge lines. I have also reserved one chapter for that marvellous eccentricity, the Listowel and Ballybunion, or the Lartigue as it was known. The final chapter brings the story up to the present.

Many people have helped in writing this book: the staffs of the National Library, Dublin, Córas Iompair Éireann, Northern Ireland Railways, Dublin City Libraries, Belfast Transport Museum, Great Southern Hotels, Noel Lewis, and Mary Kelleher who scoured the library of the Royal Dublin Society for every conceivable book on Irish railways; to all of them my thanks.

Fergus Mulligan
Dublin 1983

8

1 The Dublin and Kingstown Railway

BEFORE the coming of the railways there were four types of inland transport available: the horse, the stage coach, the canal boat and walking. Horses could only be kept by the wealthy who were the chief users of the stage coach as well; the cheapest fare from Dublin to Carlow was more than a week's wages for the average labourer and the top speed was a sedate 10 mph. Canal boats were even more expensive and slower still; the 35 miles between Dublin and Mullingar took 13½ hours before the introduction of the fly-boats.

Accounts of travel by canal varied. Sir John Carr went from Athy to Dublin in 1805 and was very impressed with the comfort, speed and cuisine offered on board: 'All the regulations of these boats are excellent. I was so delighted with my canal conveyance ... I verily think I should have spent the rest of my time in Ireland in the Athy canal boat.' Dinner consisted then of 'a leg of boiled mutton, a turkey, ham, vegetables, porter and a pint of wine each at four shillings and ten pence a head'.

A Grand Canal Company notice of 1826 contains further details of the service and the limitations on the sale of liquor: 'Wine, sold in Pints or Half-pints—and not more than one Pint to each person ... A Naggin of Spirits allowed to each Gentleman in the State Cabin, after Dinner or at Suppertime; but such allowance of Spirits not extended to women or children. *No wine or spirits to be sold in the Second Cabin.*' Obviously, the lower orders were prone to leap into the canal or molest persons of quality when intoxicated. The price list for victuals is interesting: twenty-one years after Carr's trip to Athy the charge for dinner, wine and coffee remains the same—four shillings and ten pence.

By 1845 another English visitor, a Mr Hall, came away with a less favourable impression. He describes his canal boat as 'large, awkward and lumbering ... chiefly used by the peasantry on account of its cheapness. As a mode of travelling it is exceedingly inconvenient, there is scarcely space to turn in the confined cabin'. The time was right for the entry of the railway and by 1850 there were no more passenger boats on the canals.

For some years the port of Dublin had suffered greatly from the effects of silt and was no longer the ideal anchorage it once was. So in 1817 John Rennie saw the need for a new harbour and began building wharfs and moorings at the old village of Dunleary, six miles south of Dublin. The village rapidly grew into a town and four years later was renamed Kingstown in honour of George IV's departure from the port after his disagreeable Irish visit.

The House of Commons Journal of 9 February 1825 records that a petition was received from 'several gentlemen, merchants, traders, freeholders and others of Dublin' stating that they wished 'to make and maintain a railway or tramroad from the Royal Harbour of Kingstown ... to or near Mount Street in the city of Dublin'.

There was considerable opposition from various quarters to the proposed railway, in particular coastal residents and the Grand Canal Company who, hearing their own death knell, dismissed the plan as 'an insignificant Railroad, which is neither called for nor countenanced by the mercantile interest of the city'. The plan lapsed in the face of this hostility but interest revived and after a few years a new scheme was launched. This time the railway lobby was better organised and more sure of itself. On 28 February 1831, despite a conflicting proposal for a ship canal between the two places, the Commons heard of a new group 'to be called the Dublin and Kingstown Railway Company, for the purpose of making and maintaining a Railway or Railways... from, at, or near Trinity College, in the city of Dublin, to the pier at Kingstown'.

Elaborate plans were prepared by Alexander Nimmo, a Scots engineer, showing the route at an estimated cost of £100,000 to £130,000. These were sanctioned by James Pim, later to become the key figure on the board of directors. This time the promoters wore down the opposition and on 6 September 1831 the bill received the royal assent. The restrictions imposed were many but not intolerable and at last the company was in business. One early clause was the change of terminus to Westland Row on account of the objections to the original route by the board of Trinity College and residents of Great Brunswick (Pearse) Street. The company blamed the move on 'vague fears, misrepresentations and other causes'.

The first report, issued in November 1831, spoke optimistically of the huge potential traffic on the line. Kingstown was already becoming almost a suburb of Dublin and would be a popular base for commuters as well as a destination for day trippers. Pim figured largely in these predictions; the railway was said to be 'the subject of his waking thoughts and nightly dreams' to the point that 'it seems to be chained not to his leg but to his mind'! With such single-minded devotion among its servants how could the company fail?

Together with Thomas Bergin, secretary, the D & KR had a most able pair of officials. Their first task was to arrange the Board of Public Works' loan to build the railway to a gauge of 4 ft 8½ in., the standard English gauge. This was converted in later years when 5 ft 3 in. became the Irish norm. After the requisite period of coyness the BPW agreed to a loan of £75,000 but under rather harsh conditions. Charles Vignoles was appointed engineer and prepared new plans based on those of the deceased Nimmo. Meanwhile the purchase of land along the route began and at this point a final push for a canal was made with the publication of proposals for a seaway between 'the Asylum Harbour at Kingstown and the River Anna Liffey at Dublin'. But it was too late and all interest was in the railway.

Tenders for the construction were invited and that of £83,000 (excluding permanent way materials) received from William Dargan on 26 January 1833, being the lowest by £11,000, was accepted. Dargan was already known to the company and as the directors reported, 'from his acknowledged talents and experience they have every reason to expect that the Works will be executed in the most satisfactory manner'.

William Dargan

Dargan was a native of Carlow, born in 1799, who trained as an engineer and surveyor under Thomas Telford on the Holyhead Road, where his handiwork may be particularly seen in the embankment joining Anglesey to Holy Island. Back in Ireland he worked on the Howth Road and a number of civil engineering projects including the Grand Canal and the Ulster Canal. His winning the contract for the D&KR brought him great prominence and he went on to become involved in almost every railway in the land. He built the Atmospheric Railway to Dalkey, the Ulster Railway's line from Lisburn to Armagh, the Great Southern & Western's to Kilkenny, Thurles–Cork, the Dublin and Drogheda route, the Belfast and Bally-mena, the Belfast and County Down's line to Bangor, the Midland Great Western's lines from Mullingar to Galway, Longford and Cavan and many others.

Dargan's connections with these companies were very close and he often accepted shares as payment, thus becoming involved in the actual running of the railway. His closest links were with the Dublin and Wicklow, of which he became a director and later chairman. He also had many other business interests such as canal boats, cross channel steamers, linen mills and farming. He was undoubtedly a great philanthropist and generously backed many schemes which were worth-while but could never be commercially viable. One such was the Dublin Inter-national Exhibition of 1853 which he funded almost alone. It provided a showcase for Irish goods and industry in a country recently devastated by famine, disease and emigration. Such was his popularity that a statue was raised in his honour by public subscription several years *before* his death. It stands in front of the National Gallery in Dublin.

This was the man that the D&KR board had engaged to build their railway. Dargan got to work without delay and on 13 May 1833 the directors reported that 'all the preliminary arrangements are nearly completed and the works are now in course of execution. Some progress has been made near Kingstown, at Black Rock and at Westland Row.' Even more exciting, the £75,000 loan 'has been granted in the most gratifying manner and on terms which must prove highly advantageous to the Company'.

Soon after this glowing report came the first major problem. At Blackrock it was planned to take the railway through the grounds of two prominent personages, Lord Cloncurry and the Rev. Sir Harcourt Lees. However these gentlemen refused to consider such an idea and detailed plans, drawings, pictures and models were prepared to convince them otherwise. Finally, with a promise to build a tunnel, a pair of towers with a pathway leading to the strand, piers, bridges, a bathing pavilion, a mini harbour and £3,000 and £7,500 by way of sweetener, they agreed to permit the intrusion. Most of these items can still be seen just south of Blackrock station, although the tunnel was never built. Gratefully the Company acknowledged 'the important privilege of passing these properties with an open cutting'.

Dargan's contract stated that he would complete the railway by 1 June 1834 with the added carrot of £50 for each week he was early and the stick of a £100 fine for each week he was late. He had nearly 2,000 men working and although there was some disruption in June 1833 labour relations were good; he was a fair employer and progress was quite rapid. (There were numerous complaints from lady bathers at Williamstown that during their dinner break railway labourers were inclined to strip off entirely and plunge into the sea for a refreshing swim!) By mid-July the embankment at Monkstown was finished and a month later so was the one at Seapoint. In September there was a spell of bad weather, but work con-tinued by day and night so that at the end of the year the elevating walls in the city were almost complete. However with the best will in the world it was clear that Dargan could not hope to meet the deadline and June 1 passed almost unnoticed.

At the end of July 1834 Dargan reported to the board that one line was finished and a group of directors made the return trip in a horse-drawn coach. Some weeks later the first locomotives began to arrive so that on 4 October an experimental run was made as far as Williamstown which, according to a contemporary account, was a great success.

> On Saturday the 4th of October, the first trial of the steam engine 'Vauxhall', with a small train of carriages, filled with ladies and gentlemen, was made on the line of railway from Dublin to the Martello tower at Williamstown. The experiment is said to have given great satisfaction, not only as to the rapidity of motion, ease of conveyance, and facility of stopping, but the celerity with which the train passed, by means of the crossings, from one line of road to another. The distance was about two miles and a half, which was performed four times each way, at the rate of about thirty-one miles per hour... Having joined in one of these trips, we were delighted by the perfect ease and safety with which it was performed; there is so little motion perceptible even when going at the quickest rate, that we could read or write without the slightest inconvenience.

The writer was equally enthusiastic about the quality of the engineering work.

> Of the manner in which the work has been executed, it is sufficient to observe, that the utmost solidity and severest simplicity marks the entire. The formation of the railway bed consists of layers of gravel and concrete, with longitudinal and numerous cross drains. Immense blocks of granite, at intervals of three feet, support the iron rails by means of supports called chairs; at every fifteen feet a larger block extends across and unites the two rails together, and the appearance of firmness and solidity is very remarkable in the course of construction, though at the parts which are quite finished off, nothing is to be seen except four parallel lines of iron bars, laid with almost geometrical precision.

The latter was intended to reassure the nervous passenger. The granite blocks referred to may still be seen close to their original site: they are used to support the sea wall from Merrion gates as well as on the East Pier at Dun Laoghaire.

Despite the almost universal interest in the construction of the railway there was still considerable resistance from certain vested interests. Some were people who saw their positions threatened by the coming of the railway, such as cab drivers, and those who wanted to hinder the development of Kingstown. Many of these found a spokesman in Michael Gresham, a prominent landowner and hotel proprietor of that name. He managed to block the advance of the D & KR into the town centre so that for several years the terminus was at the West Pier, near the present level crossing. He was so successful in this that a group of Kingstown citizens presented him with a silver salver in August 1833 inscribed 'as a mark of their appreciation of his spirited and successful efforts in opposing the extension of the Kingstown railway'.

The opening of the line

Meanwhile Dargan pressed on with all speed to complete the job. Being the first line in the country many problems were met for the first time. One commentator of the day remarked: 'We understand many causes have concurred to augment the difficulties and expenses of the undertaking' and indeed he spoke the truth. Finally, on 16 December the Dublin newspapers published the following item.

> Dublin and Kingstown Railway will be opened for the Conveyance of Passengers on to-morrow (Wednesday) the 17th instant. A train of carriages will start from each end of

the line every Hour, from Nine o'Clock, A.M., till Four o'Clock in the afternoon (both inclusive) at the following Fares:—

In the First Class Carriage...One Shilling
In the Second Class Carriage...Eight Pence
In the Third Class Carriage..Six Pence

Every train will include Carriages of each Class, and will stop at the Company's Station-house, Black-rock, both going and returning, to take up and set down Passengers, and in a short time it is intended to stop occasionally at some other places for the same purpose. Parcels will be conveyed from Westland-row to Black-rock and Kingstown at the following rates:—

Not exceeding one cwt..Four Pence
Exceeding one cwt. and not exceeding five cwt.....................One Shilling

No Train to start between Eleven o'Clock and Half-past Two on Sundays.

T. F. Bergin,
Clerk of the Company
Westland-row, Dec. 13th, 1834

There was no great fuss at the opening. At nine o'clock *Hibernia* puffed her way out of Westland Row amid the applause and cheers of a large crowd of spectators. Nine trains ran that day, each one packed, and over 5,000 passengers were carried.

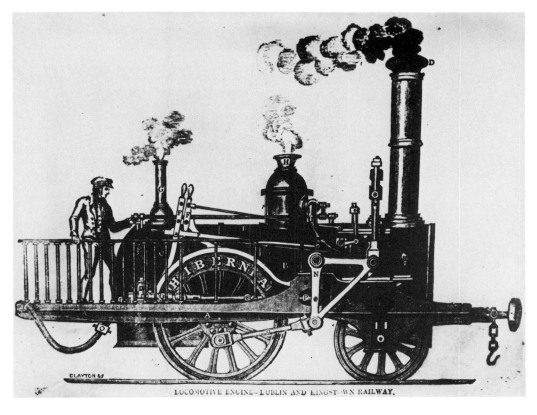

LOCOMOTIVE ENGINE—DUBLIN AND KINGSTOWN RAILWAY.

Hibernia, *the locomotive which headed the first passenger train in Ireland, 17 December 1834*

That evening there was a celebratory banquet in the Salthill hotel for the directors and their colleagues. Ireland had joined the railway age.

A few weeks before the official opening the Dublin *Penny Journal* published 'Thirteen Views on the Dublin and Kingstown Railway'. This has a detailed description of the line with an excellent portrait of what it looked like at the time.

> At present the Entrance Station is on the east side of Westland-row. The design is sufficiently characteristic of a public building without any attempt at embellishment. The chief points worthy of attention are the beautiful granite door-cases, and cornices, from the rocks near Seapoint cliffs, and the light elegant iron roof over the passengers' station ... The Railway starts at an elevation of about twenty feet from the surface, and spans in succession over each street by flat elliptical arches. For the more important streets, smaller arches for the footways have been made on each side of the principal openings.

E. L. Ahrons gave a more prosaic description when he visited Westland Row in the 1920s: 'a dingy, dirty shed with one platform'. Unfortunately some of the delightful little bridges have since had to be removed for the present Howth–Bray electrification scheme and have been replaced with ugly concrete structures (see Chapter 10). The *Penny Journal* continued:

> Hurried forward by the agency of steam, the astonished passenger glides, like Asmodeus, over the summits of the houses and streets of our city—presently is transported through green fields and tufts of trees—then skims across the surface of the sea, and taking shelter under the cliffs, coasts among the marine villas, and through rocky excavations, until he finds himself in the centre of a vast port, which unites in pleasing confusion the bustle of a commercial town with the amusements of a fashionable watering place.

Resuming a description of the route at Haig's Lane (Lansdowne Road):

> The crossing at Haig's distillery is the first accessible point to the Railway from Dublin. This being but little frequented, the roadway has been raised by gentle approaches, and passes on the level of the Railroad. A neat lodge is built, and ... gates will be kept across the Railway, and a vigilant watch kept.
>
> We next come to a handsome bridge of three arches across the river Dodder, with a side opening for foot passengers. The Railroad here approaches the surface of the country. A little further forward, and on the north side, are erecting the buildings for the repair and construction of the locomotive engines, coaches, waggons &c. and the other necessary shops and conveniences for the Company.

These workshops were later transferred to Grand Canal Street and a delightful row of railway cottages now occupies the site.

> Thus the line runs through Simmonscourt fields, crossing Sandymount lane and Sydney parade, which will be protected, like the other roads, with gates, lodges, and watchmen. At Merrion the Strand road is crossed close to the old baths, with similar protection, but on account of intrusion, the Railway from Merrion-hall on to the strand is guarded by high stone fence-walls. From Old Merrion to the place where stood the bathing places at Black-rock, the Railroad is elevated across the strand, and at high water appears like a long mole stretching into the sea.
>
> A smile will be raised at the recollection of the good-natured predictions of the direful and destructive effect the winter storms were to produce upon this attempt to force nature ... To afford additional stability and protection, an increased breadth is given to the banks seaward, which will form a delightful promenade on fine summer evenings. A cross embankment is made from opposite Booterstown lane to the Railway, to give access to passengers; and it is the intention of the noble lord of the manor to

Jones, del.   Clayton, sc.

TRAIN OF CARRIAGES QUITTING THE STATION HOUSE AT WESTLAND ROW.

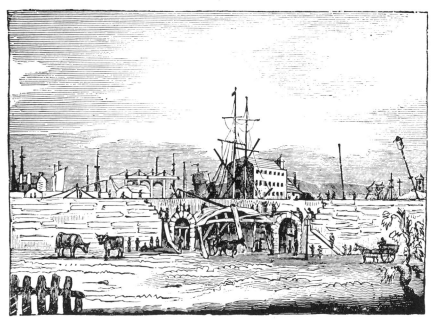

View of the Kingstown Railroad where it crosses the street near the Docks at the Drawbridge, Ringsend.

Two original woodcuts made for the opening of the Dublin and Kingstown Railway

cultivate the land redeemed by the railway operations, which will, therefore, in the course of a few months, present the appearance of a luxuriant garden, where lately was only a barren, sandy beach...

From Black-rock to Kingstown the character of the work changes continually—high walling on the land side, and open to the sea; then passing under Lord Cloncurry's demesne, between the beautiful granite pavilions erecting for his lordship; next below the noble archway or tunnel; and beyond, through a deep, rocky excavation, upwards of forty feet in depth; and below, the bridge connecting the several portions of the elegant lawn of Sir Harcourt Lees...

The house at Salthill is now converting, with vast additions, into a splendid tavern, which will rival its celebrated namesake in the vicinity of Eton college, in all, it is to be hoped, except its extravagant charges; and the hill itself will be cut into beautiful terraces and slants, and planted in an ornamental manner. To this extent, terminating on the western pier of the old harbour of Dunleary, the works of the Company are completed, and nearly ready for opening.

Even the Commissioners of Public Works, a body not noted for its exhuberance, were forced to admit that 'the undertaking as a work of art, promises to be as perfect of the kind as any that has hitherto been ever executed'. Speaking in the Commons the Chief Secretary for Ireland, Lord Morpeth, spoke highly of the railway saying: 'there was more traffic between the two places since the completion of the railway than there had ever been by road... while the owners of hackney cars, who had thought they would have been completely thrown out of bread, had actually experienced an improvement in their business'. This, Ireland's first railway, celebrates its 150th anniversary in 1984.

Fares and services

The half-hourly service was increased before long to meet the demand which was particularly heavy on holidays and at weekends. The running of trains on Sundays very soon became a thorny issue. People of strict religious beliefs considered it immoral and a breach of the sabbath. Yet Sunday was the only day of the week when most working people could escape from the grime of the city to the sea air at Kingstown. The company realised this and despite opposition from within its own ranks Sunday trains continued almost without interruption, so that by 1853 Sunday was the busiest day of the week.

As promised in the original notice an irregular pattern of stops was made at the intermediate stations: Sydney Parade, Sandymount Lane, Merrion, Booterstown, Williamstown, Blackrock and Salthill. These hardly merited the name 'station', being just a strip of gravel alongside the track from which the passenger clambered into the train. Most people travelled the whole route and Bergin notes that from the opening to 1 March 1836 a total of 1,237,800 passengers were carried, a very satisfactory result. This promising start was kept up in 1839 when 1,341,208 passengers were carried, the receipts being £34,716. Already the problem of peaks and troughs was evident, with a huge demand for transport at certain periods of the day and very little at others.

At the beginning fares of 1/-, 8d, and 6d (5p, 3½p, 2½p) were fixed, regardless of the distance travelled. However pro rata reductions were later made for shorter journeys. These were considered in the words of contemporary hotel advertisements 'strictly moderate'. The second class fare was raised a penny (i.e. half a pingin nua!) in 1839 but receipts from that class fell so drastically that the 8d fare was restored. The company showed great foresight in encouraging travel by excursion and multi-journey tickets. A dozen first class tickets could be bought for ten shillings (50p) and within two years day return tickets were being sold to commuters, day trippers, shoppers etc. at great reductions on the normal fares. Regattas, holidays, carnivals, state occasions, each was marked by the issue of special tickets which kept the trains busy. Fourpence being the change out of a shilling, for a second class ticket, to save time a large supply of groats, silver four-penny pieces, was kept handy. Then in 1840 morning tickets appeared. These were day returns available from 6–7 am only 'for the convenience of Artizans, Labourers, Bathers and others'. They cost a shilling (5p) in second class and 8d. (later 6d.) in third and were very successful.

Another early innovation was period or season tickets. In February 1835 second class annual tickets cost £12, a six monthly was £7 and a monthly £1. 10. 0 (£1.50). There were proportionate fares from other stations and first class tickets followed a year later. The latter were very worthwhile for they gave concessionary travel to the purchaser's family and free carriage of (unaccompanied) parcels.

CARRICK-ON-SHANNON.			

The Royal Canal Car which starts from Sligo every morning at 6 o'clock, leaves this at 11 o'clock, for:

		Arrives.	Fare.
		h. m.	s. d.
Drumsna	...	... 11 50	0 6
Drumod	...	... 12 30	1 0
Ruskey	...	... 12 35	1 6
Longford	...	... 2 15	3 0

In time for the Royal Canal Boat to Dublin, and intermediate Stages.

Fare from Carrick-on-shannon, including Boat and Car, to the following places:

		State.	Back.
		h. m.	s. d.
Ballymahon	...	... 4 8	4 1
Balnacareg	...	... 5 9	4 11
Mullingar	...	... 6 11	5 9
Kilcock	...	... 10 5	8 0
Maynooth	...	... 10 11	8 3
Dublin	...	... 12 5	9 3

The Car which starts from Longford every morning after the arrival of the Royal Canal Packet Boat from Dublin, leaves this at 40 minutes past 11 o'clock, for:

		h. m.	s. d.
Boyle	...	... 1 20	1 0
Sligo	...	... 5 30	4 6

C. SIDLY, Agent.

SLIGO.			

A Car starts every morning at 6 o'clock, for:

		Arrives.	Fare.
		h. m.	s. d.
Boyle	...	... 9 30	3 6
Carrick-on-Shannon	...	11 0	4 6
Drumsna	...	... 11 50	5 0
Drumod	...	... 12 30	5 6
Longford	...	... 2 15	7 6

In time for Royal Canal Packet Boat to Dublin and intermediate stages.

Fares from Sligo to the following places, including Boat and Car Fares:

		State.	Back.
		s. d.	s. d.
Mullingar	...	... 11 5	10 3
Maynooth	...	... 15 5	12 9
Dublin	...	... 16 11	13 9

☞ For Ballymahon and Athlone,

(See Longford.)

The Cars that start from Athlone every night at 11 o'clock, and from Longford every morning at 30 minutes past 8 o'clock, after the arrival of Royal Canal Packet Boat from Dublin, arrives here at 30 minutes past 5 o'clock.

G. O'NEILL, Agent.

Two pages from Bianconi's Car and Coach Lists, *1842*

One of the company's best and most reliable customers was Her Majesty's mail. The mail steamer arrived at Kingstown at 5.30 am each morning and the mails were taken by special train of one reserved coach to Dublin and from Westland Row to the General Post Office in Sackville (O'Connell) Street. In these days of instant telecommunications it is hard for us to grasp how vital to the Victorians was the penny post and its prompt delivery. You could post a letter in London (or Edinburgh) at 6 pm and be sure that barring the sinking of the mail boat it would be delivered in Dublin before breakfast. Like *The Times*, the grouse season and Ascot opening day the mail arrived unfailingly when it was supposed to.

The D & KR earned £300 per annum from conveying the mails. The schedule was very tight and the transfer of passengers and mail at Holyhead was often completed in ten minutes or less! There was the added incentive for the D & KR in that it agreed to pay the Post Office 34/- (£1.70) for every *minute* it was late.

Another regular user was the Dublin Metropolitan Police, constables, magistrates and criminals being regular travellers on the line. Such was the traffic in malfactors and the volume of complaints from upright citizens forced to share accomodation with them that two trains a day had a third class carriage set aside for such persons beginning an enforced sojourn in Van Diemen's Land, Dartmoor, the Americas or wherever. Dogs were charged 3d (1p) per journey, or their owners were, on condition they travelled in the under-seat lockers intended for parcels and luggage. On one occasion a butcher placed a joint of meat in one such locker not realising that there was a madra already in residence. The happy hound thought it was Christmas and his birthday all in one so that, as Kevin Murray puts it, 'during the journey the meat was reduced in quantity and value'. As a result the train guards were fined the value of the meat, 5/11 (29½p), for their carelessness and presented with the emaciated joint.

Westland Row is hardly a beautiful building and the facade was not improved when a hole was knocked in the front to build the connection to Amiens Street Station. However an attractive feature which is rarely noticed is the ironwork bridge over Westland Row itself. This is a fine piece of engineering whose proportions are just right and enhance what would otherwise be a very drab vista. Kingstown station was also designed by Mulvany and is much more appealing. Approaching from Dublin the terminus was to the left under a glass roof with a through platform on the right. The main buildings were at street level with a fine

A busy scene at Kingstown harbour (Dun Laoghaire) at the turn of the century

terrace overlooking the harbour. In later years the glass roof was removed and the upper level was converted to an excellent restaurant, the Na Mara, under OIE, a subsidiary of CIE which runs the Great Southern Hotels and has its headquarters in the lower part of the building. The other station which Mulvany designed was that at Blackrock, an elegant building with the clean lines of a miniature Broadstone. Ironically, the outcrop which gave Blackrock its name had to be blasted to make way for the line.

Locomotives

Being the first railway in the country the D & KR had no experience to draw on in the matter of engine design. As a result some mistakes were inevitably made. Seven engineering firms tendered for the order of six locomotives but there was conflicting advice given to the directors from various quarters. In due course three engines were supplied by George Forrester of Liverpool (*Dublin, Kingstown* and *Vauxhall*) and three by the Manchester firm of Sharp Brothers (*Hibernia, Brittania* and *Manchester*). The *Penny Journal* stated that 'the greatest mechanical perfection has been attained in these machines'. The first engine was given its trial run on the Liverpool and Manchester Railway on 27 June 1834 when it drew a train between the two cities. The tests were satisfactory and the six locomotives were shipped to Dublin. Further trials produced speeds of up to 60 mph which must have been somewhat risky given the state of the track and engines.

It was quickly found that six engines were not enough and two more were ordered from Forresters, *Victoria* and *Comet* and another from a Yorkshire company. This was the ill-fated *Star*, originally supplied to the L & MR. The latter had been disatisfied with its performance and gladly released it to the D & KR. *Star* arrived in September 1835 by which time many defects had been discovered in the Sharp engines. These troubles came to a head on 27 October 1842 when the firebox of *Hibernia* exploded, scattering red-hot coke around Kingstown station. Luckily the crew were not on the footplate at the time and no-one was injured. The locomotive was then scrapped and the other two immediately withdrawn from service, thoroughly overhauled and later sold. But *Star* gave her new owners as much trouble as she did the L & MR. Bergin made strong complaints to the makers about shoddy workmanship and bad engineering. Eventually the locomotive was almost completely rebuilt but soon after it was cannibalised for spare parts.

On 26 March 1841 the company proudly announced that it had built the first locomotive on its own premises, a fair achievement for the time. Using some of the bones of *Star* a design similar to Forrester's emerged. There was intense discussion about a suitable name for this the first Irish-produced railway engine. The temperance lobby suggested *The Irish Teetotaler* or *Father Mathew* but these were overruled by the large number of directors who held substantial interests in the liquor trade! Also rejected was the notion of holding a gala reception to mark the occasion at which the main beverage would be—tea. Finally the name *Princess* was chosen in honour of the newly born Victoria. Other locomotives to follow were *Belleisle* (the name of a visiting warship), *Shamrock* which emerged in November 1842, *Erin* a year later and *Albert* in July 1844.

These then were the first engines to run on the D & KR. The company quickly learnt to adapt and improve designs as required. One of the more obvious, but by no means the earliest, was the introduction of locomotive brakes in 1849. Up to then the means of stopping was a carriage brake which the guard operated with reverse gear if needed. Not surprisingly this led to a number of incidents.

Fifty carriages were ordered to begin with, most of which were built in Dublin at Dawsons of Capel Street and Courteney and Stephens of Blackhall Place. The wheels and axles were made in England. First class had upholstered seats for eighteen passengers, carpets and window blinds. Second class had seats for 24 persons but some were open from waist height up. Third class had toast-rack type seating for 35 without any doors or windows. Whishaw's *Railways of Great Britain and Ireland* (respectfully dedicated 'to the Railway Capitalists of the United Kingdom'), written after a visit to the line in 1839, said that 'the second class closed carriages are superior to any at present in use on any railway in the United Kingdom'. Most trains consisted of the neat arithmetical arrangement of one first class, two second class and three third class carriages. These were colour coded, as were the tickets, to aid the illiterate: first class purple, second yellow or green, third blue. If you were colour blind *and* illiterate then you had problems. Lighting was by oil lamp in first and later second and by moonlight in third. Smoking was forbidden in all except third class.

Grand Canal Street Works turned out a large number of coaches for the railway, many to a high standard. But the pride of the fleet was that built for Queen Victoria's visit to Ireland in 1849. An existing vehicle was converted, almost overnight, to bring her from Kingstown, her port of arrival, to Dublin. From reports of the time it was a most elaborate and luxurious vehicle: thick carpets, beautiful armchairs and tables, linen wall hangings and damask curtains, all of the finest Irish manufacture. Although a number of more mundane carriages lasted well into the twentieth century only one has been preserved in the Belfast Transport Museum.

The men of the D & KR

Unlike the board members of many large companies today, being a director of the D & KR was neither cosmetic nor a sinecure. There was a weekly board meeting and committees met as often as three times a week. Unpunctuality was fined, as much as a guinea (£1.05) which went towards an entertainment fund. Railway travel was free to the directors, ensuring that they could observe all and be observed. There was a strong Quaker influence on the board, no doubt accounting for its reputation for thrift and hard work, combined with enlightened self-interest. A regular feature was the breakfast meeting at the Salthill hotel which began at 6 am! This was followed by a walking tour of the line.

The company acquired the Salthill hotel almost by accident when it bought the land for the railway. With it came a large house in its own grounds. The building was leased as a hotel to a William Marsh and it soon became known as a first class eating place. There were however not enough bedrooms to make it a paying proposition and so the railway employed Mulvany to add as many as thirty extra rooms. Unfortunately Marsh's financial affairs reached a crisis and he changed his residence to the debtor's prison. Eventually an independent group bought the hotel from the railway and it continued in business until quite recently when it was demolished. The inevitable office block is about to spring up fungus-like on the spot.

As noted, a large number of labourers was employed on the construction of the line. Dargan was a fair employer but under the pressure of a strict deadline and the absence of a real safety code there were many accidents and injuries. A system of half pay operated during serious illness which in itself was revolutionary and by 1837 a relief fund was in operation. Each man paid a quarter of a day's pay per week into the fund and the company added an equal amount. Later sick benefit was increased to three-quarters pay and in case of death the company paid the funeral costs. The fund also provided generous Christmas and Easter bonuses to all employees.

The other side of the coin was that hours of work were exceptionally long. Whishaw noted that in 1839 there were 25 fitters employed in the locomotive department, earning from 9/- to 42/- per week (45p–£2.10). There were eight engine drivers earning 6/- (30p) a day, the hours being 6 am to 11 pm. In 1844 it was common for most men to work up to 110 hours per week with obvious effects on health, efficiency and safe running. Eight years later the hours were reduced to 90 for a seven day week with the odd Sunday off. By contrast the Great Southern and Western was paying the same wages for a 10 hour day, 6 day week. As might be expected many staff changed jobs. Without doubt the company's prosperity can be traced in part to this early exploitation but it must be said that this was common practice at the time and in many ways the D & KR was more generous and considerate than the majority of employers.

Like almost every railway in the land drunkenness was a major problem. One director in 1844 came across a locomotive standing forlornly and quite unattended near Merrion. He located the crew in a nearby hostelry and ordered them to remove themselves and their engine from that dangerous spot. Surprisingly they were not dismissed but fined 5/- (25p) each. Tipping was another sore point. It was strictly forbidden but impossible to eradicate, given the low wages. Travellers in the last century tended to bring vast amounts of luggage with them and an army of porters, both official and otherwise, flocked at almost every station. Most felt they were entitled to a small gratuity after hauling several portmanteaux and trunks around the place. One gentleman, a Jas Kearney, turned down the job of train guard on finding he would have to wear a uniform:

> Understanding that the situation subjects the person filling it to wear a livery dress, I must confess candidly that deference to the notions of the family and society I have sprung from, and a solicitude to excite by precept and example my children to emulation, forbid my putting on a livery dress.

The security of the line was a constant problem. The company employed elderly men to protect the various stores and buildings at night. Then in 1837 a 'night patrole' began. Two hardy men walked the entire line from Westland Row to Kingstown and back. Each man was given a weapon (a blackthorn or a musket?), a 'dark lanthorn' and a whistle. They were on duty from 8 pm to 7am but the time of their walk was not revealed until they arrived for work. Then setting out at the same time they met at Merrion to pass the time of night. Each man carried a number of wooden tallies on which he marked his passing time at Sydney Parade, Blackrock and the termini. These were then posted in the pillar box at these stations and delivered the next day to the board room of Westland Row. After an hour's rest the watchman retraced his route, repeating the whole procedure. (This primitive clocking in system is still used by modern day security men.)

Undoubtedly a twelve mile walk nightly must have been good for body and soul, especially on a summer's evening. But in January, with the waves crashing over the sea wall, the east wind howling across Dublin Bay and the rain bucketing down, it must have been a different prospect.

The system was not foolproof and abuses crept in before long. The watchmen were not posting the tallies as required but having them delivered with fictitious reports attached. The following year the method was dropped as unworkable and watchmen given a shorter stretch between stations to patrol. In any case, although the company wanted 'men of a superior class' for the job, they would hardly get strong, healthy, honest applicants who could write and tell the time by offering only 10/- (50p) a week.

Long before the opening of the line, plans were well in hand for the extension to Kingstown itself. The goal was

> the large open space opposite the Commissioners' yard... being immediately connected with the magnificent quay and landing place, now in course of construction by Government, for the accomodation of the Post Office and other steamers; and when the works are completed, passengers may step from the Railway coaches to the steamers, and again, on arriving will, with the mail bags, be conveyed from the Royal Harbour of George the Fourth to the centre of the Irish metropolis.

Once again the opposition rallied with Mr Gresham well to the fore. This time there was a long heated debate with Daniel O'Connell, no less, becoming involved. Gresham claimed that the company wanted to build a twenty foot high wall along the seafront which would block all views of the harbour. Vignoles, speaking for the railway, denied this and argued for the great benefits the line would bring on its natural extension towards Bray. O'Connell came down on the side of the company, Parliament gave its legal blessing and the way ahead was clear.

Such was the satisfaction with Dargan that his estimate of £37,200 for the section to Kingstown itself was accepted without others being sought. Dargan began work in May 1836, demolished a Martello tower at Dunleary (a pity) and ran the line in to the present terminus by May 1837 when the extension opened for traffic.

At about this time Vignoles came up with a most imaginative scheme for a trunk line between Westland Row and the harbour of Valentia, Co. Kerry. This was the earliest attempt to capture the lucrative transatlantic traffic in passengers and mail between England and America, by a shorter time at sea. Hopes were high: speaking in the Commons, Lord George Bentinck said:

> Sooner or later Valentia Harbour must be the American packet station for the whole of the Empire.

The plan involved taking the railway along the Dublin quays by means of a raised embankment and building a large harbour at Valentia. As the arguments raged over the merits of Galway v. Valentia as the most suitable packet station a John Porter entered the fray in 1847 with his book, 'A Few Observations upon our present railway system in Ireland'. He wrote: 'Surely half the money that would be required to build warehouses, docks, streets etc. at Valentia... would make first rate docks at Galway. But could there be any regular transatlantic steam-packet station more out of the way than a place like Valentia?' He had a point. Later he diluted his argument somewhat by wandering into a diatribe on the ebullient nature of the Established clergy! Needless to say the required backing for such a vast project did not materialise.

The Atmospheric Railway

A more moderate undertaking was the Dalkey extension and here the unique Atmospheric Railway made its appearance. The first experiments in the use of air as a means of transport were made in the seventeenth century and by the 1830s one Samuel Clegg had perfected a valve apparatus which greatly improved its efficiency. He approached the board of the D & KR saying he was anxious to see the system in operation on just such a line. Clegg made a very attractive offer to the directors and convinced them to try it with a further loan from the BPW.

The principle behind the atmospheric railway was a simple one: nature abhors a vacuum and by drawing the air from an enclosed cylinder it is possible to move an object through it at some speed, depending on how perfect the vacuum is. Up to a few years ago the principle could be seen in almost every department store. The shop assistant placed the customer's money with a chit in a canister. This was then inserted in a long pipe through which it was whisked to the cashier's office by means of the air being sucked out of the pipe. The change and receipt then returned to the counter with a soft plop by the same method. Another, even simpler example is drinking through a straw.

Clegg's invention involved laying a pipe 15 inches in diameter between the two rails. A valve of stout leather, strengthened with iron plates, pressed down on the pipe and protected the seal. A coat of tallow was melted into place by the passing of the train and prevented water penetration. An arm projected down from the train into the tube and it was this which was drawn along as the air was extracted from inside.

C. F. Mallet's 'Report on the Kingstown and Dalkey Atmospheric Line' for the French government (1844) mentions a number of earlier attempts, some of which are quite comical. In 1824 a M. Vallence 'enclosed piston, carriages, and passengers within a large tunnel, but his experiments were not attended with satisfactory results'. Possibly through the immediate demise of his subjects from asphyxiation.

On 26 September 1842 the BPW ceremoniously handed over the symbolic sod and twig to the railway indicating the change of ownership. Once again the opposition was active and vocal, but a compromise was reached by laying the line through a partial cutting along the sea front at Kingstown, instead of a full tunnel. The cutting was protected by attractive iron railings which are still in place.

Built by Dargan the line was a branch off the Kingstown railway, unlike today where there is through running. Almost the entire line was built on an incline with headroom, at the time, of only $8\frac{1}{2}$ feet in places. Safety standards of the day were somewhat looser than our own but one of the features of the atmospheric system was that a collision between trains was physically impossible. Five minutes before departure the boilerman at the Dalkey pumping station began pumping until he had reached the correct vacuum pressure. Meanwhile the driver had applied the brakes tightly and the passengers got on. At the signal to start the brake was released and the train moved off. At the Dalkey end a boy was employed to tell the man working the pump when the train came into sight, and he then stopped pumping. The pipe ended 560 yards short of the station, momentum being enough to bring the train the rest of the way. Of course if the load was particularly heavy the train was known to stop short or indeed run through the station and off the rails if the engineer was slow in shutting down the pump. The return trip was by gravity although a strong wind on the approach to Kingstown could be enough to halt the train before the station.

The official opening took place on 29 March 1844 with trains every half hour in each direction, at fares of 3d and 2d, there being no first class to begin with. The railway aroused enormous interest at home and abroad with visitors from all over Europe expecting great things from the system. George O'Malley Irwin, writing in his *Handbook to the County of Wicklow* (1844) said:

> We have a new and astonishing application of power opened to us, and it is impossible to anticipate all the important results to which this may lead... Were the valves and engines perfectly air-tight, a single stationary engine would give power to a line of one thousand miles as easily as to a line of one mile... There was £45 received on the Dalkey Railway on the 12th May, which at 2½d, the average fare, gives on that day, 4,320 travellers.

Brunel thought the railway was excellent and recommended the atmospheric system to the English Great Western for the Gravesend to Chatham line, while 'a committee of fifteen gentlemen of the highest character and standing in Ireland' planned a line from Dublin to Sallins along the canal banks. William Cubitt, of building fame, wanted to use it on the London and Croydon railway and Mallet prescribed it for all French railways.

There was a division of scientific opinion but the public liked the line very much. A newspaper of the day described the journey as 'most luxurious—no noise, no smoke, no cinders, no smell'. Most of the carriages had quite large glass windows, which is rather curious since the line runs through cuttings all the way, while those in use on the more scenic coastal route had few windows.

The speed potential of the atmospheric system was unwittingly tested one day shortly after the opening. An inquisitive person named Elrington was examining the apparatus when without warning the train shot off up the hill to Dalkey, reaching a top speed of 85 mph and managing to keep the rails around the many bends and twists of that section. Luckily the crew were able to bring it under control before Dalkey and no-one was injured.

The advantages of the atmospheric were speed of acceleration, safety, quiet and clean operation and savings in locomotive manufacture and maintenance. Against that there were considerable drawbacks. The system was unreliable in that, if one train stopped, all stopped, and shunting was impossible. Braking power was low and construction costs high while the pumping station had to be kept working at all times and used more coal than the equivalent steam engines. Most difficult of all was valve maintenance as a perfect vacuum was impossible. Walking along the track a person could tell a train was coming from the steady hiss of air entering through the countless small holes. More insidious were the railside rats who developed a taste for the tallow-coated leather and further reduced the effectiveness of the vacuum.

A series of breakdowns occurred in 1848 and for a time a conventional locomotive was used on the line. Even though as many as 400 bills for atmospheric railways had been prepared for Parliament, its days were numbered. With the prospect of a link up with the line to Wexford the atmospheric became an obstacle in the route to the capital. On 12 April 1854 the last train powered by air ran up to Dalkey and the line was converted for normal traction.

Today there is hardly anything to be seen of the atmospheric although the route is of course still open. Near the site of the pumping station there is Atmospheric Road and that is all. Commercially it was a failure yet the company deserves credit for pioneering effort. With modern sealing and engineering techniques, who knows that one day we may not see the system revived in these fuel-conscious days?

Victoria's visit

A large number of extra trains were run during the visit of Queen Victoria in 1849. Many thousands of spectators wanted to view the royal fleet in Kingstown

The exterior of Dun Laoghaire station designed by Mulvany. This is now a restaurant owned by a subsidiary of CIE

harbour and the railway staff worked especially hard on the occasion. In gratitude for their special efforts the company threw a grand dinner and dance for their employees in the workshops of Grand Canal Street. The paint shop was lavishly decorated and became the banquet room for the directors, officials, workmen and their sons. An enormous meal was served and accompanied by a string of toasts. When the feasting was over the men retired to the carriage shop which was transformed by floral and linen decoration into a dance hall. There the ladies joined in the frolics and at a late hour a substantial supper was served, with dancing until early the following morning. As a memento each employee received a gift of his cutlery and plate.

Railway watchdogs

It would clearly be a mistake to think that the welcome for the railways was unanimous and universal. Apart from local groups who felt threatened in one way or another by the new mode of transport there were some who cast a highly critical eye on the operations of the railway magnates. One of the earliest was William Galt who in 1843 produced a pamphlet called *Railway Reform*.

Galt was very much in favour of railways but wanted to highlight a number of serious abuses. These he considered to be: 1. exhorbitant fares (three times the

A model of the new station at Dun Laoghaire

Belgian rates); 2. ruthless profiteering and elimination of competitors; 3. the lack of any sense of public interest from the proprietors; 4. absurd inter-company rivalry of which the public was the chief victim; 5. excessive pressure on passengers to travel at a higher class by a scarcity of third class carriages, exclusively first class trains and deliberately delaying all-third trains to make the journey unendurable. Indeed the GWR of England is said to have tried 'employing sweeps to go in amongst them [third class passengers] and thus effectively drive out every man or woman who should find it in any way disagreeable to come into contact with those gentry'.

As early as 1839 the Commons had expressed its reservations about the iron horse:

> It does not appear to have been the intention of Parliament to give to a railway a complete monopoly of the means of communication. The injurious effects of the railway system on the poorer class of passenger will be more severely felt in proportion as other means of cheap travelling by stage coaches, carrier's carts etc. are gradually superseded.

Even *The Times* thundered its disapproval: 'Railway directors have at present the exercise of too much irresponsible power, and therefore imagine that they can deal with the public as they choose', a charge levelled at railway companies many times since then!

To be fair, the D & KR and the Ulster Railway (the only lines open in Ireland at the time) can be acquitted of most if not all of these charges. In fact Galt makes extensive reference to the D & KR and its effective policy of encouraging third class travel by every means, such as cheap excursions, morning tickets, and concessionary fares, many of which were aimed at that sector of the market which so many companies disdained. Galt shows the effects of such a policy in 1842 when he comments ungrammatically: 'The Company carried, without any increase in expenditure, 478,117 more passengers than what they did in 1840.'

The *Railway Times* supported his campaign but in a more restrained manner, so as not to offend the greater part of its readers:

> This practice, for certain classes of passengers will no doubt startle some of the advocates of high fares on this side of the Channel, but the success of the Kingstown Company shows that it is not too low. We should be glad to see a similar *spirit* pervading English companies, but of course, we do not counsel the establishment, upon any of our lines, of this specific charge [i.e. a farthing a mile].

Galt concludes by wishing a plague on all your third class houses: 'Nothing but the direst necessity will compel any man, however poor he may be, to travel by these legalised nuisances'.

The Bray lines

When Brunel visited the atmospheric railway in 1844 he mentioned to the directors of the D & KR that his own company, the GWR, planned to build a line into South Wales and start a new sea route from Fishguard to what is now Rosslare. There would then be a need for a line from Wexford to Dublin and he suggested that the D & KR might consider a joint venture. The Irish company had already considered the obvious extension of their line to Bray and had in fact completed a preliminary survey of the route. The GWR, anxious to establish its footing in Ireland, saw the value of an alliance with such a reputable company and through Brunel pressed for a commitment, announcing plans for a network of lines in the south–east stretching as far as Carlow and Kingstown. To this end a new company was formed, the Waterford, Wexford, Wicklow and Dublin Railway, and in turn the D & KR formed the Kingstown and Bray Railway.

Progress was hampered by the Great Famine and by the convoluted negotiations between the various interested parties. Among the items discussed was the lease of the D & KR to the WWW & DR, at an annual figure of £34,000 with a percentage of receipts over a certain figure. Finally, with Brunel as consulting engineer, work began on the Bray line in August 1847 but by the beginning of the following year had stopped. Recognising the inevitable, the WWW & DR changed its name to the more accurate Dublin and Wicklow Railway with a plan for an inland route from Bray to the capital. To add to the confusion the GWR then made known its lack of enthusiasm for the whole business.

At this point William Dargan intervened so as to get matters moving again. The sleepy little village of Bray had always been a pet project of his and he brought his influence to bear in bringing the railway to the town. He planned to make it a fashionable watering place—the Brighton of Ireland—and built a number of houses, Turkish baths, a hotel, and laid out the fine esplanade along the sea front. As a contemporary account put it: 'Under his guiding eye, and by the judicious investment of his abundant capital, a small and comparatively obscure village has been rapidly converted into a charming marine outskirt of Dublin'. Obviously the railway was essential for this.

Dargan mediated between the groups and even bought a large number of D & WR shares, anything to speed construction. Finally on 10 July 1854 the D & WR opened for business between Harcourt Road and Bray as well as the Dalkey to Bray section. The next step would clearly be the merging of the D & WR and the D & KR, but still there were problems. The route through Bray Head, Brunel's work, was already showing deficiencies and relations between the companies suddenly worsened. In October 1855, with the opening of the now converted atmospheric railway, the D & WR sent a very abrupt letter to the Kingstown company announcing that it required the use of its station there and had therefore erected a booking office on the platform. Naturally the D & KR were not amused and on several occasions evicted the poor clerk and refused to allow passengers from Bray to alight at the station. This impasse continued for several days. Normal relations were finally restored so that on 1 July 1856 the D & KR formally handed over its line to the D & WR, having postponed the lease as long as it could. From that date all services were operated by the D & WR, although of course the D & KR retained ownership of its line.

Leaving the last word to the *Penny Journal:*

By the extension of the line towards Bray and southward, the country between Kingstown and Killiney, and the beautiful valley lying between it and Bray, will doubtless be thickly studded with villas and cottages. Indeed it is fondly anticipated that this measure may be the means of introducing the railway system to Ireland...

Capital, intelligence, and enterprise, exist abundantly in Ireland; and nothing is wanting to render it the most flourishing part of the Empire, but confidence and the diffusion of information.

What can more readily bring these than the railroads, whereby the English landlord and the traveller may visit the remotest parts of Ireland with the same rapidity and safety with which he now posts down from London to Brighton.

When the landed proprietor can have the means of visiting his estates frequently and expeditiously he will perceive that to the want of employment and education are to be attributed the whole of the evils of Ireland.

2 The Dublin and South Eastern Railway

THE long awaited marriage between the D&KR and the D&WR took place in July 1856, two years after the Bray and Wicklow extension opened. The Dublin terminus was at Harcourt Road and the route inland was by Ranelagh, Dundrum and Shankill. The line was much less profitable than the D&KR section, and before long fares were increased to meet the deficit. In those days of zero inflation this remedy was worse than the disease and passenger numbers fell greatly. The D&KR protested that its line was being penalized for the inadequacy of the controlling company with high fares, poor services and infrequent connections. The new rates led to customer resistance and the revival of old forms of competition. The Dublin and Kingstown Omnibus Company began a horse drawn service between those two places in the 1860s. However, few passengers made the complete trip (the train being much quicker) and the service did not affect the railway greatly.

More serious was the arrival of the Dublin and Kingstown Steam Packet Company which, in July 1861, began a regular daily service between the Custom House Quay and Kingstown. Two ships, the *Kingstown* and the *Anna Liffey*, gave an hourly service at the very competitive rates of 9d (4p) saloon and 6d (2½p) deck class, both return. The boats were a very attractive alternative, especially in summer, and for the six years they operated, drew a large number of passengers from the railway.

Some of the line's problems can be traced to the construction of the line around Bray Head which was built by Dargan, with Brunel as consulting engineer. It is curious to speculate why, with two such eminent and skilled men involved, the line was built so near the sea front. It very quickly showed itself unable to resist winter storms despite the many short tunnels designed to protect the most exposed sections. Possibly Brunel's reputation was exaggerated, for as James Troup remarked in 1846:

> Tunnelling, which appears the most difficult task, is an ordinary mining operation; and an experienced miner, with a moderate salary, is much more competent to superintend the excavation and construction of a tunnel, than a Brunel or a Stephenson.

But the Board seemed to have no such reservations about the quality of the work for they made Dargan an additional payment of £50,000 and appointed him a director. Such munificence was also to the fore some years prior to this when the company secretary, R. M. Muggeridge, wrote to the directors requesting a *reduction* in his salary from £1,000 to £600 p.a. This corporate generosity contrasts sharply with the parsimony of the D&KR and may explain the latter's financial success compared with the poor performance of the D&WR.

The coastal route from Bray south was greatly altered in the following years as a result of erosion and slippage, and in time came to be known as 'Brunel's Folly'. The original course of the line can be clearly seen either from the train or from the elevated cliff walk which shadows the railway almost the whole way to Greystones. Past Bray Head the walk descends to follow the actual railway line where the inland diversion takes place. One curious aspect of this line was the camouflaged smoke vent which opened out on Bray Head itself. It is easy to imagine the astonishment of a Sunday stroller on seeing a gust of smoke issuing from the ground itself as a train passed silently beneath.

Harcourt Road was always intended to be a temporary terminus pending the completion of a bridge over the Grand Canal and the new station at Harcourt Street, designed by George Wilkinson. The building has a neat classical appearance with an imposing facade of Tuscan pillars, and a large arched entrance. Unfortunately the interior was less impressive, being a simple one platform affair. The new station opened on 7 February 1859, giving more direct access to the city centre.

Down into Wexford

It was always intended that the line should continue to Wexford and no time was lost in getting a contractor for the route south of Wicklow, Gorey being the next stage. To match these objectives the company decided that a change of name was required and so added the word 'Wexford' to its title. From Wicklow the line abandoned its coastal route and turned inland which, given all the headaches caused by the sea, was no bad thing. The railway opened to a point within a short distance of Rathdrum in August 1860 and to Avoca three years later. The route to Enniscorthy opened in November 1863, a number of engineering difficulties causing the dealay. Curiously enough, this remains one of the most attractive stretches of any railway in Ireland and CIE often uses delightful photos of trains crossing the Avonmore River in its advertising.

Wexford got its first railway through the activities of, among others, Arthur MacMurrough Kavanagh, the famous MP from Borris, Co. Carlow. Although born without arms or legs, the latter had a most extraordinary career and was involved, among other things, with the promotion of the Bagenalstown and Wexford Railway. It was not a great success and Kavanagh approached a number of companies with a view to a takeover. The DW & WR showed some interest in the Macmine to Ballywilliam section, seeing the possibility of extending into Co. Waterford. New Ross opened to traffic in September 1887 and lengthy negotiations began with the GS & WR for the route into Waterford itself, but it was many years before the city was reached. Also agreed about the same time was the takeover of the Wexford to Rosslare line by the DW & WR (November 1898). This was a most useful connection with the expanding port which now had a regular steamer service to Fishguard.

Linking the Dublin termini

As in many capital cities the authorities in Dublin watched the growth of a number of rival and independent railway companies with mixed feelings. Apart from such iniquitous practices as running trains on Sundays there was the more earthy difficulty of the gap between the various termini. Many plans were mooted to link them up, one of the earliest being the 'Report on the Dublin Metropolitan Railway' of 1864. It is quite short but the picture of how railways might have developed is fascinating.

Putting the problem in a nutshell, the report describes how 'the Termini in Dublin of the different lines are entirely isolated from each other, being located

Rosslare Harbour and pier, for many years the property of the F&RR&HC

chiefly near the municipal boundaries of the City'. Nor was there any link with the docks, apart from the Midland's branch then under construction. A short time before Frederick Barry had proposed a city railway from Westland Row to Island-bridge to be built twenty feet above street level. The objections were strenuous, vocal and many. The critics said that 'the handsome appearance of the city, for which it is famed, would be destroyed; that the noise of the engines and carriages..., with the blowing off of steam, would be a great nuisance; and, especially, that a Central Station on a high level above the streets would be for ever most inconvenient'. All sound, valid reasons. Barry even went so far as to construct a wooden mock-up of the Westmoreland Street viaduct which was universally condemned as hideous. Notwithstanding these objections the House of Lords approved the plan saying it was 'by far the most advantageous that has been suggested' and passed it to the Commons. Realising that the scheme would have a very stormy time in the lower house the promoters suddenly withdrew and after a time substituted a revised plan.

The new plan involved a tunnel under D'Olier Street, Fleet Street, Westmoreland Street, Parliament Street and Thomas Street to Kingsbridge. It envisaged keeping the original site for a new Central Station, i.e., between the Bank of Ireland College Green, Commercial Buildings and the quays. The new station was to be at street level in what would have been a very central position.

In addition, Harcourt Street Station was to have an underground connection across Camden Street, Kevin Street to 'pass to the east of Marsh's Library, where it is intended to construct a local station in the neighbourhood of St Patrick's Cathedral'. Other local stations were to be built at Lombard Street, Thomas Street, and St James's Gate (for Guinness). From the Broadstone a line was to run down to the river, crossing at a point 200 yards west of the Four Courts with a local station at Arran Quay.

The compilers of the Report were obviously pleased with their compromise solution, believing that it combined the best of all the plans mentioned to date. In their own words: 'The proposed system of railways will enable traffic from the interior of Ireland to pass through Dublin without difficulty or delay, and will form the shortest and most direct communication between the existing Termini and the shipping quays of the port . . . The entire length of all the railways is 5 miles, 1 furlong, and 2 chains . . . Powers have been taken in the Act to raise nearly one million pounds, which will, more than amply provide for all primary and contingent charges, including the purchase of land and buildings, the construction of the works, and the erection of the central station.'

Obviously the plan never materialised, but it is interesting to read such an articulate case for a Dublin underground system in 1864. The promoters underestimated the problems and costs of the system but it would be extremely useful today had it been built. Ironically the rapid transit plan which first appeared in the late 1970s incorporates many of the features of the 1864 proposal, even to the underground connecting the termini. Whether the cash will ever be found remains to be seen. The first steps at least have been taken with the suburban electrification.

The Loop Line

Two years later construction of a Liffey tunnel began but got no further than the first shafts which were soon abandoned. Another early scheme was the delightfully named Dublin, Rathmines, Rathgar, Roundtown, Rathfarnham and Rathcoole Railway. There was no doubt where the DRRRRRR was going but unfortunately it never got beyond the planning stage. Nothing positive happened until May 1884 when serious discussion of a link up of Westland Row with Amiens Street began. The advantages to all were clear, especially the speeding of transatlantic mail between Kingstown and Queenstown. Up to then they had been shuttled by horse drawn vans between the Dublin stations.

The chief opponent was Dublin Corporation which protested that building an overhead railway between the two stations would be 'a great obstruction and disfigurement'. The city fathers also feared that it would lead to 'the creation of nuisances and the resort of bad characters, and the commission of robberies, assaults, and other crimes'. No doubt about the disruption of the skyline: it is an ugly monstrosity and ruins the view down river to the Custom House. As for footpads, cutpurses and other persons of loose morals, the Corporation's fears were greatly exaggerated. The only people hanging around there were sheltering from the rain. (Just as the late lamented Liverpool Overhead Railway used to be known as 'the dockers' umbrella'.) Other opponents suggested a tunnel, an admirable if expensive alternative. Alas, the excessive gradients between Westland Row and Amiens Street would have made the line unworkable.

In spite of such criticisms the bill became law. Soon after both the MGWR and the GS & WR withdrew their support for reasons best known to themselves. So the debate dragged on, but construction went ahead and was completed in May 1890, to everyone's advantage except the aesthetes. Nowadays it would be possible to build a similar viaduct across the Liffey less obtrusively but at the time massive steel girders and supports were the order of the day. Undoubtedly it is a most useful stretch of line, not least because it led to a new station at Tara Street which is in fact the one closest to the city centre.

Coastal problems

Anxiety about the safety of the line around Bray Head was tragically justified in 1867 when an Enniscorthy–Dublin train left the track while crossing one of the many wooden viaducts which bridged the sea inlets. The engine smashed through the rather feeble railguard and fell 33 feet bringing a number of coaches with it. Two passengers were killed and 23 injured, some seriously. Luckily, the train landed on the inner side or casualties could have been much worse. The cause of the accident was a faulty joint in the rails and, as the inquiry found, 'the wretched manner in which the line was being relaid'. The spot was known as the Brandy Hole from its links with smugglers. Despite the clear evidence of poor maintenance (and faulty construction!) as well as attempts to improve the line just before the inquiry, there was no public outcry against the company. The line was repaired and strengthened in parts and services resumed.

Before long the board realised that extensive repairs and alterations would have to be made if the line was to be operated safely. Even so it was not until 1912 that it decided on full diversions for the troublesome sections. Erosion and the winter tides had by then become a real problem and there was genuine fear of another disaster. The railway between Killiney and Bray was the first to be tackled and was moved sharply inland from a point south of Killiney station as far as Bray. The fact that some of the original track, still visible from the point of divergence, has been washed away shows how necessary was this diversion.

Bray Head was next but this proceeded more slowly. There were problems with the contractors and the work itself was much more difficult, involving the digging of a long tunnel. Finally the work was complete and it has lasted well. Telegraph wires dangling periously across sea inlets mark the original route.

Even more problematic was the third, phase, that from Greystones to Wicklow. This line is sited actually on the seashore and is the most vulnerable of all. £250,000 was spent on the 11 mile stretch to reinforce it but even today it is a major handicap to the efficient working of the section. Massive concrete blocks have been placed on the seaward side to bolster up the line but each season it is carefully inspected to see how it will withstand the ravages of winter. An inland diversion would have been a total solution, but with amalgamation on the horizon the company was unwilling to embark on it and CIE has had trouble with it ever since.

Two short branches

As noted the railway at Kingstown and the cross-channel steamers neatly complemented each other, setting new standards in comfort and punctuality. On 23 December 1859 a new wharf was opened at Kingstown, called Carlisle Pier. It was a fine piece of work with two platforms giving direct train-ship access. Soon after new ships were introduced named *Leinster*, *Munster*, *Connaught* and *Ulster*. They were fine vessels and gave an excellent service. An anonymous female, writing her 'Recollections of Three Weeks Tour in Ireland' in 1870 described them as follows:

> We crossed to Kingstown in the 'Leinster', one of the four fine mail boats belonging to the City of Dublin company... The service is perhaps the best in the world. The boats are large, with very powerful engines, fitted up with elegance and comfort, and start punctually to a second.

It was a bad piece of work when CIE decided 100 years later to lift the tracks out to the pier, despite many denials to the contrary. However, when the ferries transfer to the new wharf passengers will be carried by moving walkway directly to the station which is very near it. Another short siding which has also disappeared is that to the Royal Dublin Society premises in Ballsbridge. There was a junction made at Lansdowne Road station and the line was extensively used for carrying horses, cattle and passengers to and from the various shows. The branch opened in 1893 and finally closed in 1971 when the RDS sold part of its premises for office development.

An interesting view of the more macabre aspects of railway operation is shown in the 1870 working timetable which carried the following notice: 'Corpses are conveyed by the same trains as Horses and Carriages, at a charge of 1s (5p) per mile for adults and 6d (2½p) for children'.

Serious competition came from the newly organised electric trams which began to operate on the Dublin–Dalkey route in 1896. So great was the effect on the railway and the loss of passengers that within five years the DW & WR was no longer paying a dividend—an extremely serious matter for all connected with it. However the leased D & KR was not affected and continued to pay a handsome 9%. Economies were made: the stations at Sandymount and Merrion were closed and other cuts in services and expenditure made. The D & KR refused to consider a reduced payment for the lease, claiming that its section was by far the most profitable and that losses were due to the expensive and, some said, unnecessary extensions to Wexford and Shillelagh. The latter was a wandering, little-used branch which left the main line at Woodenbridge Junction and ran west into County Wicklow through very picturesque countryside.

Not reaching an understanding, the DW & WR sought legislation to abandon its agreement with the D & KR. This was passed in 1903 but must have been by way of a gesture for negotiations opened again and new terms were agreed, by means of arbitrators, within a couple of years. By now the DW & WR had completed its lines to Wexford and had extended from New Ross to Waterford. Being partial to the business it felt the time had come for another change of name so that in due course the Dublin and South Eastern Railway was born, a name which it managed to keep without further adornment until the 1925 amalgamation.

Valentine's Day accident

Before that happened there took place the curious but rather serious Harcourt Street station accident. This took place on St Valentine's Day (14 February) 1900. A goods train approaching the station failed to stop, broke the buffers and went through the end wall, coming to a stop precariously perched above Hatch Street. The events of the day are worth noting for they tell us a good deal about the operating methods of a company whose reputation for safety and engineering was not high.

The train in question was a cattle special from Enniscorthy with William Hyland driving (aged 22) and Peter Jackson his fireman. Headed by engine no 17, *Wicklow*, the train made its leisurely way towards Dublin departing at 10 am. On entering Harcourt Street the driver found he was unable to bring his train under control and, as described, the engine was seen next morning with its nose high above the street, much to the amusement of passers by. Realising the train would not stop the fireman had jumped from the footplate and, as the engine was not going very fast, was unhurt. The driver, bravely but rather foolishly, stayed put and was badly injured, his arm being amputated.

An official inquiry was held without delay. Driver Hyland reported, from hospital, that he had begun work at 5 am that morning and was due to finish at 5.30 pm that evening! Apart from a short meal break at Gorey he had worked the whole day up to the time of the crash. He stated that leaving Ranelagh he applied his

The crash at Harcourt Street station, Valentine's Day 1900

brakes and estimated his speed down the incline to be about 5–6 mph, noting that the rails were quite greasy. Realising the train was not going to stop he put the engine into reverse in the belief that the buffers would stop it. The fireman confirmed all this although he did think the speed was slightly higher than normal given the load and the weather conditions.

Taking evidence from a number of witnesses the inquiry concluded that Driver Hyland's speed must have been greater than he realised on the Dundrum bank. The buffer stops were found to be dangerously inadequate—they barely checked the train (rather like some car bumpers today which are designed to resist a maximum impact of 4 mph). The report strongly recommended that they be replaced with something more substantial. The layout of the station also contributed to the accident in that there was no direct access from the up road to the goods yard. Goods trains thus had to run alongside the single passenger platform and then reverse out; at best a highly inefficient procedure.

The company took all the criticisms to heart. The buffer stops were rebuilt with steel girders, stout wooden posts and a great mass of concrete to hold the whole in place. This was just as well for a few years later there occurred what would certainly have been a repetition. Hydraulic buffers were set in place and a direct crossover to the goods yard was built. Finally all goods trains were ordered to stop at Ranelagh to secure their brakes before descending into the terminus.

Driver Hyland returned, in time, to Bray depot where he worked in the office; Jackson left his job immediately after the accident. Number 17 got a great deal of attention and, using an enormous winch, was lowered to the ground. Then by means of temporary rails, the first set being transferred to the front as soon as the wheels cleared it, the locomotive ran under its own power down Hatch Street, up Earlsfort Terrace and back to the goods yard via Adelaide Road. It was then repaired and put back in service. Number 17 suffered further derailment indignities which will be described later.

The Civil War

Most railways in Ireland suffered from the ravages of the bitter Civil War of 1922–3 between those who accepted the Treaty with Britain and those who wanted to continue the fight. This was a crippling blow to the new state; in Dublin alone the total damage is estimated to have been £100,000,000 and the effects of the war are still felt today.

The National Government retained control of the railways and used them frequently for transporting troops and armaments but this did not stop Irregular forces from commandeering trains when they needed them. As the Army advanced into the south and south–west the retreating Republicans used guerrilla tactics to disrupt communications. Railways became 'a legitimate target', at first when they were carrying Free State troops but later on any occasion and without warning. Trains were ambushed, fired on, burnt out, derailed. Bridges and viaducts were blown up, signal boxes and stations gutted, stretches of rails removed and telegraph wires cut. Railway staff were subject to threat and intimidation, risking their lives to keep the trains running. As in every organisation in the country political opinion on the conflict was divided but all agreed that the service had to be maintained.

Waterford and Wexford were particularly affected by the war and, operating in those counties, the D & SER suffered more than its share of the troubles. As with most companies the railwaymen, in particular drivers and firemen, kept working under extremely dangerous conditions, as one incident, in July 1922, may help to illustrate.

A series of attacks had been made by Republican forces in the Wexford area and a large force of Free State soldiers had captured a number of the raiders. These were being transported to Dublin on a special train which was also carrying the mails. At Killurin the train was ambushed and the National troops jumped down on to the track to return fire. Having little cover, the officer in charge ordered the driver to bring the train forward into the station where it would have more protection. But the driver, being a Republican and probably knowing the attack was to take place, claimed the brakes were jammed and that he was unable to move the engine. After half an hour the raiders withdrew leaving three Free State soldiers dead alongside the track.

It was found that the brakes were working perfectly and the driver was arrested on a charge of complicity in the soldiers' death. A second raid was only just avoided near Killiney and at Harcourt Street shots were fired for several minutes as a final attempt to release the Irregular prisoners was made. The original driver was tried but later released.

Engine no 17, the one that took a nose dive through the end wall of Harcourt Street station, was the centre of attention later in 1923 when it was derailed by Anti-Treaty forces near Palace East. Fortunately there were no serious injuries but the locomotive lay on its side at the top of a steep embankment. As before, it was feared that any attempt to lift it back on the rails would send it sliding down, causing even more damage. It seems to have had a liking for temporary rails for once again the solution was to lower the engine down the embankment and run it along the roadway as before. In this way no 17 was steamed for about a mile to a point where the road came level with the track and it could be levered back onto conventional track.

The last raid was in February when a train was sent off driverless, again near Palace East. It was intended to derail it but on this occasion the engine and carriages kept on the rails, apart from one set of wheels which ploughed up a mile of track and was completely destroyed. By the end of April it was time for the damage to be assessed, hostilities being more or less at an end as far as the company was concerned. Twenty locomotives had been either destroyed or damaged, with 131 carriages and wagons likewise. A claim for £84,000 was made to the Government while, on top of this, £163,000 had been awarded for disruption suffered in the period of state control during and after the First World War.

Amalgamation

Calls for amalgamation of all railways in Ireland had been heard in the mid-eighteenth century but now circumstances took over where argument and persuasion had failed. The period of state control, the astronomic rise in wages and costs, the eight hour day, road competition and the disruption of the troubles all highlighted the need for central control if the railway system was to survive. The first effort was the wooing of the Cork, Bandon and South Coast Railway by the GS & WR; the MGWR followed suit and thus the Great Southern Railway was born. The D & SER was prepared to join a grouping with the Great Northern but not the GS & WR, it being proposed that there be two overall concerns for the northern and southern halves of the country. But the time for such delays was long past and the only sensible solution—a merger of all railways operating wholly in the state—was imposed. From 1 January 1925 all such lines were run by the Great Southern Railways, including the D & SER.

Centralised control had an immediate effect. A number of lines were singled, in particular that between Wicklow and Newcastle, while Bray station, the source of an increasing commuter traffic, was elaborately rebuilt. A most useful innovation was that of colour light signalling between Amiens Street and Dun Laoghaire. This is semi-automatic, controlled from Westland Row and came into operation in 1936. Most of it is still in use but will be shortly replaced. Somewhat less useful was the electric signal cabin at Harcourt Street which was hardly a dire necessity given the station still had only one platform.

In 1928 Sandymount and Merrion stations were reopened in the hope of increased commuter traffic, but this was not a success and they closed again five years later. At the same time experiments with new forms of motive power were beginning. One of the most durable was that of battery powered railcars built to the design of Dr Drumm of University College, Dublin. The first vehicle began operating in February 1932. It was heavy: 70 tons plus 15 tons of batteries and carried 140 seated passengers. A similar car entered service that summer. The

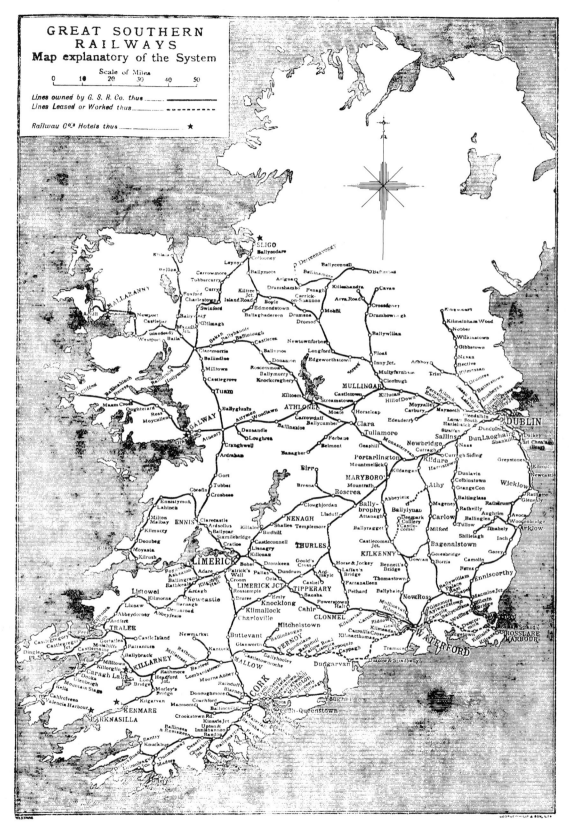

Map of the GSR from the 1931 annual report

The first Drumm battery railcar no. 386 on trial in 1930

batteries needed to be charged at the end of each run and were a regular sight on the Bray lines, along with two more also built at Inchicore in 1939. Despite their drawbacks the electric railcars were extremely useful during the periods of fuel

One of the Drumm battery trains which began running in Dublin in October 1939

DUBLIN (Harcourt Street).

Distance from Dublin	STATIONS		WEEK-DAYS.												
			11	12	13	14	15	16	17	18	19	20			
				PAS.	PAS.	Mixed		PAS.	PAS.	PAS.	PAS.	PAS.			
Mls.			a.m.	a.m.	a.m.	a.m.	p.m.	p.m.	p.m.	p.m.	p.m.	p.m.			
—	**DUBLIN** Harcourt St.)	dep.	...	9 55	...	11E 0	...	...	1s 0	1E10	1 30	2s 5	...	...	...
¾	Ranelagh ...	,,	...	9 59	...	11E 4	...	...	1s 4	1E13	1 34	2s 9	...	...	...
1¼	Milltown Halt	,,	...	10 2	...	11E 7	...	...	1s 7	1E15	1 37	2s12	...	...	...
3	Dundrum ...	,,	...	10 7	...	11E15	...	...	1s12	1E19	1 42	2s17	...	...	...
5¼	Stillorgan Halt	,,	...	10 13	...	11E21	...	...	1s18	1E24	1 48	2s23	...	...	...
6	Foxrock ...	,,	...	10 16	...	11E26	...	...	1s21	1E26	1 51	2s26	...	...	...
7¼	Carrickmines W	,,	...	10 19	...	11E29	...	...	1s24	...	1 54	2s29	...	...	...
9¾	Shankill ...	,,	...	10 24	...	11E34	...	...	1s29	...	1 59	2s34	...	...	...
12¼	BRAY ... {	arr.	...	10 30	...	11E50	...	...	1s35	...	2 5	2s40	...	...	...
	{	dep.	...	...	...	...	...	1E28	1s51	...	...	...	...	...	...
17	**GREYSTONES**	arr.	...	...	...	...	...	1E40	2s 3	...	...	...	...	...	...

The Harcourt Street line from the 1947 working timetable

shortage, especially up to and including the last war. They were finally withdrawn in July 1949. It might be said that Dr Drumm's invention has not received the acclaim it deserves and with spiralling fuel costs we may yet see its reintroduction in a modified form.

The old D & SER section continued without significant changes until full nationalisation took place under the banner of Córas Iompair Éireann in 1945. A number of inquiries into future rail policy were held some of which painted a gloomy picture. The 1950s saw a steady decline in the use of suburban trains out of Dublin partly as a result of the phasing out of trams and the introduction of faster bus services. The inevitable inquiry came up with the equally inevitable findings: loss-making branch lines to be closed, the number of stations reduced and buses to be used as feeders. Still passenger numbers declined with the greater use of private transport, but no-one expected major changes on what were the D & SER lines.

Harcourt Street closure

Then in 1958 the bombshell dropped. CIE announced that after a 'detailed survey' it had decided to close the line between Harcourt Street station and Shanganagh Junction where it joined the coast route near Bray. It was a colossal blunder, a decision of paralysing stupidity and shortsightedness. No other closure in Ireland has generated such antagonism and bitterness for the protests were not of the token variety associated with the ending of services on a minor branch line; there was universal condemnation of the decision then and later.

Dublin at the time was just beginning its vast urban expansion with new housing estates appearing all round the city. Petrol however was still cheap and most people drove to work. CIE justified itself by saying a shrinking number of passengers were using the service and as many travelled from Bray they could therefore go to Westland Row. A totally inadequate bus service was substituted, no 86, which took twice as long as the train then and, later, three times as long. It was then cut back to terminate at Cabinteely.

Despite a heated controversy in the newspapers and on the air, CIE went ahead with the closure from January 1 1959 and quickly lifted the rails hoping that this would end the matter. But every six months or so the closure comes up for discussion and the decision is roundly condemned. The name of C. S. (Tod) Andrews is frequently linked with this fiasco; whether he is personally responsible or not this whole business and the many closures around the country in 1963–4 took place during his reign as chairman of CIE. These included the Macmine to Waterford line (New Ross–Waterford staying open for goods only), Bagenalstown to Palace East and eleven stations on the remaining lines. Suburban services had been almost halved and Sandymount, Sydney Parade, Booterstown and Salthill stations closed several years before this and still the company's losses mounted. Fortunately the land on which the Harcourt Street service ran has not been sold which shows a vein of sanity. The bridges have been removed although the fine cut-stone viaduct over the Dodder at Milltown remains.

With growing traffic chaos in the city the turn in suburban services came and has been increasing steadily since. A number of stations were reopened in the 1970s (Sydney Parade, Booterstown) and services at peak hours increased. For many trains it is standing room only. Outmoded stock is still being used and yet most commuters have nothing but praise for the way train crews continue to provide a regular service despite storms or strikes. The electrification promises to greatly improve the service with peak time trains every few minutes and late night trains as well.

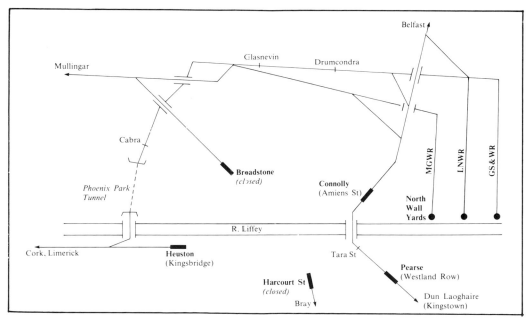

The Dublin railway network as at 1983

It is noteworthy that Ireland's first railway, the Dublin and Kingstown, despite being run by another company, kept its independence right up to the 1925 amalgamation and that it should be part of the first line to be adapted under the new electrification scheme. Long may it continue.

3 The Great Southern and Western Railway

WITH a total mileage at its peak of 1,150, this was the largest of the Irish railway companies: in its own words the 'Premier Line'. As the name suggests its trains ran to most of the south and south–west of the country from its Kingsbridge headquarters.

In 1842 a group of Dublin businessmen, seeing the success of the D & KR and the Ulster Railway, was granted leave to construct a line between the capital and the ancient town of Cashel in Co. Tipperary. This was to be the first stage in a trunk line to Cork with branches to all the major towns of Munster. The town with its majestic Rock became so closely associated with the GS & WR that for many years the share stock of the company was known as 'cashels'.

The relatively slow development of railways in Ireland made the GS & WR project all the more welcome. In 1841 *The Times* commented:

> It is much to be regretted that the concurrence of various causes, political and financial, has prevented the capitalist from turning his attention to Ireland; and in no respect could his capital be more usefully employed, so far at least as regards the country, than in the construction of railways.

Demise of the Grand Canal

The sentiments were admirable but before they could become a reality a bitter dispute arose between the fledgling concern and the Grand Canal Company whose waterways would be quite obsolete once the railway was built. In 1844 a pamphlet appeared, challenging the Dublin–Cashel line of the GS & WR which claimed that it spelt ruin for the canal (as indeed it did). The Grand Canal Company proposed a desperate compromise to share the fruits of railway expansion which would allow it to build an atmospheric line from Dublin to Sallins with the latter an interchange with the GS & WR. This involved a terminus at Portobello, the canal basin and double tracks parallel to the waterway.

An unusual solution to the impasse was suggested by James Pim in a letter to George Carr, chairman of the GS & WR. He felt the two companies should merge to build a joint line from Sallins to Galway along the Grand Canal banks. At a notional £2,000 per mile he felt 'there can be no rational doubt of its early and complete success'.

The following year the railway came back with a stinging dismissal of such plans. In a pamphlet, entitled rather innocently, 'Remarks on the Dublin Terminus of the Cashel or Great Southern and Western Railway', it claimed that building a terminal station at Portobello would involve great demolition and enormous disruption of roads and traffic to and from the city. Fair enough but less easy to defend was the argument that 'a terminus at Portobello would be more expensive to make—and when made, would be inconvenient to the public, and disadvantageous to the city'. The great handicap to Kingsbridge (Heuston) station has always been its remoteness from the city centre.

Nonetheless the company rose to the challenge of isolation by saying that its terminus was 'on the centre line of the city', i.e. the Liffey. This of course is not the same as being in the centre, for Celbridge in Co. Kildare is on the centre line too. The quays, it claimed, gave 'two, open, level, and straight lines of approach' to the station which was near the Smithfield cattle market and within easy reach of the Custom House Quay by boat. Again the accessibility claim could be challenged: there was severe congestion at Watling Street Bridge on the south quays caused by a narrow archway known as the Richmond Tower. Instead of having it demolished the railway eventually paid for it to be removed intact to its present site and it now stands as a delightful castellated entrance to the Royal Hospital at Kilmainham.

Finally, to seal the dispute, the GS&WR argued that a double line of track along the canal would be difficult and expensive to build, requiring a large number of new bridges. Also impractical was the notion of basing the goods depot at James's Street and that for passengers at Portobello. There is a touch of overkill in the arguments of the railway lobby but they did have the stronger case and the outcome was clear from the start. In brief: the canal company folded.

Mapping the route

Having disposed of this little problem the company got on with building its railway. John MacNeill had prepared a preliminary report on the route in 1844, estimating the cost including the Carlow branch at £1,300,000 or £11,000 per mile with a schedule of two years. The cost was optimistic, for even taking account of lower land prices and construction expenses all round, it was one sixth of the amount estimated for the London to Birmingham line which was 12 miles longer. Interesting to read are MacNeill's suggestions for extensions. He proposed a line from Holy Cross to Limerick (never built) and Cashel to Clonmel (this became Thurles–Clonmel). Then to the horror of the Midland Great Western Railway he advocated a frontal assault on their territory with a line from Celbridge to Mullingar and even as far as Galway! The Irish railway companies had a generally unspoken gentlemen's agreement to keep within their own territory, hence the geographical accuracy of their titles. This was nothing short of an invasion and caused bad feeling for many years to come, although the GS&WR got no nearer than a branch from Portarlington to Athlone.

Construction began in January 1845 and with the celebrated William Dargan as one of the chief contractors progress was good. Trains began operating to Carlow on 4 August 1846 and to Portlaoise in June 1847. Three months later Ballybrophy was on the railway map and this was the scene of one of the first recorded railway murders in Ireland. John D'Arcy, a labourer on the line was charged that on 13 November 1847 he 'did kill and murder, one Michael Smith, by striking him with a stone of no value on the left side of the head'. D'Arcy had fled and joined the army in Cork to escape the law, but he and the military had a violent disagreement. He boasted of the murder to all and sundry so that in due course he was arrested, tried and executed at Ballybrophy on 23 March 1848.

Thurles got its trains on 13 March 1848 and here too we may deviate to record the majesty of the law in action. For Thurles saw the arrest of the fenian William Smith O'Brien on 5 August that year. A London and North Western Railway guard on temporary assignment in Ireland pointed him out to the police who moved in force to arrest him. The informer returned to England with his reward and bought a public house on the proceeds. But it is said he was his own best customer and died from over-indulgence of his beverage.

O'Brien must have been a regular traveller on the line as well as being a literary chap with classical leanings. He is the author of a pretty little sonnet entitled 'Lines written in the railway train while proceeding from Ballybrophy to Dublin, January 29 1848'. It is rare enough for Clondalkin to keep company with spondees and dactyls.

> Nunc via nos ducit iucundo ferrea motu
> Atque aestus currum pellit pollente vapore,
> At odor insuavis nares offendit et aegrum
> Efficit e nostris unum qui Maior habetur.
> Progredimur ceterum cursu fervente rotarum.
> Haud mora! Transimus civitatem Virginis almae.
> Iam sanctae Brigidae antiquam accedimus aram.
> Iam sese attolit Clondalkin in aeltera turris
> Ardua, iamque nobis Dublini marmia clara
> Apparent, statimque domos et templa videmus.
> Finis opus, dixit sapiens, sic nosque coronat.
> Nunc via finita est—finitum carmen habemus.

Loosely translated:

> The railway draws us on with soothing motion as heat propels the engine, billowing smoke. But the unpleasant smell makes one of us sick, Major by name. Still we rush on, the wheels spinning round. There is no delay as now we pass the town of the gentle virgin (Portlaoise) and arrive at the venerable shrine of holy Brigid (Kildare). Already the lofty tower of Clondalkin looms up and the buildings of Dublin are plain to see. At once we spy her churches and houses. 'The end is the work's crown' said the sage and so it is. Our journey is over and we have finished our poem.

Returning to more prosaic matters: the Famine was by this time at its height and many poor wretches kept body and soul together by working on the line. Official help was very slow but one effort was made by Lord George Bentinck when he appealed to the Commons in February 1847 for government funds to speed up railway construction. In particular he sought £500,000 for the GS & WR to employ 50,000 labourers.

Another active campaigner was John Porter who, in the same year, published his 'Observations upon our present railway system in Ireland'. Porter stated that construction costs were much lower in Ireland than in England because of the flatter landscape, lower wages and the ability to draw on the experience and errors of English companies. He strongly advocates railway investment and castigates landowners 'for they require not merely a high but an exhorbitant price for their half-cultivated acres, as if the Railway was rather an enemy or a stranger to be plundered, than their best friend to be welcomed'. He goes on:

> I believe that Ireland without railways means Ireland without manufactures, without industry, without any commercial life or spirit . . . and our gauge of five feet three inches is much better than the English gauge of four feet eight and a half inches.

Public opinion in railway directors, he says, is low and argues for a central railway board in Dublin instead of referring almost every decision to London as was common up to then. Porter believed that mismanagement was rife, saying that within months of the Carlow line opening road competition from carmen revived spectacularly on account of a rise in railway fares. He finishes with a *cri de coeur* against faceless administrations: 'A corporation of men has neither a soul to be damned, a body to be kicked or a name to be honoured'!

With trains running to and from Thurles, the GS & WR was within fifteen miles of its original planned terminus at Cashel. But curiously enough the company decided to by-pass the town whose name was linked so closely and became almost synonymous with it from the earliest days. By coincidence the Waterford and Limerick was planned to include the town but was also diverted at the last minute. It was not until 1904 that the GS & WR built a branch from Goold's Cross. The station nestled quite spectacularly at the foot of the Rock and, as a further extension was planned, it was a temporary building. But the ad hoc facilities became permanent and, despite the tourist potential, the branch was never a success and closed in 1947.

Kingsbridge

What sort of a terminus did the Premier Line build for its headquarters? It was and remains a magnificent building. Twenty plans were submitted and that of the English architect, Sancton Wood, was accepted. D'Alton's *Memoir of the GS & WR* (1846) describes it as 'one of the handsomest structures in the Metropolis, consisting of a noble centre, with wings and clock towers, all built of granite, and all according to the design of Mr Woods, a celebrated London architect'. D'Alton goes on:

> The principal front... consists of a central pile, two stories high, the lower rusticated, from which spring Corinthian pillars supporting the cornice which surmounts the upper storey; at each side are wings the height of the basement storey, from which rise handsome clock-towers.

Some compared it to a renaissance house and Charles Hamilton Ellis, the distinguished railway writer, said it was among the most meritorious railway buildings in Europe. There is no doubt the granite facade has lasted well and it dominates the approach from the city centre. Fortunately there are no office blocks nearby to spoil the effect. The main passenger entrance is still imposing with its fine detail and the eight exterior columns. The train shed was designed by John MacNeill with 2½ acres of roofing, 72 cast iron pillars and 150 gas lamps. New platforms have been added, the gas lamps are gone and there is a useful if rather ugly destination board over the departure area but apart from that the interior is remarkably unchanged. There is no need now for the gantries which once transferred carriages from one platform to another but no 1 platform is still known as the 'military platform' from the number of troop trains which left from it. There are several barracks in the area and it was possible to deliver squadrons of soldiers directly to this (uncovered) platform for onward shipment without bringing them into contact with more refined travellers in the main station area.

En route

Inchicore was the main engineering works for the railway and remains the same for CIE. The buildings were also designed by Sancton Wood in a mock tudor style and have a very distinctive appearance—almost folly-like with their towers and battlements. The works now cover 73 acres and over 1,000 people work there.

Within the area is the Inchicore Model School, founded by the GS & WR for the education of the workers' children. Wood's handiwork can be seen in the stations between Monasterevan and Limerick Junction, all of which are quite different yet with the characteristic slender windows and diamond glass.

The line crosses the Curragh outside Newbridge with its own station near the racetrack. The company built a new stand for the owners, designed by Wood, in gratitude for being released from the obligation to build walls the length of the Curragh preventing horses being startled or worse by passing trains.

Past Inchicore is the suburban station of Clondalkin now closed but ripe for development as there is a large housing estate there. Like Kingsbridge it was designed by Wood and, as D'Alton describes it in his 1846 *Memoir*, is 'a handsome specimen of the Elizabethan style of architecture, in which all the station-houses on the line are constructed'. Equally keen was the *Irish Railway Gazette* which said it was

> an exceedingly handsome edifice. We may state indeed that they are all finished, and have been designed with a view to permanence and utility. The accommodation they contain is most ample; and while they are really beautiful structures, they are simple in their details, and most substantially built.

Meanwhile Dargan won the contract for the section from Thurles to Cork at a cost of £600,000, his largest project to date and an indication of his supreme reputation. Luckily the appeal to Lord Bentinck was successful and the company was granted £500,000 by way of a loan. In this way the construction could continue at a great pace and Limerick Junction was reached on 3 July 1848 where the Waterford and Limerick Railway made a connection. There was a big celebration at this point despite the disturbances of the time.

Limerick Junction has an almost worldwide reputation as the classic Irish railway station, some of it more than justified. Its quaintness lies in the eccentric working it requires on account of the layout; how it survived virtually unchanged as a mainline junction well into the second half of this century is a mystery. For a start it is about 21 miles from Limerick and is in fact in Co. Tipperary, but its chief fascination derives from the layout. Until 1967 every train which stopped there had to complete at least one reversal to reach the platform. Isolated from any village (the nearest is Tipperary town three miles away) it consists of a long island

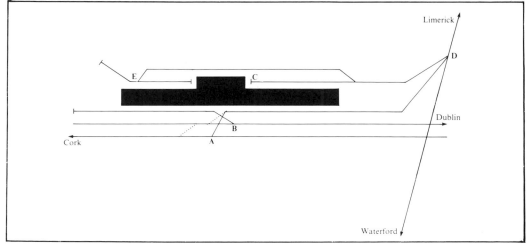

Limerick Junction before layout changes in 1967; the new track is shown by a dotted line

platform with a series of bays and crossovers. A Dublin–Cork train ran through the station well away from the platform until it was past point A. Then it reversed back over the track until it came alongside the upper half of the platform. Cork–Dublin trains ran past point B and then reversed back to the opposite end of the station so that the two trains ended up facing each other. A train going from Waterford to Limerick ran completely past the station and then reversed back into the bay platform at C. However a Waterford bound train performed the greatest gymnastic tricks. Leaving the main line at D apparently heading for the bay platform it swung away at the last minute, ran round the main buildings heading for the nearby siding and having passed point E then completed the obligatory reversal into the other bay platform. Thus it ended up facing Cork and had to repeat the procedure the other way round to continue to Waterford.

Generous timetable margins were allowed for all these manoevrings so that it is not surprising that a first class buffet room developed at the Junction since so much time was spent there. Of course such arrangements could not continue for ever and in 1967 a number of alterations were made which eliminated many but not all of the reversals. Trains to and from Cork can now get direct access to the platform but still end up facing each other. There is also a link now so that Dublin to Limerick trains need not call at the Junction at all.

Writing of these changes the *Railway Magazine* said that, while purists and strict conservationists might object, no railway could continue to exist in a syrup of

Preserved GS & WR engine no. 186 on a steam excursion at Dun Laoghaire. Built in 1879 it is now owned by the RPSI

preservation. Today the Junction is not as busy as it once was, but at certain times of the day in summer it is thronged when trains from Dublin, Tralee, Limerick and Waterford converge on the place at the one time. If the line from Waterford closes then all that will change. There is a delightfully witty and readable account in an article entitled 'A Day the Junction', *Journal of the IRRS*.

Work on building the stretch from Limerick Junction to Mallow was also fast and, despite the unsuitable ground, finished on 19 March 1849. Immediately south of the town the line crosses the River Blackwater and here a large ten arch viaduct was built. From there to Cork the railway runs through difficult country which called for a great deal of excavation work. Even so the first special to a temporary station at Blackpool outside Cork ran on 18 October doing the trip from Dublin in 5½ hours. Eleven days later the first regular service to Dublin began with two through trains in each direction; the faster did the journey in 7 hours while the other stopped everywhere and took 12 hours, no less.

At the same time work went on digging the tunnel (1,355 yards) into the city of Cork, a slow laborious business. It was not until 3 December 1855 that trains began running through the tunnel, down the steep incline to a terminus at the quays. This was replaced by the present station in 1893. It is an attractive red brick building, quite unlike the first terminus at Penrose's Marsh with its white limestone and the row of Doric columns. Arriving there the passenger from Dublin bursts from the long, dripping tunnel into the bright, airy station which is built on a sharp bend. There was once a railway hotel attached but this is now used for offices. In the main passenger entrance there is a fine old locomotive on display, dating from 1848. It is a Bury 2-2-2 no 36 and stands on some original GS&WR rails. As one of the best examples of early railway engineering in the country it is well worth seeing.

Cork suburban lines: Youghal and Cobh

West from Cork ran the self-explanatory Cork and Youghal Railway, originally sanctioned in 1854, and opened in 1860–1. The same company built the short branch to Queenstown (Cobh or 'Cobb H' as it was known to British sailors before the last war). Closely involved with it was a maverick businessman by name D. Leopold Lewis, a devotee of the grand gesture. To inspire confidence in his shaky ventures (he was twice bankrupt already) he offered to buy back any shares purchased, at the original price plus 40%! He went on to throw a huge banquet for the workmen on completion of the line, bought a steamer on the Blackwater and the entire town of Youghal from the Duke of Devonshire. At this point the bubble burst and he went bankrupt for the third and last time: here endeth the career of D. Leopold Lewis.

Unfortunately the C&YR crashed at the same time as Mr Lewis but by now the GS&WR was well on the way to buying it, at a bargain price as it turned out.

Youghal is a pleasant town and a popular seaside resort. It lost its regular passenger service in 1963 but up to a few years ago there were passenger trains on Sundays in summer from Cork. These have had to be suspended because of CIE's shortage of rolling stock. The Cobh branch is a very pleasant excursion, passing as it does over a pair of viaducts to reach Great Island on which the town is situated. From the middle of the last century transatlantic liners began to call there to pick up mail and passengers, greatly adding to the traffic on the line. Mail trains from Dublin began to run through to the port from 1876 and continued to do so until

1922. Most famous of these was the *American Mail* which cut several hours off the journey from London to America. It involved changes at Holyhead, Kingstown and Cork; no great problem for the much encumbered travelling Victorian with his host of valets and servants.

The train from Kingsbridge took $4\frac{1}{2}$ hours to Cork where all transferred to a boat for the run to Cobh until the opening of the railway. A further simplification took place when the Dublin loop line opened in 1892 and the *American Mail* ran (picturesquely) from Kingstown to Queenstown. By then the journey had been cut to four hours and as well as the express to meet the Cunard liners there was a second weekly service for the White Star Line, owners of the ill-fated *Titanic* which was built in Belfast and whose last port of call was Cobh.

There was intense competition for the mails contract both for its revenue and prestige. Punctual running was vital and these trains took precedence over all others. One passenger a Mr Piza, with exceptionally urgent business in America left London for Queenstown on 15 December 1892. He chose to go via Kingstown but on arrival there missed his connection for Cork. Being in a hurry he decided the only thing was to hire a train to get him to Cobh in time for the sailing. A charge of £44.10.0 was quickly agreed with the GS & WR which supplied an engine and one carriage without delay. Mr Piza sat back in his private train which did the run in 3 hours 25 minutes but on reaching Cobh, to his dismay, there was the *SS Teutonic* slowly steaming out of the harbour. Not to be outdone Mr Piza immediately hired a fast tender and set off in hot pursuit after the liner which was then at half speed. He succeeded in reaching it and was cheered aboard by his fellow passengers.

The liners ceased to call in 1914 after the mail stops were transferred to Holyhead and Fishguard. Cobh still has quite a busy commuter service from Cork with up to 14 trains a day in each direction. Unfortunately there are disturbing rumours of possible closure but given the other transport deprivations in the Cork area it is hoped this will not happen.

In the same year that Youghal saw its first trains the GS & WR also opened its branch from Mallow to Fermoy. The line was 17 miles long and was built by Dargan although on this occasion he underestimated the cost by more than half, largely accounted for by the substantial viaduct at Kilcummer. For many years this was the route of boat trains between Rosslare and Cork until its closure in 1967 when services were diverted through Limerick Junction. Fares for the through journey continued to be worked out as per the original route. From Fermoy there ran the 12 mile branch to Mitchelstown which opened in 1891 and merged fully with the GS & WR in 1900.

More significant was the junction at Fermoy with that curious animal the Fishguard and Rosslare Railways and Harbours Company. This was an example of railway control spanning the Irish Sea through the expansionist activities of the English Great Western Railway (see below).

Rails into the Kingdom

West from Mallow ran the Killarney Junction Railway to the famous tourist resort of that name. Once again Dargan was in action and this time his sums were more accurate. The line opened in 1853 and before long tourists were flocking in by train, many to stay at the celebrated Railway Hotel which is today known as the Great Southern Hotel and excellently run by a subsidiary of CIE. It was the first railway hotel and opened on 11 July 1854. Further on was the Tralee and Killarney Railway which left from a junction some distance from Killarney station. The latter was meant to be a terminus—obviously the promoters felt that further into Kerry one dared not go. So once again there is a strange reversal procedure although not quite as strenuous as at Limerick Junction. The Tralee train arriving from Mallow pulls in as normal at the platform. On departure it must reverse about ¼ mile back down the track clear of the junction. It can then proceed on its way up a steep incline which sweeps away to the right past Killarney station. The reverse applies for trains in the other direction.

The GS & WR invested large sums in both these companies and took them over completely in May 1860. The route is through wild and beautiful country with gorse bushes brushing against the carriage window as the train hurtles through jagged limestone cuttings with the Kerry mountains as a backdrop. There are a number of stops on the way at beautifully kept little stations in the middle of nowhere where a few people get on and fewer get off. It is a constant amazement to find the brassy commercialism of Killarney in the middle of this wild and lonesome beauty.

'A magnificent undertaking'

The year 1860 is a good point to take stock of just what the GS & WR had achieved. It had built 350 track miles and was well on the way to establishing itself as one of the best run railways in the country. Morale among staff was high for employment prospects on the railway were good and the men took pride in their work. Wages were above average and even then clerical staff worked only an eight hour day. For unskilled workers there was a thirteen hour day. Even so, with an average of ten trains a day passing through, life in a country station should not be compared with a cotton mill or a steel works. There was plenty of opportunity for extra-curricular activities, some of which landed the participants in trouble. For example, the stationmasters at Thurles and Templemore were severely reprimanded for slipping off to Cashel together for a flutter on the races during a slack period. Worse, they had travelled by train without paying their fare! Other distractions were dogs, cards, gaming and of course the Demon Drink. The company issued repeated notices and threats of fines, suspension and dismissal for anyone found under the influence. While specifically forbidding staff to keep pigs or goats in their cottages it was generous in response to dedicated service and in welfare schemes was well ahead of its time.

The number of directors had been cut from 27 to a more manageable 16, which made for an efficient and profitable railway, so the overall impression of most visitors was favourable. Sir Charles Roney came to Ireland and wrote his little book *How to spend a month in Ireland* in 1861. He travelled a good deal on the railways, particulary the GS & WR and had this to say:

> Irish railways have hitherto given much better dividends to their shareholders than railways with similar receipts in England or Scotland, the reason being that the working expenses are less in proportion to receipts . . . But it should be stated on the whole, the speed is less, and there are fewer trains running than on English or Scotch lines of railway.

Even more fulsome was *The Irish Times* which in 1867 described the GS & WR as 'a magnificent undertaking of which Ireland should be proud. . . . Everything about it is as solid as granite . . . it is admirably managed'. High praise indeed.

Unfriendly rivals

Less inspiring was the constant bickering with other companies, in particular the Midland Great Western. The GS&WR had always had an eye on the west as a source of traffic and had prepared plans for a line at least as far as Athlone. This was, at that time as now, an important business centre, one of the main Shannon crossing points and had a large military presence for speedy despatch to the turbulent parts of Connacht. Such was the traffic in personnel and equipment that the original 1850s rails could be seen until quite recently in the artillery loading bays. The potential in railway services was worth arguing over.

A split at board level had produced the MGWR and relations between the two groups remained poor. Many of the battles were fought in Parliament: when one company produced extension plans the other immediately slapped down a counter proposal. Accusations flew back and forth of traffic poaching and the two bodies went to extraordinary lengths to divert passengers and goods over their own lines. For example the MGWR at one time issued excursion tickets from Dublin to Killarney deep in its rival's territory. The journey involved taking the (MGWR) train to Athlone, a steamer (the MGWR owned *Duchess of Argyll* or *Artizan*) from Athlone to Tarbert and thence to Killarney by road. This whole affair took two days, no less, while the ordinary GS&WR train from Dublin took about six hours. The latter did manage to push its stunted branch as far as Athlone but it never reached its potential. The line forked off the route to Cork at the pleasant station of Portarlington. This has the tallest signal cabin in Ireland, built it is said to spot a MGWR invasion while it was still far off.

The row came to an ignominious end in the noted year of 1860 when respective territory was delineated like the fifteenth century treaty which divided the new world, east and west between Spain and Portugal by an imaginary line down the length of the Atlantic. On a smaller scale the MGWR was to have the area north and west of a line between Dublin, Kildare and Athlone; the GS&WR agreed to take the territory south and east of it. Partition often causes problems in Ireland. In addition, each company promised not to sneak off and grab the moribund Grand Canal without telling the other.

Limerick had always been a goal of the GS&WR route planners and the fact that the Waterford and Limerick Railway got there first in 1848 did not dampen their enthusiasm. It was quite a large city and an important maritime and industrial centre—many of the uniforms worn by both sides in the American Civil War were made there. There were the inevitable dreams of the city becoming the main trans-atlantic packet station and the 1836 promoters canvassed Limerick as having no shortage of 'good houses for the billetting of troops before and after sea voyages'. Naturally the residents were not so keen on sharing their homes with battalions of homesick and/or seasick soldiers and the scheme failed.

The GS&WR decided to launch the assault by a flanking manoeuvre. The Roscrea and Parsonstown (Birr) Junction Railway was promoted with GS&WR backing for a branch off the Cork line at Ballybrophy and opened as far as Roscrea in October 1857. Then abandoning all subterfuge the company announced its plan to extend to Limerick. The W&LR objected but to no avail, and from 1 June 1864 trains ran from Limerick to Nenagh operated jointly by the GS&WR and the W&LR, an uneasy alliance which lasted up to the amalgamation.

In the same area was the line which of all Irish railways must be the prime candidate for inclusion in the roll of Heroic Failures. This was the Parsonstown and

Portumna Bridge, known as the 'stolen railway'. It began its shaky existence in 1861 when the Earl of Clanricarde gained authority to build the 12 mile branch. The public was slow to match its verbal support with ready cash so the promoters resorted to lending money to buy shares and bribery to gain the backing of certain people. Two contractors tried and failed to complete the line until the third made it in 1868. After grudging approval from the Board of Trade inspector the line was leased to the GS & WR for ten years. Two trains only ran each day at around 6 am and 9.30 pm, hardly timings which would attract a host of passengers. In addition the line stopped a mile short of Portumna because the bridge in the title was unsafe to carry rail traffic. The ten years' operation were a disaster and the GS & WR could not get rid of a liability, which cost it £2,000 a year in losses, fast enough. The owners blamed the larger company but could not force it to renew the lease so that the minimal service stopped and the creditors swarmed in to get whatever was left. A vast and almost coordinated campaign of looting and pillage began: sleepers, rails, signals, signposts, ballast, footbridges, even Portumna station buildings disappeared one night! That finished the P & PBR.

Kerry branches

With the increase in traffic following the opening of the lines to Killarney and Tralee the GS & WR turned its attention to extensions towards the coast of Kerry. As mentioned in Chapter 1, Charles Vignoles had planned an extravagant route from Dublin to Valentia but nothing had come of it. Nonetheless the idea of such extensions was sown and permission for a line to Killorglin was granted in 1871 although construction did not begin for another twelve years. The branch opened to Killorglin in 1885 from a junction at Farranfore. To promote the extension the government offered to finance the continuation to Valentia and so, not surprisingly,

Loo Bridge station on the Kenmare line

the GS&WR lost no time in starting work. The terrain was extremely difficult and many tunnels and earthworks were needed. The main town on the route was Cahirciveen and the line followed the south shore of Dingle Bay. There were spectacular views on the branch as the railway clung to a narrow ledge cut into the hillside. The line opened to Valentia on 12 September 1893 and the station had the distinction of being the most westerly in Europe; it was near the berth for the ferry to Valentia Island with its telegraph station and meteorological office. Surprisingly, services on the line lasted until 1960, a good deal longer than many branches with heavier traffic. Today the path of the railway can still be seen from the road with its fine bridges and honeycomb of tunnels through the rock.

The Kenmare branch left the main line at Headford Junction and ran for 20 miles through equally difficult country. It too was built with state funds and work started in December 1890. The line was completed three years later and had even fewer stations of any size than the Valentia line. The chief traffic potential was seen to be from tourists and fish, both of which were hooked in great quantities in that part of Kerry. Unfortunately they were also rather seasonal and erratic so that periods of great activity alternated with a slump in the demand for transport. The only truly reliable source of revenue was from cattle specials which ran in connection with the regular cattle fairs. Nonetheless the railway built a fine hotel at Kenmare, later to become a Great Southern Hotel which only recently passed from CIE ownership. The GS&WR advertised the town as the starting point for 'the Prince of Wales Tour' of the Kerry peninsula and offered many excursion tickets and inclusive offers to attract passengers to this beautiful part of the country.

Dublin connections

Being a mile from O'Connell Bridge the directors of the GS&WR soon found that despite all their publicity to the contrary Kingsbridge Station was a little removed from the city centre. (Today buses are used to carry train passengers on the final stretch.) In addition the lack of connection between the five Dublin termini added to the company's isolation. So when plans for a link up were first mooted the GS&WR was a strong supporter. The MGWR was quick off the mark and opened its Liffey branch in 1864 so as to ease the transfer of cattle arriving from the Midlands for onward shipment from the quays. The obvious solution was for the GS&WR to link up with its former enemy and share the line along the Royal Canal to the river. A further willing partner was the English London & North Western Railway which had a short spur at the North Wall and welcomed the idea of access to the south and south–west.

The branch left the main line just short of Kingsbridge, crossed the Liffey at a pleasant tree-lined spot and tunnelled under the Phoenix Park near the Wellington Monument (described by George IV as 'that overgrown milestone'). It went under the Royal Canal and emerged near Cabra where extensive sidings were built for the cattle market. From there it joined the MGWR line and ran down to the warehouses and the docks. The line opened in 1877 and soon after the GS&WR ran a service to connect with the L&NWR steamers operating between Holyhead and the North Wall.

The English company had its own station in Dublin, an unusual design which reflects its cross-channel origins. Nearby it also ran its own hotel to fortify passengers before or help them recuperate after the sea voyage. It is an attractive building but has suffered some neglect over the years and is now British Rail's headquarters in Ireland. (A good way to see it between the warehouses is from across the river: 5p on the Liffey ferry.)

This arrangement continued more or less satisfactorily for a number of years, although the GS & WR was not wild about paying a large annual rent to its old rival. The company was relieved, therefore, when in 1894 an independent group announced plans for a suburban line from Glasnevin to the North Wall. Support for it was lacking so in 1897 the board at Kingsbridge decided to build the line which was ready in 1901. It runs parallel to the Midland's but, unlike it, it is raised well above street level. The next stage was to join the line out of Amiens Street (Great Northern) and this took place in 1906. Thus the GS & WR was connected with almost every line in Dublin.

Early in the century there was a short-lived suburban service between Kingsbridge and Amiens Street stations. Seven trains ran daily in each direction, calling at Drumcondra and Glasnevin. But for some reason they were little used, perhaps because of poor connections or different commuting patterns and they were withdrawn before long in 1907. Drumcondra has gained a new lease of life as the base of the Irish Railway Record Society and both stations may be reopened as part of the urban transport development scheme. Few passenger trains use the complete branch although up to a few years ago the boat train from Dun Laoghaire ran to Connolly and on to Heuston via the GS & WR link line. Of course the branch is greatly used by goods trains from the yards at the North Wall.

Rosslare lines

Mention has been made of the Fishguard and Rosslare Railways and Harbours Company. In 1882 an independent company opened the line between Waterford and Rosslare then confusingly known as Greenore. The enterprise was not a great success and by 1894 services were being provided by the F & RR & HC, to be taken over in turn by the GS & WR four years later. At the same time the latter company was approached to take over the Waterford, Dungarvan and Lismore Railway which was by then in financial difficulties. A number of other companies became involved in the Rosslare–Mallow connection so that in the end no less than seven bodies were responsible for its construction. In 1906 the first regular packet service started between Fishguard and Rosslare, the pier area was greatly developed and trains were run to meet the sailings on both sides of the channel. The stations between Rosslare and Waterford are unusual in that they are all built to an island platform design which is quite rare in Ireland. Thus right up to the amalgamation the line from Fermoy to Wexford was shown on the GS & WR map as a leased line. Indeed when CIE regrettably decided to close part of the route in the late 1960s there were endless legal complications which arose from the fact that it was owned jointly by CIE and British Rail, the successor to the GWR.

The main incentive for the GS & WR's sponsorship of this project was to capture the valuable traffic from England to the south of Ireland. The mails contract came up for renewal regularly and there was fierce competition for it. A similar urgency led to the building of the City of Dublin Junction Railway in 1891 and although the GS & WR kept its involvement to a minimum it benefited greatly from the direct link between Kingsbridge and Westland Row. Incidentally one of the advantages of the ugly iron bridge over the Liffey is that while crossing it the passenger has a delightful aerial view up and down the length of the river.

The Waterford and Limerick Railway

The first railway authorised for construction in Ireland was the Waterford and Limerick Railway which received parliamentary approval in 1826, a year after the Stockton and Darlington. The line was not built at that time and the Dublin and Kingstown was the first railway to open in 1834. However there was a sizeable company in existence with the original name which ran its first trains between Limerick and Tipperary on 9 May 1848. A succession of engineers worked on the line including Vignoles and the construction work was by Dargan. At Tipperary work halted for two years before Dargan was instructed to proceed to Waterford. He reached the city in 1854 and regular services began running to Limerick whose station was ready in 1858. It is a spacious building of grey stone and unlike the Waterford terminal is very close to the city and has plenty of facilities for freight, parking and buses. South from Limerick was the Foynes branch and the North Kerry line. The companies which built these lines were partly controlled by the W&LR and the GS&WR. Also prominent among the shareholders was Dargan who saw great potential in the port of Foynes. When the railway reached the town in 1858 he ran a steamer there, the *Kelpie*, from Kilrush and Tarbert. Dargan hoped that Foynes would one day be the American packet station (of course!) but this never came about. After a few years the *Kelpie* was sold off and became a blockade runner in the American Civil War, then at its height and was sunk while engaged in that dangerous occupation.

The link up with the GS&WR at Tralee was finally made in December 1880, all services being provided by the W&LR. The takings were never outstanding as there were few towns of any size on the way and the coastline seems to have been almost deliberately avoided. Three trains daily were more than enough to meet traffic demands. Another company operated by the W&LR was the Tralee and Fenit Railway whose eight mile branch opened on 5 July 1887. It too had its financial problems and before long had lost its nominal independence.

Right from the start the W&LR had exceptionally close links with the GWR at Paddington. The English company was keen to develop lines in the south and south–west of Ireland which would draw traffic away from the rival concerns at Liverpool and Holyhead and in this it was quite successful. It helped the growing W&LR with generous loans and reduced tariffs which was just as well because strict economy was the keynote to the Irish company's operations. Staff, engines, carriages, wagons, repairs, all were cut to the minimum. If a locomotive broke down and could not be speedily fixed the service was simply cancelled rather than leasing a replacement from another company. Staff were forced to accept lower than average wages with further cuts from time to time. Needless to say, morale was low and the turnover high.

By contrast with this parsimony the company was ready to extend its route mileage by taking over other lines at the drop of a hat. The board members and senior officials changed almost as regularly as the ordinary staff and it was only with the arrival of William Malcolmson that a truly professional approach was adopted. He was a forceful if rather eccentric character who challenged inefficiency and sloppiness wherever he saw it. He also objected to running trains on Sundays and presented a free pass for three years to a local MP who supported his view.

In other ways the company was quite forward thinking. Fourth class travel was introduced by the issue of return tickets at $1\frac{1}{2}$ times the single fare but in open wagons. Free travel was offered to the Protestant Orphans' Society as well as food

Limerick to Ennis, Tuam and Sligo.

Distance from Limerick	UP TRAINS	Sectional Running 1 Pass.	Sectional Running 2 Goods	WEEK DAYS arr.	dep.	4 Mail Goods arr.	dep.	5 Pass. arr.	dep.	6 Tuam. Goods arr.	dep.	7 arr.	dep.	8 Pass. arr.	dep.
Mls.				a.m.	a.m.	a.m.	a.m.	a.m.	a.m.	a.m.	a.m.	p.m.	p.m.	p.m.	p.m.
—	**LIMERICK** W ¶ ●	**0**	**0**	...	...	...	**3 40**	...	**8 50**	...	**10 30**	...	...	...	**4 10**
	,, Goods Yard	...	...	...	...	...	...	...	...	...	...	...	...	...	...
4	LONGPAVEMENT HALT ¶	10	18	...	...	...	...	9 2	9 3	...	...	...	...	4 22	4 23
9¾	CRATLOE HALT ...	14	20	...	...	...	...	C.	R.	...	...	...	...	C.	R.
13	SIXMILEBRIDGE ...	6	9	...	...	...	...	9 27	9 28	11 21	11 35	...	...	4 47	4 48
16½	BALLYCAR ... +W ¶	6	14	...	...	...	...	9 36	9 37	11 53	12 9	...	...	4 56	4 57
19¾	ARDSOLLUS	6	13	...	...	...	...	9 45	9 46	12 26	12 38	...	...	5 5	5 6
22¾	CLARECASTLE ¶	6	10	...	...	...	...	9 54	9 55	12 52	1 9	...	...	5 14	5 17
24¾	**ENNIS** ... W ¶ ●	**3**	**7**	...	...	**5 15**	**6 14**	**10 0**	**10 5**	**1 20**	**3 30**	...	...	**5 22**	...
32½	CRUSHEEN ... ¶	16	27	...	...	...	...	10 23	10 24	4 1	4 25	...	...	...	...
36¾	TUBBER	7	13	...	...	...	...	10 33	10 34	4 42	4 55	...	...	...	...
42¼	GORT ... W ¶	11	14	...	...	...	...	10 47	10 51	5 13	5 55	...	...	...	...
49	ARDRAHAN ... ¶	10	20	...	...	...	...	11 3	11 5	6 19	6 50	...	...	...	...
55	CRAUGHWELL + ¶	11	16	...	...	...	...	11 18	11 23	7 10	7 35	...	...	...	...
60¼	**ATHENRY** ... ¶ ●	**10**	**17**	...	...	**8 5**	**9 25**	**11 35**	**3 10**	**7 56**	**9 10**	...	...	...	...
70	BALLYGLUNIN ¶	17	26	...	...	9 55	10 10	3 29	3 30	9 40	9 50	...	...	...	...
76	**TUAM** ... W ¶ ●	**11**	**18**	...	...	**10 32**	**12 30**	**3 43**	**3 48**	**10 12**	..	...	...	...	...
80¾	CASTLEGROVE N	8	12	...	...	12 46	12 55	3 58	3 59	...	...	...	...	...	...
85	MILLTOWN (Galway) ¶	9	13	...	...	1 12	1 37	4 10	4 11	...	...	...	...	...	...
88¾	BALLINDINE ... ¶	7	12	...	...	1 53	2 12	4 20	4 21	...	...	...	...	...	...
93¼	**CLAREMORRIS** W ¶ ●	**9**	**13**	...	...	**2 29**	**3 30**	**4 32**	**4 55**	...	...	...	...	...	...
102¾	KILTIMAGH ... ¶	21	30	...	...	4 4	4 25	5 18	5 20	...	...	...	...	...	...
110½	SWINFORD ... ¶	16	22	...	...	4 51	5 10	5 38	5 40	...	...	...	...	...	...
117¼	CHARLESTOWN + ¶	15	21	...	...	5 35	6 22	5 57	5 58	...	...	...	...	...	...
120¼	CURRY ... N	9	12	...	...	6 38	6 43	6 9	6 10	...	...	...	...	...	...
124	TUBBERCURRY W ¶ ⊛	9	13	...	...	7 0	7 45	6 21	6 26	...	...	...	...	...	...
129	CARROWMORE N	11	15	...	...	8 4	8 14	6 39	6 40	...	...	...	...	...	...
134½	LEYNY ... + ¶	12	14	...	...	8 32	8 44	6 54	6 55	...	...	...	...	...	...
139	COLLOONEY ... W	8	12	...	...	9 0	9 15	7 5	7 6	...	...	...	...	...	...
140¾	BALLYSODARE ¶	4	6	...	...	9 25	10 0	7 12	7 15	...	...	...	...	...	...
145¼	**SLIGO** ... W ●	**10**	**15**	...	...	**10 20**	...	**7 27**	...	...	...	...	...	...	...

W—Water Column. ¶ E.T. Staff Station. ⊛ Engine Turntable. N—No Telephone Communication.
C.R.—Stops to pick up or set down when required. +—See page 1A.

	16 S. L. & N. C. RAIL CAR		17 SATS. ONLY S. L. & N. C. MIXED		18 S. L. & N. C. RAIL CAR		19 S. L. & N. C. GOODS		20 S. L. & N. C. MIXED	
	a.m.	a.m.	p.m.	a.m.	p.m.	p.m.	p.m.	p.m.	p.m.	p.m.
BALLYSODARE ¶	...	8 55	...	11 55	...	4 0	...	6 30	...	10 10
SLIGO ... W ●	**9 5**	...	**12 5**	...	**4 10**	...	**6 45**	...	**10 25**	...

The Limerick–Sligo line and the SL&NCR from CIE's working timetable of 1947

and clothes destined for the victims of the 1870 Franco-Prussian war and while employees' wages were low there were generous premiums for low coal consumption which was always considered a greater priority than speed.

The Burma Road

Like the North Kerry line, the long west coast route from Limerick to Sligo was built by a bewildering array of companies. It was of course in the heart of MGWR country and that company viewed the arrival of the W&LR with the deepest suspicion. In 1859 the Limerick and Ennis Railway opened for business, closely followed by the Athenry and Tuam and the Athenry and Ennis Junction. Not being so adept they succeeded in getting the W&LR to take over their operations which with its expansionist policy the company eagerly did. Next on the scene was a body with the unwieldy title of the Athenry and Tuam Extension to Claremorris Light Railway; it was light in everything except name. Pushing northwards, connection was made with the MGWR at Claremorris and at Collooney.

An heroic failure

The Athenry and Ennis Junction had a most unfortunate history. From the start funds were in short supply and not having been paid for some time the contractor, not unreasonably, stopped work. Following an injection of capital the company handed over a large sum which the contractor fell upon, resumed work for a short while and then went bankrupt. A second contractor was engaged but seeing the number of obstacles to the job he too fell by the wayside. So the company decided that the only way to do something was to do it oneself and so completed the line on its own. Meanwhile Malcolmson of the W&LR was asked to join the board and provide the service on the line which he gladly did.

However, no sooner was that formidable character ensconced than a number of disputes broke out between lessor and lessee. The infant company asked the MGWR to help get rid of the W&LR dominance, which it was delighted to do. But the promised help was not forthcoming and the Athenry and Ennis Junction found itself alone.

The line opened in 1869 with a ramshackle collection of worn out rolling stock. The public had little faith in such vehicles and within a year financial problems had come to a head. So great were its debts that the Co. Clare sheriff seized an entire train and would only let it depart with the bailiffs riding on the footplate, which must have been a great nuisance for the driver and fireman. Not to be outdone the Co. Galway sheriff did the same thing at Gort a few days later. It is a fact that you cannot take possession of a train twice over and an unseemly contretemps arose between the two forces of law and order, each claiming prior right of ownership. While the bemused passengers and crew looked on a fight developed in which the Galway officers triumphed. They took over the train but would not allow it to proceed (for fear it would slip back into Clare no doubt!).

Arranging for disposal of the company's assets it was found that the rolling stock was still owned by the finance company and had to be returned to it. In fact the only item of any value owned by the A&EJR was a tired old engine. So bad was its condition that there was only one interested purchaser—the A&EJR! So the company bought back its own locomotive and within a short time was able to resume services as if nothing had happened. The A&EJR was indeed an Heroic Failure.

Passenger services over the Limerick–Sligo line operated by the W&LR took over seven hours for the 145 miles. This leisurely pace could have been improved but not by much for the route was made at the minimum cost with many sharp bends and constant rises and falls. There was a low population density on the route so two trains daily was more than enough. The MGWR was met at Collooney, south of Sligo and this town of 500 souls had at one time no less than three separate railway stations: the MGWR (still in use), the Sligo Leitrim and Northern Counties and W&LR which was dubbed Collooney South to reduce the confusion.

The company's tracks officially ended here although it had running powers into Sligo over the MGWR. There was a similar ambiguity about Athenry. A passenger arriving there who looked out of the carriage window saw a platform sign reading Athenry and Tuam Junction. But if he glanced at the opposite platform it read Athenry and Ennis Junction. It was relative to the direction you were going or that the company expected you to go.

Naturally the MGWR vehemently opposed this southern intrusion when the W&LR took over the Limerick to Sligo line. It failed in this as in its opposition to the merger of the W&LR with the GS&WR but it had the small compensation of being allowed to run a daily goods service from Athenry to Limerick. Having built the Claremorris to Collooney extension the W&LR was so pleased with itself that it decided its long straggling L-shaped line should have a new title reflecting its expanding operations and so from 1896 it was known as the Waterford Limerick and Western Railway.

Connections on the west coast line were surprisingly good. At Collooney the SLNCR services were met, but surprisingly not for passengers heading north. Goods services were heavier with a large number of cattle trains being run from the west onto the SLNCR for transfer to northern ports and shipment to Britain. At Limerick there was a link with the boat train from Rosslare and with MGWR services at Claremorris and Athenry.

The amalgamation of the WL&WR which took place in May 1901 had many effects on both companies. A number of directors joined the board at Kingsbridge and of course the increased mileage made the company by far the biggest in the country. An immediate problem was the condition of the rolling stock and permanent way of the WL&WR which was well below the standards of the larger company. Maintenance had been allowed to suffer in the interest of economy and one of the first tasks was to bring both up to the normal level. Travel between Dublin and a number of WL&WR stations improved greatly with faster timing, more trains and better connections.

The years up to the First World War were ones of reasonable prosperity for the company with passenger figures in 1910 breaking the three million mark. However the war brought a change. Unlike in Britain the Irish railways did not come under state control until 1916. Then the Irish Railway Executive Committee was established with the general manager of the GS&WR, E. A. Neale in charge. This body remained in control until August 1921. The war years and after were highly significant for the railways. Greater troop and munitions movement brought extra traffic but costs doubled and in some cases trebled in a few years. Undoubtedly many working on the lines were underpaid but fares were not allowed to keep up with expenditure and although compensation of over £750,000 was paid by the government this went nowhere near meeting all the costs involved. Maintenance, for example, had virtually come to a halt.

Also problematic was the period of conflict leading up to the Anglo–Irish Treaty of 1921. As on so many railways the men were active on the Volunteers' side and refused to work any train carrying British troops. Large scale suspensions and closures followed. Much more disastrous was the Civil War period, for being the largest railway the GS&WR suffered the most frequent attacks of Anti-Treaty forces wishing to disrupt the government of the new state. Again railway staff did their best to keep services going despite constant danger to themselves and threats to their families; most were tired of fighting and more concerned about leading a normal life than about the finer points of constitutional law at issue.

Note to the secretary of the C & LR from Kingsbridge, August 1921

The sabotage of the railway was thorough and by the end of 1922 nearly a third of all lines were unworkable. Trains were commandeered by both sides, often with a requisition note of questionable value and the Government forces used a number of armoured trains in the south and south–west to counter-attack against anti-Treaty forces. So effective was the disruption that when the Free State offensive was launched in Munster a B & I steamer had to be used to get the troops to Cork. The Railway Defence and Maintenance Corps was then formed to patrol the country's lines and repair the damage.

When hostilities ceased in 1923 services began to return to normal as compensation was received from public funds. By then it was clear that the status quo could no longer continue for in many ways the damage was irreparable. The previous year the Cork Bandon and South Coast had set an example by merging with the GS & WR. While the Drummond Commission had called for such mergers as far back as 1836 and there had been many calls since then, this was the first step towards full nationalisation which was of course the only way railways could survive. One suggestion was for a grouping of northern and southern lines but this came to nothing at the time. The government pressed for complete amalgamation saying that legislation would be used against those who held back; these were mainly the smaller concerns who rightly feared they would lose their identity in the new group.

In April 1924 the GS & WR with the CB & SCR merged with the MGWR to form the Great Southern Railway with the D & SER following on 1 January 1925 from which date the Great Southern Railways were born. The smaller companies then joined the fold during that year. Although the GS & WR officially disappeared from 1924 its spirit has survived in more than just the similarity of names. The operational methods were continued for many years and most of the stations still open have scarcely changed over the years. Kingsbridge is hardly altered for thankfully CIE has not followed the hideous practice of British Rail in making every station identical with plastic signs and strip lights. All in all Sancton Wood, Dargan and the other founding fathers would have little to complain of the remainder of the Premier Line.

Services

Dublin being the company's headquarters and the main centre of population most GS & WR trains ran to and from the capital. Between Dublin and Cork/Limerick there were five or six trains daily in each direction, with about three on most other routes. The fastest trains to Cork were those connecting with the Holyhead steamer and the Irish Mail from London Euston. The journey time ranged from seven hours in 1849 to 3 hours and 55 minutes in 1925, ensuring the delivery of letters from England in Cork by noon. Until the end of the last century only first and second class passengers were carried with an extra charge. From 1897 third class carriages were added and the following year first and second dining cars. There was also a night mail, similarly timed to meet the steamers which took about six hours for the journey. It was on this service that travelling post offices (TPOs) were first introduced in 1855. The idea was that urgent letters could be posted in a special box attached to the carriage for delivery at any town on the train route. Then in 1879 a sleeping car for first class travellers appeared, a rarity on Irish railways given the short distances involved.

Passengers on other services were less well catered for. Third class travel was for many years not encouraged by the GS & WR as on many other railways and at one time third class passengers to Cork had to endure a twelve hour journey on the 'Parliamentary' train. This was so called from the act of 1844 which required the running of at least one third class train on each line daily at a fare no greater than a penny a mile. This commendable piece of legislation was to protect the poorer traveller who was for a long time actively discouraged. Despite poor connections, frequent changes and very slow running third class travellers quickly took to the trains. In 1859, $9\frac{1}{2}$ million people had travelled by train, three-quarters of them on the GS & WR and with steadily increasing revenue from third class the journey time of the 'Parliamentary' had been cut to 7 hours in 1905 and then to $6\frac{1}{2}$ hours.

Hotels and catering

With the rise in tourism the GS & WR decided to become involved in catering and the hotel business. The Railway Hotel at Killarney was one of the first railway hostelries in the world and has always been a first class hotel. Other hotels were run by the company at Caragh Lake, Kenmare, Waterville, Parknasilla, Cork, Dublin and Limerick Junction. Some were operated directly, others under licence to outside contractors.

When the Killarney Hotel opened it received a great deal of publicity. A newspaper of the day had the following account.

> On Monday last [11 July 1854], this splendid establishment was opened for the public accommodation under the active and energetic management of Mr Schill, a German.... This building, which is not fifty yards from the railway terminus contains over one

The Radio Train headed by ex-GS&WR no. 405 leaves Mallow for Killarney

hundred beds at present but which will be easily doubled when the wings are completed. All the other accommodations and appliances of the hotel are of the first and most complete order. The furniture and fittings, though still somewhat incomplete, promise to be the most commodious and elegant. Nothing is tawdry.

The hotel, it seems, lived up to its promise for in 1870 there was an account written by an English visitor who encountered that Irish phenomenon a 'soft rain'.

> We entered Killarney like drowned rats. What elysium to find ourselves in that most comfortable and well appointed of all hotels 'the Railway'! What luxury to have a comfortable bath, and to feel dry and civilized once more, as we took our places at the well-provided table in the large saloon! My advice to anyone about to proceed from Cork to Killarney by Bianconi car is—'Don't'.

How pleasing for the company to have its hotel praised so highly *and* to have its transport rivals slated in the same paragraph! Alas the natives only barely come up to scratch, for the writer notes: 'We found the common people in the south very polite, and tolerably intelligent'. Indeed her account of the road journey with piles of luggage, no seats, badly shod horses and swarms of beggars would drive anyone to take the slowest 'Parliamentary' in preference.

It is said that the land for the hotel at Killarney was granted without charge to the GS&WR by the Earl of Kenmare on condition that certain trains waited for him if he was late. Be that as it may the clientele was certainly exclusive. One hundred years after the opening (1954) the Great Southern Hotel group (the present owners) issued a booklet which graphically describes the place.

> Solid, luxurious in its jewel-like setting, it provided the proper background for the stately crinoline-and-antimacassar period. Victorian characters straight out of the

novels of those years—and frequently engaged in writing them!—paraded solemnly across its halls and drawing-rooms, slept voluminously in its feather-stuffed Four Posters, and wined and dined almost gluttonously from the herioc table d'hote.

Making allowances for the rhetoric this is probably a fairly accurate description.

A number of refreshment rooms at stations were also run by the company and by 1900 there were 12 of these in all. They served various items from light snacks and drinks to full meals and were divided according to class. On the train there were similar facilities with little difference between first and second class. Thus for 3/6 (17½p) the hungry traveller got soup, fish, entree, joint, sweet and dessert—which must have helped to pass the journey. (Nowadays the fare is more limited but even so eating on a CIE train is still very pleasurable and at a fairly reasonable cost.) If your appetite was less voracious you could have a luncheon basket, ordered in advance at the station of your choice for 3/- (30p). This contained half a chicken, ham, or tongue, bread, cheese, claret, beer or mineral water. It included cutlery, crockery and that most necessary item, a corkscrew. As with luggage the Victorians did not do things by halves.

Fares and tickets

The nineteenth century was an era of strict class division and nowhere was this more evident than on the railways. Few people expected or wanted the working class to travel by train in any number, hence the great reluctance to provide third class coaches on many trains. Gradually economic realism dawned on the railway proprietors and they no longer saw themselves as serving only 'the quality'. Thus

A modern train en route from Dublin to Waterford. Note the distinctive station architecture

half of all the passengers carried in 1850 were third, but by 1913 the number had risen to 93% of the total. Single fares were fixed at a little over 2d, 1½d and 1d per mile. Incredibly these fares remained practically unchanged from 1850 to 1918, while today we are used to fare increases of 15–20% *every year.*

Return tickets were sold at 1½ times the single fare and luggage was carried on a scale similar to air travel today: 112 lbs first class, 84 lbs second, 56 lbs third. Unlike today, rail travellers of the last century tended to bring with them a fleet of trunks, boxes and cases as social life required several changes of clothes in the one day. Excess luggage was carried on the roof of the carriage secured with leather straps.

Initially special trains were not actively promoted although there were some for race meetings and events like the Dublin Horse Show. One enterprising gentleman who helped to change that was the Rev. Mr Bagot, a clergyman from Kildare who was clearly a latent travel agent. He organised a great number of trips from his area all over the country. With fares at less than half the normal single Rev. Bagot attracted large numbers of people who could not normally afford train travel. In one year over 11,000 travelled on his excursions. Other more up market trips consisted of a Shannon cruise with rail travel to Banagher, steamer to Killaloe with lunch on board and train back to Dublin, all for 13/- (65p). A similar offer is made nowadays by CIE involving the regular train to Carrick-on-Shannon, a special bus to Lough Key Forest Park with lots of time to explore it and a

Preserved GS & WR Bury 2-2-2 no. 36, built in 1848, now on display at Cork station

delightful cruise back to Carrick over one of the most spectacular stretches of waterway in the country for the return train to Dublin. No meals are included but the trip is first class value. Other GS & WR special offers included a rate of ½d per mile for the destitute on their way to the workhouse and a flat fare of 10/- (50p) for convicts travelling from anywhere in Ireland to Spike Island prison in Cork. We can take it these were single tickets.

Even more active than Mr Bagot in promoting rail travel was a gent whom the minutes refer to as 'a Mr Thomas Cook of Leicester', who ran a number of trips over the line for the benefit of his English customers. However Mr Cook's credit worthiness seems to have been questioned for in 1852 the company would not allow him to run any more excursions until previous outings had been paid for.

There was no delay in advertising and launching a parcels service; it began in 1846. Those under 1 lb were carried anywhere on the network for 6d (2½p) including delivery to any address within two miles of the GPO in Dublin and Cork and one mile in other towns. With the contraction of the railways this service has been used less but there is today a lively traffic in express parcels which travel by regular passenger train. Another way it has survived is in the provincial bus service. For a modest sum the driver will take a personal interest in your parcel and nurse it all the way to its destination in Donegal or Kerry. Strangely, CIE tends to keep very quiet about this excellent facility.

Locomotives and engineers

The GS & WR ordered 40 locomotives from engineers in Liverpool and Manchester to designs common at the time. One of these, no 36, has survived as mentioned above and is now on display at Cork station. These were maintained and altered at Inchicore giving the staff there valuable experience in the principles of locomotive construction so that the first home produced engine no 57 emerged in 1852. To advance this programme a number of skilled engineers were brought to Ireland and each in turn had considerable effect on the engines built during his term. One of the most formative influences was in fact an Irishman, Alexander McDonnell who had worked abroad for some years and arrived at Inchicore in 1864. Up to then locomotives had been produced to a wide variety of designs so McDonnell set out to standardise these based on the one most suitable to the company's needs known as the 101 class. He had great success in raising the standard of work so that the locomotives were as good as any produced in these islands. McDonnell was a good organiser and could not stand sloppiness and disorder. He was a tall man with greying beard and hair and one evening he was walking home when he spotted a former railway watchman staggering along the street 'with drink taken'. The engineer reprimanded him saying: 'I'm surprised at you and you an old policeman.' The watchman was quick to reply 'Is it oul' you're calling me? Mebbe I'm no oulder than yerself, you an' your oul' grey beard!'

When John Aspinall arrived from Crewe in 1875 he found Inchicore a hive of activity. H. A. V. Bulleid, later himself to be CME there under CIE, wrote a charming biography of him full of life and anecdote as well as the technical know how you would expect. As he says, together with McDonnell and Aspinall the GS & WR 'comfortably held its place as the leading Irish railway'.

In 1879 it was a celebration year at Inchicore. McDonnell and his two assistants Aspinall and Ivatt (who came from Crewe two years before and was then based in Cork) had produced 100 of the 144 locomotives in the programme. To mark the occasion there was a dinner dance at the works to which the staff and their wives were invited. McDonnell spoke at the dinner, congratulating his engineers on the range of their achievements: Mrs Aspinall and Mrs Ivatt were both pregnant at the time.

Another significant character was Robert Coey who became works manager in 1886 and chief mechanical engineer ten years later. He was responsible for designing and building a number of express locomotives then badly needed to replace outdated machines on the mail trains. There were 26 in all, numbered up to 340 and incorporating a number of ideas he had picked up at the GWR works in Swindon and in the USA. There were also a number of other goods and passenger engines to emerge during his regime, most of which were highly successful.

The company built two steam railcars, i.e. a small carriage permanently attached to its own locomotive. These were *Sprite* and *Fairy* which emerged from Inchicore in 1857 and 1894. They were used for inspecting the network and as pay carriages. A paymaster and his assistant travelled in each leaving Dublin on alternate Tuesdays and returning the following Saturday. Wages were paid fortnightly and at each station the employees mounted the steps at one side, received their money at a small rear window and went down the other side. No doubt this was one train which was greeted ecstatically. At 8 each morning the pay train left its overnight stop and finished the day's run in mid afternoon. Surprisingly given the amount of cash they carried in remote areas robberies were few until the Civil War when attacks became more frequent. The pay carriages ran up

Waterford–Dublin container train passing Jerpoint Abbey

a huge mileage until the time when the GSR introduced a new system of paying wages.

Carriages

The original first class coaches of the GS & WR were fine compartment carriages, solidly built in Dublin with good upholstery and oil lamps. Each had four compartments and at the time were considered the height of luxury. Second class had five compartments with 15 inch wooden seating for ten people. The partition was barely high enough to stop you cracking your head against that of your neighbour in the next compartment. Two oil lamps gave light to the whole coach. Third class was very primitive but no more than on most railways at the time. Plain wooden seats with 18 inch backs were provided (twelve hours to Cork!) and occasionally when carriages were in short supply cattle wagons were substituted. Presumably the cattle were not present at the same time. There was no lighting in third and no heating in any class.

By 1871 cushions had made a reluctant appearance in second class and fifteen years later this indulgence had even spread to third. First class had by then new upholstery of luxurious standard in red leather and second had fully sprung seats and window blinds. There was some debate about the latter improvement as it was feared that many marginal passengers would transfer from first to second and from second to third. The extravagance of it all was particularly opposed by the company chairman on these grounds.

Lavatories were first provided in 1882. We may pity the third class passenger on a long journey but it should be remembered that there were frequent and lengthy stops at almost every station. At the outbreak of the First World War sycamore and mahogany were used in first class with green cloth upholstery and electric lights. Sycamore walnut and white oak were the features of second class coaches, along with green flowered tapestry seat covers.

Dining cars made their appearance on 1 June 1898 on the Cork mail train and were extremely lavish in their decoration. They were lit by electricity, cooking was by gas and they were later extended to the Rosslare boat trains. Even more impressive were the state cars built by the railway. The first was in 1851 for the use of the Lord Lieutenant in his progress around the country and renovated for the visit of Queen Victoria ten years later. It was a most luxurious vehicle, 28 feet long with curved glass windows at either end. The interior consisted of an anteroom, salon and boudoir. A new state carriage was constructed for Edward VII in 1903 and is the finest piece of coaching work produced at Inchicore. It was 50 feet long with a smoking room, reception room and Queen's room. The decor of each room by the Dublin firm of Sibthorpe was quite distinct and highly elaborate in style as was the mode of the day. After the establishment of the state the coach was disused for a long time until in 1961 CIE completely refurbished it and put it back in service. It was in superb condition and was used by the President and visiting dignitaries such as the Belgian Queen on an extended holiday in Ireland. It is delightful to think that such an excellent piece of GS & WR craftsmanship has survived.

The more mundane carriages were painted in dark purple with yellow/vermillion lines and gold lettering with red shading. The company crest, composed of the arms of Dublin, Cork, Kilkenny and Limerick surrounded by a collar with the company's name, was displayed on the side of each coach.

4 The Midland Great Western Railway

THE Midland Great Western Railway was the third largest in Ireland and is frequently called the most Irish, not by reason of any particular eccentricity but because it was the least influenced by English companies in operation or construction. It was said that the Midland, as it is commonly called, was mostly used by politicians, priests, farmers and people who had a horse to sell, and this is not a million miles from the truth. As early as 12 October 1836 Alexander Nimmo had presented his engineer's report to the proposed Great Central Irish Railway at Mullingar. He proposed various lines for the stillborn GCIR, including one from Dublin to Kells and Belturbet to connect with the Ulster Canal. His projection of the Sligo line was quite accurate, suggesting the great potential of Ballinasloe Fair and the Arigna mines, later served by the Cavan and Leitrim. Nothing came of this plan.

The Midland was born out of controversy. A row blew up in the GS & WR board room when an independent group of directors proposed building a line to Athlone and Longford. The GS & WR felt that this was its own territory and the result was the incorporation of the MGWR on 21 July 1845 with authority to construct a line to Mullingar and later to Galway. Unfortunately the splinter group splintered and went on to propose a rival scheme to Galway via Athlone. This company called itself the Irish Great Western Railway and received the delighted support of the GS & WR, provided the line ran through its station at Portarlington. Each company raced to get parliamentary approval for its own scheme and suffered boost and setback in turn.

One of the reasons for this great rivalry was the haste to be the first company to reach Galway, then confidently predicted to be *the* future port for all transatlantic traffic between Europe and America. At that time almost any harbour with more than a couple of fathoms at high tide was fondly imagined and promoted as a packet station. The potential traffic from Galway in passengers, goods and mail would be large steady and lucrative. Thus in 1850 George Willoughby Hemans was commissioned by the company to prepare a report on the feasibility of Galway as such a port. Clearly Mr Hemans' brief was well defined for he cannot recommend it too highly. The chief reasons in its favour, he said, were the fact that the railway was almost there, the extensive dock facilities in situ and its nearness to the American coast.

He goes on to query the suitability of Queenstown and adds 'it is doubtful whether a line could be made from any existing Railway to either Berehaven or Valentia for much less than a million sterling'. This was in case Vignoles' plan should be resurrected. Finally he proposes that Howth would be a much better port than Kingstown for Holyhead. The report was clearly intended for the post office, shipowners and industrialists with regular traffic to and from America.

To reinforce the message the company decided on a dramatic action. The steamer *Viceroy* was chartered the same year for a trial run between Galway and Halifax or New York. All went well and she set off to zip across the Atlantic and thus clinch the argument once and for all. Unfortunately the ship went down off the American coast and the same can be said of the development of Galway as the chief Atlantic port in Ireland.

Returning to the actual building of the line: the original act authorised the company to purchase the Royal Canal and this proved a useful acquisition. Messrs Jeffs won the construction contract for the first 26 miles to Enfield at a cost of £70,000, a reasonable figure by all accounts. The Lord Lieutenant, Baron Heytesbury cut the first sod at the Broadstone on 8 January 1846 and had a street in Dublin 8 named after him. The sod-cutting took place in the garden of the Royal Canal Company's house and there was a reception inside to celebrate the occasion. This house, 1 Railway Terrace, later became the house of the GSR's Running Superintendent and now provides overnight accommodation for CIE staff away from home.

Work began in earnest and as one account written in 1850 notes, the construction of the line across the bogs of the central plain 'has offered Mr Hemans, the engineer of the line, much scope for the excercise of his skill'. In fact by following the course of the canal to within 15 miles of Mullingar, extending bridges and viaducts to pass over waterway and railway, the company was able to avoid a great deal of expense and a large part of the first section is quite level. Nonetheless subsidence and drainage were later to be a problem.

The route opened for traffic on 28 June 1847 and all appears to have gone well as the *Freeman's Journal* reports:

> Yesterday the above line of railway was opened for public traffic as far as Enfield . . . Altogether four trains left the terminus at Broadstone during the day. The carriages, particularly the first and second class are got up in a very superior style.
>
> In some of the first class carriages there are beds fitted up something after the fashion of berths in steam packets, and there are other carriages for the exclusive use of ladies when they travel alone and do not want to enter mixed trains . . . Everything passed off with the utmost success and to the satisfaction of all parties concerned.

The Broadstone

Meanwhile work had continued designing and building a terminus in Dublin which was suitable for the main route to the west. In 1846 Hemans had reported to the board on a suitable location.

> At the Broadstone Harbour, which is scarcely half a statute mile from the Post Office, an area is now cleared, wherein you may build the most commodious and spacious passenger station in the United Kingdom, occupying a splendid and commanding situation, and capable of being connected hereafter, if found desirable, with the most extensive depots for every species of railway stock.
>
> The passenger approach, via Dominick Street, will be direct and convenient, and from the close proximity of this Station to Smithfield, a cattle disembarking shed can be made for the supply of that market, communicating with the main line behind the principal station and distant only five hundred yards from the Market Place.

In the same year John Skipton Mulvany supplied plans for the Broadstone terminus. The board described them as being to 'a very handsome and suitable design' but postponed the expenditure so as to speed up the opening of the line to traffic. Mulvany was a distinguished architect who had already designed Kingstown station and would later plan Mullingar, Athlone and Galway. The work was completed in 1851, the design being intended to convey stability, solidity and above all safety to the as yet quite nervous passenger/investor. In the 1850 *MGWR Guide* it is described as 'a chaste and truly noble erection, in granite, combining in its details the peculiarities of the Egyptian and Grecian style of architecture'.

It is a most imposing building with a large projecting entrance block and two sturdy lamp standards. Down one side there is a magnificent colonnade where cab drivers sheltered while waiting the arrival of the trains. The station had two platforms with four carriage sidings between them and nearby the extensive workshops and sheds of the Midland. Also in the area the company built a number of houses for its more senior staff; these are in the suitably named Great Western Square, a delightful gated park with red brick houses surrounding it. It is a most pleasant spot.

Not long after the opening the Midland found itself the centre of public attention by having a murder on its premises. On 14 November 1856 a Broadstone cashier, George Little, was found in his office with his throat cut. A large sum of money was missing. Despite police investigation and the services of a French clairvoyant no progress was made with the case although most of the money was recovered not far from the cashier's office. Then the following year a Mrs Spollin walked into a Dublin police barracks and said her husband, a porter on the MGWR, had committed the murder. Spollin was arrested and tried but eventually acquitted for lack of evidence. There the mystery remains to this day.

With regular services operating to Enfield the company pressed on with its extensions to the west and north-west. Kinnegad was reached on 6 December 1847, and from there it was decided to leave the canal and strike across country to Mullingar which opened to traffic on 2 October 1848.

Towards Galway

The dispute with the GS & WR and its minion the IGWR continued without abate. While the Midland sought parliamentary approval for the line to Galway the rival group planned a line from Portarlington to Athlone, believing that it would thus be at a decided advantage in reaching Galway first. The legal ups and downs resulted in the Midland getting sole approval for the extension to Athlone while at the same time the Commons heard a proposal on 4 February 1847 for a line from Longford to Sligo from the 'Great Midland and Western Railway' i.e. the MGWR. Having got approval by the acts of 1846–7, the Midland lost no time in pushing its line west towards Galway and was gleeful when the railway had crossed the Shannon and it had its station at Athlone. The GS & WR was at this time no nearer than Tullamore and the sparring continued with charge and countercharge. For example, in 1858 the Midland advertised a rail and steamer ticket from the Broadstone to Limerick, then served by the W & LR. Leaving Dublin at 7.45, passengers arrived at Athlone about four hours later to travel by boat to Killaloe. A horse bus completed the journey to Limerick at 6.45 pm. Fares were 12/6 and 6/-, first and third, compared with 23/9 and 10/9 for the more direct journey on the GS & WR which took 6 hours compared with 11½. As each company unveiled its extension plan the other replied with a rival proposal. Finally, by means of a fine girder bridge across the Shannon, the Midland announced the opening of the through route to Galway from 1 August 1851.

MIDLAND GREAT WESTERN RAILWAY OF IRELAND.

OPEN TO GALWAY.

TIME and FARE TABLE for DECEMBER 15th, 1853.

DOWN TRAINS.

Miles from Dublin	STATIONS. Hours of Starting.	7. 0 Morn. 1, 2, 3, Class.	10.30 Morn. 1, & 2 Class.	4. 0 Aftern. 1, 2, 3, Class.	5. 0 Aftern. 1, 2, 3, Class.	MAIL. 7. 15 Even. 1 & 2 Class.	10. 0 Night Goods &c.	10.30 Morn. 1, 2, 3, Class.	MAIL. 7. 15 Even. 1, 2, Class.	1st Class. s. d.	2nd Class. s. d.	3rd Class. s. d.	4th Class. s. d.	Two wheels. s. d.	Four wheels. s. d.	One Horse s. d.	Two Horses. s. d.	Three Horses. s. d.
	TRAINS LEAVE	H. M.	H. M.	H. M.	H. M.	H. M.	H. M.	H. M.	H. M.									
—	DUBLIN, at	7. 0	10. 30	4. 0	5. 0	7. 15	10. 0	10. 30	7. 15									
4¾	Blanchardstown,		*10. 40		* 5. 10			*10. 40		0. 10	0. 8	0. 4	0. 3					
7	Clonsilla,	* 7. 20	10. 50	* 4. 20	5. 25			10. 50		1. 0	1. 0	0. 7	0. 5					
9	Lucan,		*10. 55	* 4. 25	* 5. 33	7. 36		*10. 55	7. 36	1. 3	1. 0	0. 9	0. 6					
11	Leixlip,		*11. 0	* 4. 32	* 5. 40	7. 42		*11. 0	7. 42	1. 6	1. 3	0. 10	0. 7					
15	Maynooth,	7. 40	11. 16	* 4. 42	5. 54	7. 52	10. 45	11. 16	7. 52	2. 6	2. 0	1. 3	0. 10	5. 0	9. 0	5. 0	9. 6	13. 6
19	Kilcock,	7. 50	11. 25	* 4. 52	6. 6	8. 2	11. 0	11. 25	8. 2	3. 0	2. 6	1. 6	1. 1	7. 0	11. 6	7. 0	11. 6	16. 0
21	Ferns Lock,		*11. 30	4. 58				*11. 30		3. 6	2. 8	1. 8	1. 2					
26¼	Enfield,	8. 5	11. 45	5. 10	6. 30	8. 20	11. 35	11. 45	8. 20	4. 0	3. 0	2. 0	1. 4	9. 0	13. 6	9. 0	15. 0	20. 0
30¼	Moyvalley,		*11. 55	* 5. 22		* 8. 28		*11. 55		4. 8	4. 0	2. 6	1. 10					
36	Hill of Down,	8. 20	12. 15	5. 37		8. 40	12. 10	12. 15	8. 40	5. 8	4. 10	3. 0	2. 2	12. 0	18. 6	12. 0	21. 0	28. 0
41¾	Killucan,	8. 35	12. 35	* 5. 55		8. 52	12. 35	12. 30	8. 52	6. 8	5. 8	3. 5	2. 7	14. 0	21. 0	14. 0	24. 0	32. 6
50	MULLINGAR arrives at		12. 50			9. 15		12. 52	9. 15									
	leaves at	8. 55	12. 55	6. 25		9. 20	1. 10	1. 5	9. 20	8. 0	6. 8	4. 2	3. 0	17. 0	25. 6	17. 0	30. 0	40. 0
58	Castletown,	9. 15	1. 15	6. 50		9. 38	1. 40	1. 25	9. 38	9. 0	7. 6	4. 10	3. 4	19. 6	30. 0	19. 6	35. 0	49. 0
62	Streamstown,		*1. 22	* 7. 0			1. 52	*1. 52		*9. 0	8. 3	5. 0	3. 6	21. 0	32. 0	21. 0	37. 6	52. 0
68	Moate,	9. 35	1. 35	7. 15		9. 58	2. 40	1. 45	9. 58	11. 0	9. 0	5. 6	3. 9	22. 0	34. 0	23. 0	41. 0	56. 0
78	ATHLONE, arrives at	10. 0	2. 0	7. 45			3. 30											
	leaves at	10. 20	2. 10			10. 22	5. 45	2. 15	10. 22	12. 6	10. 0	6. 0	4. 0	26. 0	39. 0	26. 0	47. 6	64. 0
91½	BALLINASLOE,	10. 55	2. 40			11. 5	6. 25	2. 45	11. 5	15. 0	12. 0	7. 0	4. 6	31. 0	46. 6	31. 0	55. 6	76. 6
101¼	WOODLAWN,	11. 30	3. 20			11. 26	7. 20	3. 20	11. 26	16. 6	13. 3	8. 0	5. 0	34. 0	51. 0	34. 0	61. 0	84. 6
113½	ATHENRY,	12. 0	3. 50			11. 55	8. 5	3. 50	11. 55	18. 0	14. 6	9. 0	5. 4	38. 0	57. 0	38. 0	68. 6	94. 6
121	Oranmore,	*12. 20	* 4. 15			12. 10	8. 40	*4. 15	12. 10	19. 0	15. 3	9. 6	5. 9	40. 0	60. 0	40. 0	73. 6	100. 0
126¼	GALWAY,	12. 40	4. 30			12. 30	9. 15	4. 30	12. 30	20. 0	16. 0	10. 0	6. 0	42. 6	63. 6	42. 0	76. 6	106. 0
		P.M.	P.M.	P.M.	P.M.	night.	A. M.	P. M.	night.									

UP TRAINS.

Miles From Galway	STATIONS. Hours of Starting.	MAIL. 12. 0 Night. 1 & 2 Class.	8. 0 Morn. 1, 2, 3, Class.	8. 15 Morn. 1, 2, 3, Class.	8. 30 Morn. 1, 2, Class.	12. 0 Noon. Goods, & 2, 3, & 4 Class.	4. 0 Aftern. 1, 2, 3, Class.	4. 0 Aftern. 1, 2, 3, Class.	MAIL. 12. 0 Night. 1, 2, Class.	1st Class. s. d.	2nd Class. s. d.	3rd Class. s. d.	4th Class. s. d.	Two wheels. s. d.	Four wheels. s. d.	One Horse. s. d.	Two Horses. s. d.	Three Horses. s. d.
	TRAINS LEAVE	H. M.	H. M.	H. M.	H. M.	H. M.	H. M.	H. M.	H. M.									
—	GALWAY,	12. 0			8. 30	12. 0	4. 0	4. 0	12. 0									
6¼	Oranmore,	12. 15			* 8. 45	*12. 20	* 4. 15	*4. 15	12. 15	1. 0	0. 9	0. 6	0. 3	4. 6	6. 6	2. 0	3. 6	5. 0
13	ATHENRY,	12. 30			9. 5	12. 55	4. 34	4. 34	12. 30	2. 0	1. 6	1. 0	0. 8	4. 6	6. 6	4. 6	8. 6	11. 6
25	WOODLAWN,	12. 57			9. 40	1. 45	5. 4	5. 4	12. 57	3. 6	2. 9	2. 0	1. 0	5. 6	8. 0	16. 0	16. 0	22. 0
35	BALLINASLOE,	1. 26			9. 55	2. 25	5. 21	5. 21	1. 26	5. 0	4. 0	3. 0	1. 6	11. 6	17. 0	11. 6	21. 0	29. 0
48¼	ATHLONE, arrives at	2. 0			10. 20	3. 20	5. 55	5. 55	2. 0									
	leaves at	2. 5	8. 0		10. 30	3. 40	6. 15	6. 15	2. 5	7. 6	6. 0	4. 0	2. 0	16. 6	24. 6	16. 6	30. 0	41. 0
58½	Moate,	2. 22	8. 25		10. 55	4. 25	6. 38	6. 38	2. 27	9. 0	7. 0	4. 6	2. 3	20. 0	29. 6	19. 6	36. 0	49. 6
64¼	Streamstown,		* 8. 40		*11. 10	* 4. 55	* 6. 57	*6. 57		10. 0	8. 0	5. 0	2. 6	21. 0	31. 6	21. 0	38. 6	52. 6
68¼	Castletown,	2. 45	8. 50		11. 30	5. 15	7. 7	7. 7	2. 50	11. 0	8. 6	5. 2	2. 8	23. 0	34. 6	23. 0	42. 0	57. 6
76½	MULLINGAR, arrives at	3. 7			11. 50		7. 30	7. 30										
	leaves at	3. 12	9. 10		12. 0	5. 45	7. 25	7. 30	3. 12	12. 0	9. 4	5. 10	3. 0	25. 6	38. 6	25. 6	46. 6	64. 0
85	Killucan,	3. 31	9. 30		12. 18	6. 15	7. 49	7. 49	3. 31	13. 4	10. 4	6. 2	3. 5	28. 6	42. 6	28. 6	51. 6	71. 0
90¾	Hill of Down,	3. 44	* 9. 42		12. 32	6. 40	8. 3	8. 3	3. 44	14. 4	11. 2	7. 0	4. 2	30. 6	45. 6	30. 6	55. 0	76. 0
96	Moyvalley,		* 9. 55		*12. 49		* 8. 19	8. 19		15. 4	12. 0	7. 6	4. 2					
100	Enfield,	4. 6	10. 5	8. 15	12. 55	7. 20	8. 30	8. 30	4. 6	16. 0	12. 6	7. 10	4. 5	33. 6	50. 0	33. 6	60. 6	83. 6
105¼	Ferns Lock,		*10. 20	* 8. 30	* 1. 7		* 8. 45	*8. 45		16. 6	13. 4	8. 4	4. 10					
107½	Kilcock,	4. 23	10. 25	8. 36	1. 11	7. 55	8. 53	8. 53	4. 23	17. 0	13. 6	8. 6	4. 11	36. 0	54. 0	36. 0	64. 6	89. 0
111½	Maynooth,	4. 32	10. 40	8. 50	1. 22	8. 15	9. 4	9. 4	4. 32	17. 6	14. 0	8. 9	5. 2	37. 6	56. 0	37. 6	68. 0	93. 6
115½	Leixlip,	4. 41	*10. 50	* 9. 5	1. 32		* 9. 18	*9. 18	4. 41	18. 6	14. 9	9. 2	5. 5					
117½	Lucan,	4. 46	*10. 55	* 9. 11	1. 37		* 9. 24	*9. 24	4. 46	18. 9	15. 0	9. 3	5. 6					
119½	Clonsilla,		*11. 0	* 9. 17	* 1. 42		* 9. 32	*9. 32		19. 0	15. 2	9. 5	5. 8					
122	Blanchardstown,		*11. 10	* 9. 25			* 9. 41	*9. 41		19. 2	15. 4	9. 8	5. 9					
126¼	DUBLIN,	5. 15	11. 30	9. 45	2. 0	9. 0	10. 0	10. 0	5. 15	20. 0	16. 0	10. 0	6. 0	42. 6	63. 6	42. 0	76. 6	106. 0
		A.M.	A.M.	A.M.	P.M.	P.M.	P.M.	P.M.	A.M.									

NOTE.—When the Time in the Table is marked thus [*] the Train will only stop to set down Passengers, when application has been made to the Guard at a preceding Station; or take them up when the Station Master shews the Red Signal. *Flag Stations are printed in Italic.*

The Goods Trains cannot be insured to arrive punctually at the Stations, but will be as nearly punctual as possible.

N.B.—The times of Arrival of the other Trains at the various Stations named are not guaranteed.

Communication between Galway, Ballinasloe, Athlone & Mullingar with England, via Holyhead

First and Second Class Passengers can now be Booked through by this route to the following Stations on English Railways, at the subjoined Rates, which include the Sea Passage money between Kingstown and Holyhead, as also the Fares on the Dublin and Kingstown Railway:—

	LONDON 1st Class. £ s. d.	LONDON 2nd Class. £ s. d.	BIRMINGHAM 1st Class. £ s. d.	BIRMINGHAM 2nd Class. £ s. d.	MANCHESTER 1st Class. £ s. d.	MANCHESTER 2nd Class. £ s. d.	CHESTER OR LIVERPOOL 1st Class. £ s. d.	CHESTER OR LIVERPOOL 2nd Class. £ s. d.
To or From GALWAY, and......	3. 16. 0	2. 14. 0	2. 18. 0	2. 0. 0	2. 4. 0	1. 16. 0	2. 0. 0	1. 11. 0
" BALLINASLOE and	3. 13. 0	2. 11. 0	2. 14. 0	2. 0. 0	2. 0. 0	1. 12. 0	1. 15. 0	1. 7. 0
" ATHLONE and......	3. 11. 0	2. 9. 0	2. 12. 0	1. 18. 0	1. 17. 0	1. 10. 0	1. 12. 0	1. 5. 0
" MULLINGAR and....	3. 8. 0	2. 6. 0	2. 8. 0	1. 16. 0	1. 13. 0	1. 6. 0	1. 8. 0	1. 1. 0

The Single Journey Tickets are only available on the day of issue and the two following days. The journey may be broken at Dublin, Holyhead, Bangor, Crewe, or Chester.

RETURN TICKETS ARE ISSUED AT ABOUT A FARE AND A HALF.

Those to and from London are available for 14 days after the date of issue, i.e. the journey must be completed within the 15 days. Those to other Stations are available for Seven days after the date of issue, completing the journey within the Eighth day.

DEPARTURES OF THE STEAM BOAT FROM KINGSTOWN FOR HOLYHEAD:—
9. 0 a.m., Sundays excepted.

First and Second Class by Express Trains between Chester, Birmingham, and London.

Mondays, Wednesdays, and Fridays, a Steamer leaves KILLALOE for ATHLONE to meet the 4. 0 o'clock UP Train, Dublin, 10. 0 p.m., and Returns from Athlone every alternate day, Steamer leaving at 10. 30 o'Clock, Morning.

MGWR timetable sheet for the Galway line, December 1853

Galway station with the Great Southern Hotel, formerly Railway. The former line to Clifden can be seen where it tailed off to the left

The new line was a major development for the west. The company may have been over-optimistic in its prediction that 'this most magnificent line of railway is destined to become sooner or later the ordinary route for passengers and merchandise from Great Britain towards the North American continent' but its effect was revolutionary. Before the railway heavy goods took four days to get from Galway to Dublin but now the train could bring them in ten hours. Galway became the most popular starting point for touring Connemara which was thus opened up to a commercial activity it had never known before.

Every effort was made to attract visitors and natives to use the new line. Just as fly boats had run from each temporary terminus while the railway was under construction so now the Midland published timetables giving horse-drawn car connections from almost every station. Perhaps more than any other line in Ireland this one changed the lives of the people living near it. Emigration, whether seasonal or permanent, was a regular feature of the congested districts, especially after the horrendous famine years. The railway brought a new mobility to people who had to travel to earn a living.

The year after the Galway line opened the Midland made a bid to gain control of the Grand Canal. Since it already controlled the Royal Canal the GS & WR felt this was an attempt to corner the market in that if its rival managed the purchase there would be competitive services running far into its southern territory. On this occasion it was successful and the MGWR had to be satisfied with a seven year lease.

Speed was not a prime consideration on the Midland; one train which took 5¼ hours for the 126 miles to Galway had its passage ironically described as 'a rush across Ireland'. Another noteworthy who experienced the company's rather flexible timetable was Lord Halsbury, the English Lord Chancellor. He arrived at a small country station in good time for his train's departure and sat patiently in the carriage while the appointed time came and went. Finally in desperation he called the guard and told him he had to catch the mail boat from Dublin, asking when would the train be going. The guard was quite unconcerned and replied they would probably be moving before long and to have patience. 'Do you know who I am?' spluttered Halsbury. 'I am the Lord Chancellor of England.' The railwayman was unruffled by his distinguished passenger and answered: 'Well sir, she couldn't get started any sooner if you were the County Court judge himself!'

In anticipation of the boom in tourist traffic to the west the Midland decided to build its own hotel in Galway. This was the Railway Hotel (later the Great Southern) which has a commanding position overlooking Eyre Square and is linked directly to the terminus. It was intended to be a luxurious building for the most discriminating and affluent visitor. Mulvany designed it and the station also, although it must be said that it is one of his less successful buildings, being curiously devoid of character. However, there is a sense of magnificence about it

Enfield, a typical MGWR rural station

today with its more recent additions. It seems that the management of the hotel some years after the opening was rather deficient, for one tourist wrote a critical account of his stay there.

> On arrival in Galway, we put up at the Railway Hotel, kept by Mr Bergin, an obliging man, who has in the hotel almost more than he can manage. It is a large and most peculiarly constructed building—is sadly out of repair, and ought to be put in order by the Railway directors, who, for the company, are the owners of the property. It was built for the American packet trade, and on the largest of large ideas even of the Irish.

Allowing for the patronising tone of these remarks it appears that the visitor had some grievance and had discovered like many tourists since then the difference between the advertisement and the reality.

The Principal Line

The second line of the Midland was the branch from Mullingar to Sligo. This had received parliamentary approval as far as Longford in 1845 but with the rush to Galway and disputes with its southern neighbour the company was delayed in opening up the north-west. The line was opened to Longford in 1855 and two years later formalities for building the remainder were cleared. Construction took over five years and Sligo got its first trains on 3 September 1862. This long delay is all the more surprising when it is considered how frequently the town featured in proposals during the 1840s with the birth of such non-starters as the Sligo, Ballina and Westport, Enniskillen and Sligo Railway. This was of course the period known as the railway mania, when Parliament was swamped with proposed lines between every town and village in the country. (For example five schemes were

Edenderry, Co. Offaly, the terminus of the short branch from Enfield

launched at the same time for a railway between Cork and Fermoy!) Part of the reason for this was the lower cost of construction in Ireland as a result of falling land prices and wages in a mainly rural country.

The Sligo branch was known to the Midland as the Principal Line, to distinguish it from the route to Galway which was the Main Line! It was single tracked from Longford to Collooney and near Mullingar lay Inny Junction, the station for the branch to Cavan which opened on 8 July 1856. Inny Junction was unique in that there was no road access to it whatever and the nearest town was several miles away. It was literally in the middle of nowhere. The two platforms were suitably enough on an island from where connections ran to meet the Great Northern service from Clones. Further up the Sligo line was the tiny station of Clonhugh, built for one of the directors whose estate of the same name was nearby. The minuscule waiting room still stands but of course the station is long since closed.

In 1858 the GS & WR had at long last got authorisation for its extension from Tullamore to Athlone and within a year and a half the line was complete. There was a through line to the Midland station but the larger company decided to keep the Shannon between them and built its station on the east side of the river. Yet with all the battling to get there the new route never attracted more than a small percentage of the traffic going west. It is ironic therefore that many years later CIE have found it extremely useful to divert trains to Galway and Westport along it and thus ease the pressure on the Mullingar line.

Also out of Athlone was the branch to Mayo first promoted by the Great Northern and Western Railway, a company whose short-lived career need not detain us. Soon after construction began the 1860 agreement was signed between the GS & WR and the Midland bringing to an end years of strife. The MGWR was thus free to continue its extension towards Claremorris.

The line opened to Roscommon on 13 February 1860 and to Claremorris on 19 May 1862. Westport, the next target, was not reached until 1866, and Ballina from a branch at Manulla Junction in 1873. Claremorris became a junction when the WL & WR arrived in 1894 while thrusting northwards to Sligo. While disliking such intrusion there was little the Midland could do other than negotiate for running powers over part of the line. Claremorris is today quite a busy station especially during the summer when a large number of trains run to the nearby shrine at Knock. Specials run from all over Ireland and this is yet another reason for not building an airport there.

Consolidation: the Tatlow years

With its main lines complete it is time to look at how the railway was run. The picture which emerges in the 1860s is not a rosy one. Whether the long running dispute had drained the company it appears that things were not going well. Joseph Tatlow, who became the company's able general manager writes in his biography *Fifty Years of Railway Life* (1920) that with a top heavy board of fifteen directors and petty corruption 'in 1864 the railway was in a very bad condition, wretchedly run down and woefully mismanaged'. He quotes Ballinasloe Fair as an example of the kind of problems he faced.

In 1860 over 80,000 sheep and 20,000 cattle passed through this fair, much of it by rail. So great was the business done that each year a large force of railwaymen, headed by the chairman and several of the directors descended on the town for the week. Tatlow gives a lively account of the proceedings.

We established ourselves in quarters that were part of the original station premises... To be able to entertain friends and customers of the company was one of the reasons, probably the main reason, why the directors passed the fair week at Ballinasloe. Their hospitality was not limited to invitations to dinner, for guests were welcomed, without special invitation, to breakfast and lunch and light refreshments during the day.

It was an arrangement which gave pleasure to both hosts and guests and was not without advantage to the company. A good dinner solves many a difficulty, while the post-prandial cigar and a glass of grog, like faith, removes mountains.

It was not all plain sailing and socialising for Tatlow recalls a particularly harrowing occasion: 'Throughout the day I was besieged by grumbling and discontented customers: want of wagons, unfair distribution, favouritism, delays were the burden of their complaints, and I had to admit that in the working of the Ballinasloe fair traffic, all was not perfect.' He recalls that the locomotive engineer carved 23 notches in the ceiling beam of his room, one for each annual visit; it would be interesting to know if they are still there. Such was the influx of railwaymen that dormitory coaches were brought from Dublin to accommodate them.

Morale was obviously low among the staff, reflected in an uncaring approach to their work. It was this mental attitude which Tatlow had to tackle. One Isaac Latimer, author of *A Holiday Run by Rail and Road in Ireland* (1871), gave his impression of the railway in some detail.

All along the Midland Great Western Line (to Sligo), the growth of potatoes, which in many cases were over-run with weeds, there was no attempt made by the station masters to ornament their grounds by growing flowers, or in any manner contributing to their adornment.

The Midland has a most enterprising English manager (Tatlow), who has had a large experience in railway affairs and he might perhaps do something in the way of encouragement to bring about a better state of things.

Mr Latimer goes on to describe the problems arising from inter-company rivalry or even downright hostility.

The run from Galway to the lakes of Killarney is rather a slow business. The railways do not appear to work so much in accord with each other as might and should be done in the interest of trade, of the tourists and of the companies themselves.

Hence to get from Galway to Limerick, a distance of 69 miles, the traveller occupies six hours and a half, and he can get no further than that in a day unless he is off at an early hour at which few men, and still fewer women, care to rise... There are stoppages on the way.

Latimer does not fully understand the rivalry between the Midland and the WL & WR on that route, two companies who never got on very well and whose trains often connected only by accident. Similarly the very early start necessary indicates the working hours of the farming community at the time. However he does have a word of praise for the state of the buildings on the line to Limerick: 'the railway stations are cultivated and ornamented with flowers, which grow luxuriantly'.

Part of the Midland's problems must surely have been in the type of managers employed. For example, E. B. Ivatts wrote a memo on the selection of railway staff which shows an exceptionally high degree of imbecility.

A man with a prominence of the forehead just over the eyes will make a quick ticket collector. By passing the finger up the front of the nose to where the nose joins the forehead, in some men, the skull at this point, which may be termed the root of the nose, will be found to protrude, and, in some cases, form quite a lump.

Men of this type are quick, ready and observant, and most good detectives have this development. If the hair of the head and whiskers also is fine in texture and quality, so will the owner be the more incisive and perfecting in character.

Mr Ivatts is clearly a devotee of that discounted Victorian fad phrenology, the study of bumps on the head to determine character, but where he gets his notion on the significance of hair type is a mystery. It is terrifying to think that such a man occupied a senior position on the company's staff.

Even with such handicaps Tatlow lost no time in working on the Midland to bring it up to the required standard. He was responsible for building a good deal of new rolling stock, improving the permanent way and introducing staff discipline so that before long the railway was the equal of any in Ireland.

Western branches

Being quite self-contained the MGWR built only a few branch lines off its main routes. One of these was the Killeshandra branch which left the Cavan line at Crossdoney and ran the 7 miles to its terminus. This route opened on 1 June 1886, twelve years after the Sligo and Ballaghadereen Junction Railway began its service from Kilfree Junction. This nine mile branch was operated by the Midland and later fully absorbed by it.

One branch which survived an amazingly long time was that from Attymon Junction to Loughrea. This unremarkable line was built without any major engineering difficulties under the baronial guarantee scheme and opened for traffic on 1 December 1890. The line operated, like so many small Irish railways, in an area of diminishing traffic density and was unusual in that almost to the end it had trains of mixed passengers and goods, connecting with the Galway–Dublin services at Attymon. There was one intermediate station at Dunsandle. It was a typical branch line in that nothing very startling happened in its history apart from the odd flash of scandal such as the summons to Dublin of the Loughrea station master some years ago to explain the disappearance of a wagon load of coal. The same man was later warned that he was not to 'have anyone residing in his house'. This may have been just his brother from Clare or was the station house turning into a sink of vice and iniquity? We will never know for three years later there is a reference to him as the 'ex-station master'. Either he was transferred, sacked or deceased but no more is heard of him.

When the inevitable closure noises were heard in the 1960s under C. S. Andrews' contraction policy there was particularly vocal protest from the local community and amazingly this time the outcry was successful. The line survived as one of the last steam haunts in Ireland, largely through the enthusiasm of the people who worked it. The development of Tynagh mines at this time brought a good deal of traffic on to the line for although most of the ore was shipped by road much of the engineering equipment was delivered by rail to Loughrea. Another unusual source of income was film making. *Alfred the Great* was filmed in the area and there was great movement of cinema equipment and personnel through Loughrea station at the time.

However the days of the branch were numbered despite the best efforts of the staff to encourage usage of the line. On my last visit just a few months before closure Loughrea station was smart and clean with a neat house and lots of CIE promotional material prominently displayed on the approaches to the station. Similar in many ways was the 13 mile branch between Claremorris and Ballinrobe

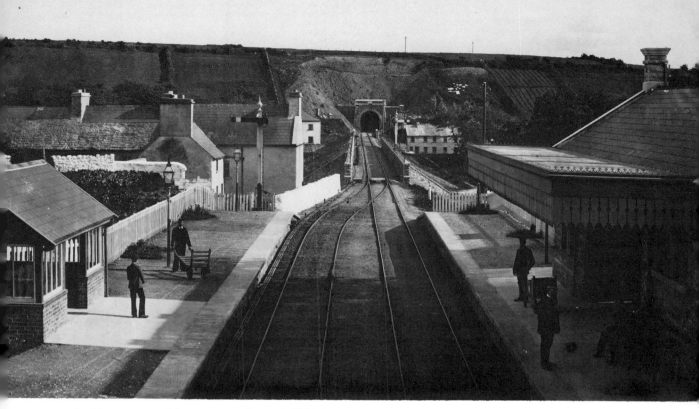

A tidy scene at Newport on the Achill line. Compare the station buildings with those of the Listowel and Ballybunion Railway

which opened on 1 November 1892. It too was built under baronial guarantee and although an independent company, was worked and virtually controlled by the Midland. Further west was the dramatically beautiful branch to Achill on the coast. It was built with a grant from the Board of Public Works and ran around Clew Bay from Westport to end at the mainland next to Achill Island. The countryside was harsh and poor but the expectations from tourist traffic were high and the company built a fine hotel at Mulrany for visitors to the area. There was only one other station at Newport and the three trains daily were sparsely used in winter time. There was one through coach to and from Dublin which joined the train at Westport and in turn was linked up to the service from Galway at Athlone.

The land in Achill has always been poor and in times past the only living to be had in that beautiful area was from fishing or tourism. As a result there has always been heavy emigration, much of it seasonal to meet the labour demands of farmers in Scotland and England. Local tradition has it that in the seventeenth century Brian Rua Ó Cearbhain predicted the coming of the railways, belching smoke and fire, and said that the first and last trains at Achill would carry the dead as passengers. It so happened that on 14 June 1894 a hooker left the island carrying a large number of young people on their way to catch the Glasgow steamer from Westport. They were going to find work at the harvest in Scotland and when the boat capsized thirty of them were drowned. Although the railway was not yet open for service a special train was run to bring the dead home to Mulrany. Then in 1937 a group of Achill labourers were burnt to death in a fire near Glasgow and the bodies, ten in all, were brought home for burial. Once again a funeral train ran on

The Corrib viaduct outside Galway station

the Achill line and two weeks later the railway closed.

Equally spectacular was the 49 mile branch from Galway to Clifden, the routing of which caused some early problems. The Midland wanted to build the line along the coast through Spiddal in order to serve what few centres of population there were and to get the trade in fish. The Board of Works favoured an inland route through extremely poor countryside and since it was putting up most of the money for the project its view prevailed. Construction began in 1891 and was completed on 1 July 1895, quite a long time for the distance involved. The hold ups were caused by a tunnel, a cutting at Oughterard and building a viaduct across the Corrib whose stone supports can still be seen in the river near Woodquay. The company made great efforts to publicise the line and attract foreign visitors to the area and to Clifden in particular. Handbooks and tourist guides were published regularly, like most railway companies, describing the delights of Connemara and the west. One such book issued in 1900 described the Achill and Clifden branches as follows: 'They are of full gauge, as substantially built as the rest of the system and have station accommodation of quite unusual quality—bright, artistic and simple.'

To encourage tourism the company ran its own buses between Clifden and Westport so that a round trip could be made taking in both branches. Other enticements were the 'Tourist Express', a through service from Dublin which ran non-stop from Galway to Clifden. A fine hotel was built by the company at Recess which was, like the stations, a fine solid building and in 1903 hosted King Edward VII on his visit to Connemara. But traffic in the low season was light to say the least and the coming of the car spelt the end for the Clifden line which ceased operating on 27 April 1935. Again the closure has attracted a certain folklore in that it is said the rails when lifted were sold to a German firm of engineers who

Recess station in the heart of Connemara

later used them to make bombs for the Blitz. The truth may be more prosaic for the rails probably went into store at the Broadstone. Today driving towards Clifden the line of railway can be seen almost the whole way marked by the many bridges and viaducts which are still in place.

Developments in Dublin

In Dublin the Midland was quick to see the need for direct access to the port of Dublin for its cattle and freight business. It was the first company to act on this

The pleasant station at Clifden with a train about to depart for Galway

and opened its Liffey branch to the quays in 1864, running from Liffey Junction to the quays. All goods traffic was handled at the goods yard there and delivered to the Dublin consignee by road. Soon after, with business booming, the company decided to expand the station at the Broadstone and in 1870 acquired part of the grounds of Grangegorman prison to build further sidings and an engine shed. In the course of construction the area was found to be a burial ground dating from the cholera epidemic of 1832. A further improvement was the building of a new approach road to the station which greatly eased access. Unfortunately this involved the alteration of the fine old Foster acqueduct which brought an arm of the Royal Canal down from Phibsboro and across the top of Constitution Hill. This was built at the beginning of the nineteenth century and was dedicated to John Foster, Lord Oriel. The Midland added an iron superstructure across the acqueduct which led to a canal basin in front of the Broadstone. This in turn had its own pontoon bridge which could be swung aside for the rare passage of boats. In the middle of this century the basin was filled in and the acqueduct removed on account of the traffic congestion it caused.

While the troubles with the GS&WR were sorted out by the 1860 agreement this did not spell the end of the Midland's disagreements with other companies. On one occasion this led to a fracas known as the battle of Newcomen Junction. The City of Dublin Junction Railway, having built its loop line across the Liffey, was authorised to make a branch to the MGWR's line at Newcomen Junction. But the latter objected strongly, saying the position of the line 'would be unsafe and unworkable'. Joseph Tatlow recounts the whole silly business:

> The promoters insisted; the Midland were obdurate. The promoters invaded the Midland premises, knocked down a wall and entered on Midland land. The Midland gathered their forces, drove back the attacking party and restored the wall. Again the attack was made and again the wall was demolished and rebuilt. And so the warfare continued, until at length an armistice was declared.

In the end a compromise was reached by the intervention of the Railway Commissioners but not before there were a number of sore heads about the place. It must be said that the objections of the Midland were not totally unreasonable for the line as built running from the canal up to Connolly Station has an extremely steep gradient and could in the days of less than 100% effective brakes have been quite dangerous.

Further expansion

County Meath was an area where the Midland was able to acquire one or two lines without going to the trouble of building them. In 1858 the Dublin & Meath Railway had proposed building a line from the GS&WR at Lucan to Navan and Athboy. By a combination of judicious emoluments and sleight of hand the Midland was able to divert the branch so that it left from its own line at Clonsilla, a major achievement. The D&MR had running powers over the route into the Broadstone and began running its trains in 1862 from Navan. It also built another line from Kilmessan to Athboy in 1864. The Navan and Kingscourt was another small independent company which built its 11 mile line in 1865 to join with the Great Northern and the Midland at Navan. From June 1869 the Midland took over the D&MR and the N&KR followed in 1888.

A less successful attempted takeover was that of the Athenry and Ennis Railway in 1892. This would have been a very useful connection as Ennis was a busy market town as well as being the junction for the West Clare Railway. Of course this would break the tacit agreement about respective territory and, as Tatlow says, 'to the Waterford and Limerick the bare idea of giving up possession of the fair Ennis to their rival the Midland was gall and wormwood'. The inquiry into the proposed sale had its lighter moments. One witness who was weary of being questioned was asked what would happen if an animal strayed on the line as a train approached and replied: 'It would excercise its running powers.' The Midland was confident of the outcome but in fact the decision of the committee went against them. 'Fortune' as Tatlow noted stoically, 'is a fickle jade and at the last she left us in the lurch.'

Thus with its lines substantially complete the Midland continued on its modestly prosperous way. The company's engines were unusual in that almost all were given names as well as numbers, many surviving well into the 1950s. The livery was emerald green which changed briefly to a royal blue for a few years but reverted to the old colour shortly afterwards. Another uncommon feature of the early locomotives was the upward flare of the engine cab making identification easy. From the First World War black was the preferred colour. Since it did not have any notable suburban working, apart from an irregular service to Maynooth, the Midland had few of the small tank engines normally seen on such workings. In fact there were four basic designs which were used throughout the company's independent life. Ashtown was one of the stations on the route to Maynooth which had been a halt for the Phoenix Park races and was opened fully in 1906 in an effort to boost commuter traffic. It closed in 1934, was reopened temporarily for the papal ceremonies in 1979 and now has a permanent service on the revived Maynooth line which CIE operates with additional stops at Clonsilla and Leixlip. Traffic is light at the moment but hopefully will improve with new rolling stock and a more frequent service.

Carriages

The coaches of the MGWR were quite distinctive, as Francis Head found when he took a second class ticket to Maynooth in 1852, described in *A Fortnight in Ireland.*

> On reaching the station I found a train of rich, dark blue carriages equal if not superior to any I have seen on the Continent of Europe. Each was composed of a first coupe handsomely lined with blue cloth with two second class carriages painted in the interior drab colour. In both were four seats covered with new glossy morocco leather. The glass windows, above which were Venetian shutters painted in two shades of light blue, had neat linen curtains chequered in blue and drab.

On a later trip to Athlone he decided to sample first class and is very favourably impressed with the sense of space and such useful items as a small hinged table.

> I next discovered a sliding door by which the coupe could be divided into two chambers and on continuing my search I observed several indications of another hidden luxury, which unbuttoning a hasp, proved, to my great astonishment, to be two comfortable double beds and hair matresses, in which two couples, closing the intermediate door, might separately sleep as comfortably and as innocently as if they were at home.

Another outstanding vehicle was the Dargan saloon, presented to the company by the famous contractor when he had completed the line from Athlone to Galway in 1851. It was carefully preserved by the Midland and used on special occasions for

VIPs such as the Empress of Austria who travelled in it during her extensive hunting forays in Co. Meath. It is now thankfully preserved in the Belfast Transport Museum. Tatlow says of it:

> In 1891 it was nearly fifty years old and was handsome still. The panels were modelled on the old stage coach design, and a great bow window adorned each end.

Less luxurious were the famous old six-wheelers which were used on all the company's branches and local services for third class passengers. They lasted a remarkably long time under the GSR and could occasionally be seen up to a decade or two ago.

Troubled times

The Midland suffered its share of the Troubles although not as much as other Irish lines. During the Anglo–Irish conflict the 'Blacksmith of Ballinalee', Sean McEoin, seems to have been frequently involved with it. On one occasion a train guard, Jack Murray, tells of being roused from his bed early one morning to work a special from Broadstone to Longford and back. When he got to the station he found the train consisted of ambulance coaches, fully staffed with doctors and nurses. Its purpose was to bring to Dublin the dead and wounded from McEoin's ambush of Auxiliaries at Clonfin. Later on, in March 1921, the military learnt that he would be travelling unaccompanied on the 5.40 am train from the Broadstone. As the train pulled into Mullingar McEoin looked out of the window and saw the station was swarming with soldiers and Black and Tans. Deciding to shoot it out he began firing before the train stopped but was badly wounded and taken back to Dublin to the military hospital, now St Bricin's, and later imprisoned in Mountjoy.

The Civil War, largely a war of semantics, was as disastrous for the Midland as it was for the other railway companies. Derailments, burnings and hijacks were frequent although the disruption never reached the peak it did on the GS&WR. When the plans for railway amalgamation were announced the Midland was a willing partner and being one of the largest concerns had an influential voice in the newly formed GSR. Among the early casualties of the new regime were the lines to the far west. The Killala branch closed in July 1934, Clifden lost its service on 27 April 1935 and Achill in September 1937. Apart from these and a number of branch lines the Midland is largely intact at the time of writing with regular services to Sligo, Galway and Westport and a more limited one to Ballina.

A more significant closure was that of the Broadstone station in 1937. Being a little removed from the centre of the city the GSR decided to transfer all services to the west to Amiens Street and Westland Row stations. But the building was not to disappear at once for the railway workshops were to be expanded and developed. Glasnevin Junction was adapted to allow through running to Amiens Street and, from 17 January, all services ran through to Westland Row. It was a nostalgic occasion but not totally unexpected. When the last train arrived early on the morning of 17 January to the accompaniment of numerous detonators the driver was mobbed by an enthusiastic crowd who celebrated the station's passing with a jar or two, the whole event being recorded by RTE radio. Today the main part of the Broadstone is somewhat altered and a large part has been turned into a bus garage. The line has been lifted as far as Liffey Junction but is otherwise intact and who knows we may one day see trains running into the old terminus of the most Irish of the railway companies.

5 The Great Northern Railway

ONE of the first projected railways in Ireland was the 'Leinster and Ulster Rail Company' which met in January 1825 to build 'rail roads between Dublin and the North, particularly Belfast, and the intermediate Towns, with Branches'. The company never got farther than the drawing board and it was nine years later before the first line opened, the Dublin and Kingstown. Nonetheless the 1825 scheme shows that the promoters saw the potential from a rail link of the administrative and industrial capitals of Ireland.

In 1836 the government-appointed Drummond Commission met to report on the best way of bringing the benefits of railways to Ireland. It suggested that the most suitable method for a country of such relatively sparse population and low industrial development was for a fully integrated system of lines. This conclusion did not of course have the force of law and it was not until 1925 that the amalgamation took place However fifty years before that a number of companies operating in north and north–east Ireland did merge to form the Great Northern, the first of which to appear was the Ulster Railway.

The Ulster Railway

Construction of the UR between Belfast and Armagh began in 1837 and was slow even by the standards of the time. It took two years to build the $7\frac{1}{2}$ miles to Lisburn, the weather being atrocious and conditions difficult, but the line was solidly build and it opened on 12 August 1839. It was clear that despite the number of companies becoming involved at some time there would be through services between Dublin and Belfast as planned in the 1825 proposal. So almost immediately the question of gauge arose. The Dublin and Kingstown had adopted the English gauge of 4ft $8\frac{1}{2}$ in. but the UR, wanting to do things on the grand scale, decided to go for 6ft 2in.

The Belfast terminus at Great Victoria Street was a fine sturdy building with two platforms and three tracks. When the first locomotives were delivered at Belfast docks there was great excitement and soon after notices appeared in the papers announcing the opening as far as Lisburn. There was one intermediate station at Dunmurry with fares at 1/- first (5p) and 6d ($2\frac{1}{2}$p) second irrespective of the distance travelled. With seven trains in each direction over 3,000 people travelled on the first day without mishap. There were no third class carriages provided for some years possibly because of government opposition on the grounds they 'would only encourage the lower orders to wander aimlessly about the country'.

However enthusiasm for the railway was not quite universal. Among the protestant population in the north the sabbath was inviolable and when certain ministers of religion learnt that trains would run on Sundays they denounced this

Great Victoria Street station in Belfast (GNR)

A diesel multiple unit on the former GNR line near Lisburn

monstrous evil in no uncertain terms. One gentleman hurled anathemas from the pulpit like thunderbolts. He accused the newly arrived Ulster Railway of 'sending souls to the devil at sixpence a piece', adding for good measure that 'every sound of the railway steam whistle is answered by a shout in Hell!' Apart from the moral dangers of Sunday travel there were other fears. Landowners near the line claimed that the smoke would kill the birds, the noise would drive cattle and sheep into a frenzy, the horse would become an extinct species, cows would withhold their milk and sparks would set fire to every house, factory and cottage for miles around. With all these dangers pending it is surprising that railways were not banned by law.

The railway managed not to destroy the entire fabric of life in Ulster and the first stage was considered by almost everyone to be a success. Portadown was clearly the next target and the company was confident it could raise the capital to fund the extension. But by now investors were backward in coming forward and the directors were forced to approach the Board of Works for a loan, as their worthy predecessors the Dublin and Kingstown had done. The government did not rush to advance the readies but £20,000 was eventually handed over and Dargan got to work building the line. Portadown was reached in 1842 and there it stopped for a while.

A question of gauge

Meanwhile further south the Dublin and Drogheda Railway (see below) were about to cross the Rubicon if not the Boyne and had decided on a gauge of 5 ft 2 in. The UR shot up in protest like a startled pheasant claiming that as their gauge of 6 ft 2 in had been decided by a royal commission all others should fall in with it. The D&DR demurred and announced it was going ahead with track laying. Various figures from 3 ft to 7 ft were suggested so an arbitrator was called in, Major General Pasley RE, who being the very model of a modern major general tackled the problem with military efficiency and impartiality and came up with a compromise of 5 ft 3 in. It was as well to get the problem sorted out early on and this gauge was later enforced on almost all Irish railways by law. Regauging began immediately and cost the UR nearly £20,000, although two-thirds was met by compensation.

The Cyclops, *GNR Locomotive no. 135*

Having disposed of the gauge dilemma all eyes were on Armagh, the next desti-nation. The area around Portadown is particularly marshy so progress was again slow. There was also a certain amount of station hopscotch around the Bann but from 1863 a permanent site east of the river was chosen. Armagh was finally reached in 1848; within ten years Dargan had brought the railway to Monaghan and in 1863 to Cavan where it joined the MGWR and thus a roundabout Belfast to Dublin link was made. Meanwhile plans were well advanced for the UR to run services between Portadown and Dungannon, built by Dargan in 1858 and thus provide a rail link between Belfast and Derry.

Services

By 1863 the UR had a substantial mileage in operation. One continuing omission was third class accommodation, all the more so given the high number of people working in the shipyards and linen factories around Belfast. Third class wagons (without seats) made their grudging appearance in the 1840s but in case they became too popular they were only used on one train each day at 2pm, a useless time of day for working people but enough to meet the minimum legal requirement. The question of third class travel was a recurring problem for the UR as for many other lines. On the one hand the company wanted to keep their services the preserve of the wealthy and yet they could not afford to ignore the fact that third class travel was an increasing proportion of the total receipts. One UR director said that in running third class wagons 'first class passengers had dropped down to second class, while the dirty coats went further down to the third class among the great unwashed', a common complaint. This kind of thinking prevailed until 1848 when third class was no longer run exclusively with goods trains.

It was this very class division which led to the death of a train guard or police-man in 1842. The company employed guards to sit on a roof seat above each coach. On this occasion a third class passenger who was tired of the rigours of his class decided to slip into the relative comfort of a second class carriage. The guard stood up to order him back and was hit by a road bridge under which the train was travelling at 25mph. His skull was fractured and he died soon after.

The 1860s were a time of great leaps forward. Gas lights appeared in UR carriages in 1863 and contemporary accounts were very enthusiastic. 'Anyone who visits the Ulster Railway station can contrast the splendidly lighted carriages of the Ulster with the dingy conveyances used on the main line between Belfast and Dublin.' But for some reason the experiment was not a success and was in time abandoned. A year later third class were allowed to purchase return tickets, a grudging admission that even if the unwashed do go away they would probably only come back again.

The Dublin and Drogheda Railway

Impetus for a link between Dublin and Drogheda came from one Thomas Brodigan, a Drogheda landowner who called a public meeting to press for the building of a railway to the capital. Everyone agreed in principle on the advantages of such a line but harmony dissolved when it came to discussing the route it should take. Some favoured the coastline while others pressed for a diver-sion inland claiming that the fishing villages of Co. Dublin were undeveloped and that following the coast would mean building several expensive viaducts. The parties were also divided on the choice of terminus: some thought that a spot opposite the GPO in Sackville (O'Connell) Street was ideal for speeding mails on the line and for the city centre. Others pushed for a site in Prussia Street and others still in what is only slightly less remote 'the waste ground near the Basin at Blessington Street' adjacent to what was later the Broadstone.

The services of an engineer, William Cubitt (a familiar building name today) were engaged to assess the alternatives. His report on the Great Northern Trunk Railway appeared in 1836 and he opted for the coastal party. He estimated the cost at £650,000, half of which would be taken up by cuttings and embankments. For some reason he advocated tunnelling for part of the line thereby making a saving of £150,000. He also had a sting in the tail for the board in case it got too penny pinching: 'It would be better not to make a Railway at all for the present, than to make one inferior in plan and execution to what the science and practice of the present day would admit to be the best.'

Naturally the inhabitants of such towns as Navan were aggrieved and they speedily rejected Cubitt's report. The bill for the railway as planned by him was challenged throughout its passage but was finally passed on 13 August 1836. No sooner had work begun in 1838 than a royal commission delivered itself of a revised verdict saying that the inland route might be preferable after all! Work stopped until further backing was received and a new bill shepherded through Parliament by Daniel O'Connell. Dargan resumed construction according to the original plan in October 1840 and Amiens Street was chosen as the Dublin terminus, a third of the capital for the whole project coming from Manchester businessmen. After such a stormy beginning the building of the UR seems like a picnic.

Dargan made steady progress and in 1844 the first trial runs took place. On 18 March a special train ran to Drogheda with 565 passengers aboard including Earl de Grey, the Lord Lieutenant. Coastguards fired off their cannon as the train progressed up the line as if to mark the success of the coastal party and that evening there was a buffet and ball in John MacNeil's house in Rutland (Parnell) Square. By May 23 the works were nearly ready and O'Connell was feted in the course of a special run to Drogheda and back.

Amiens Street Station

The following day Earl de Gray laid the foundation stone of Amiens Street Station. Inside were 'the current coins of the realm from a farthing to a sovereign, *Saunders' News Letter* and the Freeman's Journal of the day', as well as a history of the company (of necessity rather brief), directors' reports and a vellum manuscript giving an account of the opening. Hopefully when some future property speculator demolishes Amiens Street to make way for an office block he will remember to rescue these items from the rubble. The usual banquet followed, this time under the arches of the station, and at 3 pm all went up to see the first train depart.

The terminus was built at a cost of £7,000, the material being Wicklow granite. The architect was William Deane Butler and he produced a plan for a striking building of Italianate style. Opinions differ about it; some say it is the least satisfactory of the Dublin termini while others agree with a contemporary observer who said it 'easily carried off the palm for architectural excellence'. Most would admit that it has a graceful facade with towers and pinnacles which give it an almost folly-like appearance. Of more pragmatic concern is that for thirty years

The Italianate façade of Amiens Street station c. 1900

passengers had to struggle up a long flight of stairs to reach the platforms until the ramp was built opposite Store Street. Recently a new entrance for access to suburban trains was opened by CIE, saving the long trek up the mainline platforms to catch a local train. This has made the station a lot easier to negotiate, especially at peak times.

Being built at an elevation there are a large number of bridges on the line—no less than 75 arches between Amiens Street and the Royal Canal. The embankments referred to earlier were at Malahide, Rogerstown and Gormanstown, with bridges over the Tolka River, the Howth Road near Dollymount and at Balbriggan, all of which must have added a good deal to the cost of construction. These works have lasted remarkably well with only occasional restructuring.

Services

In 1844 there were three types of train on offer: the mail which ran at 30 mph and stopped only at Malahide and Balbriggan; the quick, which was a bit slower, and the mixed which had three classes, goods wagons and took a very long time. Third class was provided on mixed trains only. On the mails and the quick fares were 4/6 first and 3/- second (22½p, 15p) and on the mixed they were 3/6, 2/6, 1/6 (17½p, 12½p, 7½p). If you were an infant and unable to walk you travelled free and if a dog the charge was half the third class fare. A number of people were issued with free passes including such gentlemen of conflicting interests as Mr Cairnes, a successful brewer, and Fr Mathew the temperance preacher. The company was also one of the first to issue return tickets at 1½ times the single fare. It was however a bit slow in taking goods traffic, most of it being for onward shipment, and the Boyne remained a major obstacle for many years.

With its line operating smoothly the D & DR next turned to the question of extensions. The small fishing village at Howth, situated at the end of the long embracing arm of land around Dublin Bay, was by then being promoted as a rival packet station to Kingstown. The line was approved in 1845 and opened on 30 May 1847. Although Howth never again became a cross channel port there has always been a busy service for commuters and day trippers (holders of return tickets once got a free cold bath, if they wanted it). For its next line the company decided to turn inland and headed for Navan, to placate those who were put out at not being on the main line. There the Dublin & Meath line was crossed running up to Kingscourt. The D & DR continued its route to Kells and terminated at Oldcastle which opened for traffic on 17 May 1863. The D & MR had running powers as far as Kells and was thus able to offer a quicker more direct route between Kells, Navan and Dublin than via Drogheda. When the D & MR was absorbed by the MGWR in 1869 an agreement was made with the D & DR on the division of receipts for the section.

The Dublin and Belfast Junction Railway

With trains operating between Dublin–Drogheda and Belfast–Portadown there was an outstanding gap between Drogheda and Portadown. Thus the D & BJR was formed to link the systems on 6 April 1844 with its 63 mile line. The first and most apparent obstacle to this was crossing the Boyne at Drogheda and on account of the expense this was delayed as late as possible, a motive which was roundly criticised at the time since it caused great inconvenience for passengers and goods. One caustic newspaper of the day said: 'Their reason is the the bridge will cost money, but will the time ever come when it will not cost money?'

The title of the D & BJR was a little misleading in that it went nowhere near either Dublin or Belfast, but that is a minor point. The first section to be opened was that between Drogheda (north of the river) and Dundalk on 15 February 1849 despite the usual problems of a shortage of funds and slow contractors. A loan of £120,000 was negotiated from the government of the day for the next section between Dundalk and Portadown which after heavy rock blasting and the raising of the giant Bessbrook viaduct was completed on 10 June 1852. This viaduct is a huge structure with eighteen arches and at its highest is 140 feet from the ground. In this way were Belfast and Dublin linked, apart from the Boyne crossing which symbolically and actually kept the two cities apart. Transfer passengers faced a tedious and time consuming prospect of getting off at one station, making their own way across the river and ascending to join another train on the other side.

Eventually work began on the bridge but it was a difficult task given the engineering skills of the time. Designs had to be constantly modified in the face of technical problems and one pier had to be sunk 43 feet below the water to find a solid foundation. A temporary wooden structure opened with strict controls for the 1853 Dublin International Exhibition (largely funded by Dargan) and two years later on 5 April 1855 the stone viaduct opened for normal traffic. The stonework is basically unchanged since then and it is a magnificent sight when viewed from ground level along the quays. Indeed the rail traveller has an equally spectacular view on leaving Drogheda for Belfast as he can look down inside the funnel of ships moored at the quays!

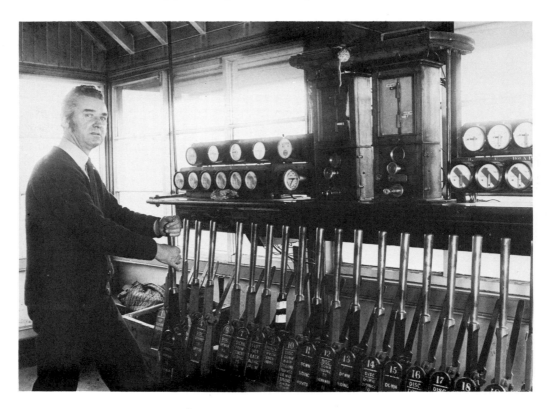

Drogheda signalman using the old manual levers at the station's north cabin before automation

It is as well that Drogheda has such a fine piece of work to boast of for it does not always feature among Ireland's most attractive towns. As early as 1866 G. S. Measom wrote of it in his *MGWR Guide* as having 'a strong fish-like smell, and altogether so dirty and uncomfortable, and with such miserable accommodation, that the tourist will not feel inclined to linger in the town any longer than necessary'! Such vehemence *could* be ascribed to a desire to direct the Belfast bound passenger over the MGWR's route via Cavan although the connections were almost non-existent. Be that as it may you see the town at its best from the Boyne viaduct.

With the construction of the two viaducts the D & BJR was almost at the end of its financial resources although it did lease and run a short line between Scarva and Banbridge. It also made a contribution of £20,000 to the cost of a line between Clones and Cavan, as did the D & DR and the UR. It is not surprising therefore that some years later a train was seized for non-payment of rates. Trains are not very disposable items and the one which the collector chose to impound was by chance one on which six grand jurors were travelling on urgent business to Dundalk. The rates official stuck to his guns and would not allow the train to proceed without payment despite the concerted efforts of its six distinguished passengers. Finally an unseemly pooling of funds took place, the money handed over and the train allowed to depart. No doubt the official was either exiled to Buncrana or else became Collector-General. The whole affair shows that the D & BJR was in a tight position and in fact expenditure was kept to a minimum for the rest of its independent life.

The Irish North Western Railway

This company derives from a tangled web of schemes roughly based on the Dundalk region. The chief constituents were the Dundalk and Enniskillen Railway with a terminus at Barrack Street, Dundalk and the Londonderry and Enniskillen, that unfortunate company which ranks high on the immortal list of failed enterprises. The turning of the first sod at Barrack Street on 15 October 1845 was marked with great ceremony. Shareholders marched through the town 'wearing white ribbons on their left breasts', a symbol whose meaning has been lost in the mist of history. A temperance band followed these worthies to the chosen spot. There the chairman, Lord Roden, turned the first shovelful and handed the company secretary a piece of clay and a twig to indicate the company's ownership. What the secretary did with these objects is not recorded.

With such an expeditious launch progress was disappointingly slow on account of the shortage of capital. It took the company almost nine years to reach Ballybay (17 July 1854) and the line struggled into Enniskillen on 15 February 1859. Yet despite its impecunious state the minds of the D & ER directors were constantly absorbed with possible extensions in the erroneous belief that increased mileage equals increased profitability, a fatal mistake. Cavan was the chief goal and the first stage was the branch to Cootehill, which opened on 18 October 1860. There the line stopped for the UR was by then well advanced in building its own line to Cavan and the Cootehill branch remained, an uneconomic stretch pointing forlornly in the direction of the company's dashed hopes.

A renowned feature of the D & ER was the square crossing at Dundalk where it traversed the Dublin to Belfast line. Railways abhor perpendicular crossings almost as much as nature abhors a vacuum. They are considered dangerous and uncontrollable, which accounts for their rarity. Most engineers would build a trailing junction with points and signals or else raise one line above the other, certainly at such a busy station as Dundalk with trains coming in from Enniskillen, Armagh, Greenore, Belfast and Dublin. In fact the junction was remarkably free of accidents, possibly because of the almost excessive caution of those using it. Another example of such a crossing is Limerick Junction.

Possibly the least efficient if not the most dangerous railway ever to operate in Ireland was the Londonderry and Enniskillen. This began its disastrous career in 1845 with misguided authority to build the 60 mile line between the two places in its name. Its troubled history is a catalogue of routing squabbles, legal battles (invariably lost), low receipts, shoddy track, derailments, absence of maintenance, canal competition, untrained staff and poor management. The board tried to run their company from London and from the start could not decide on the route the line should follow. John MacNeil and George Stephenson disagreed on the path between Strabane and Omagh and even over the siting of the Derry terminus. Stephenson's route was chosen, but a few years after opening the terminus was moved nearer the city centre. Stephenson's influence on the running of the company seems to have been minimal—perhaps he got out before it destroyed his reputation. How the Board of Trade ever gave permission for the line to open is a mystery but there is some evidence that the company did start running trains before all the specified improvements had been made. The line between Derry and Strabane opened on 19 April 1847 and to Omagh five years later. True to form Fintona was reached in 1853, a year before Parliament gave its permission to begin construction.

The Fintona tram

Fintona was the junction for the famous horse drawn tram which ran (or strolled) down the three-quarters mile branch to the town. For the whole of its existence the branch was worked in this way and the horse was possibly the most pampered in Ireland. The tram was open on top with three classes and the vehicle introduced in 1883 lasted until closure. Third class fare in the 1950s was one penny. In recent years Dick (the horse) was much visited by enthusiasts including a number of American soldiers stationed nearby during the last war, when it was very busy. It was common then for a soldier to have a quiet word with the driver, a packet of sugar or cigarettes would change hands and the horse would find a yelling rider on his back for the trip. Dick was tolerant of such liberties and quite smart for he knew exactly how many trips he had to make each day; without prompting he would know whether to walk to the other end of the tram or to the stable if that was the last run of the day.

Mergers and takeovers

The L & ER staggered on, a hazard to the public, until 1859–60 when it was approached by the D & ER with a lease proposal which it leapt at in relief. This unforeseen expansion prompted the adoption of a new name by the D & ER, more fitting to its higher destiny: the Irish North Western Railway. It was advisable to drop the name L & ER as soon as possible anyway.

Westward from the Enniskillen–Omagh line ran the Enniskillen and Bundoran Railway, a 35 mile branch running into south Donegal and the seaside towns of Ballyshannon and Bundoran. This opened from Bundoran Junction, a lovely tree-lined affair built as a triangle, on 13 June 1866. Permission to extend to Sligo, an obvious destination, was obtained in 1862 but the line was never built and Bundoran remained the terminus and the destination of the popular *Bundoran Express*. This line was operated by the INWR and therefore ripe for takeover.

The Annaghmore elopement

The final link in this railway jigsaw which became the Great Northern Railway (Ireland) was the Portadown, Dungannon and Omagh Railway which opened between 1858 and 1861. This provided a new route between Belfast and Derry nearly 50 miles shorter than going via Clones. The line was the scene of the spectacular 'Annaghmore elopement' in 1858, a touching little episode straight out of the pages of a Victorian novel.

A few miles from Portadown is the small town of Annaghmore, behind whose station was and is a public house for the consolation, convenience and refreshment of travellers. This hostelry was run by two comely maidens of the distinguished name Telford, the daughters of a local farmer. A regular driver on the line, now sadly closed, was one John Hardstaff and as is the nature of these things he developed a great interest in one of the Misses Telford. The father heard of the romance and cruelly forbade his weeping daughter to see her engine driver again. Thus the couple were forced to meet in secret and decided that on the evening of 9 September they would run away together. The plan was that the girl would join her lover on the last train to Dungannon, which he was driving that night.

However it is very hard to keep these things to yourself and before the train pulled in the Telfords had got word and were out in force to prevent her escaping to wedded bliss in Dungannon. With the support of Reilly, the porter, Mr Telford prowled the station as the train arrived. But by this time the determined girl was climbing into a carriage from the track, assisted by her intended. At last the train began to pull out but realising she was aboard the malevolent Reilly switched the points so that the train swung off the main line into a siding. It ran down the 85 yards, smashed through the buffers and ended up in a bog. The young lady, seeing the train was going no further and in the heat of the moment, opened the carriage door and leapt dramatically from the train. She would have been better to stay put for she ended up with water up to her waist and stuck fast in a boghole from which predicament she had to be rescued by Hardstaff. Both then retired sheepishly to the station house to dry off.

The story ends happily, for the next day, as Col. Ross notes drily in his official report: 'She succeeded in placing herself and her box under the care of John Hardstaff, by a train of which he was not the driver, as would doubtless have been the preferable course in the first instance.'

It was a relief to all concerned when the D & ER, no goldmine itself, took over the L & ER to form the INWR. Although it made a fair effort the INWR was never free of financial problems. After 1862 no dividend was paid to investors and the company admitted it was 'in a Condition of pecuniary Embarassment'. In other words it was broke so that news of the Northern Railway merger must have been music to its ears.

The Great Northern Railway (Ireland)

The first mention of an amalgamation of the above companies was made as early as 1847 but there was strong resistance to the idea from many of the independently minded companies new to the business of running a railway. The UR was particularly opposed to any such merger so that the D & DR and the D & BJR were the first to agree to join forces in 1875 to form the Northern Railway of Ireland. This move was widely welcomed as changing trains twice on the fairly short Dublin–Belfast run was considered a great nuisance and connections were not always guaranteed. The following January the sickly INWR joined the fold and on 1 April 1876 the UR, dropping all pretence at coyness, came in with the other three to form the Great Northern Railway Company (Ireland).

An early problem for the new company was a surfeit of directors on the joint board, it being several years before mortality, dissension and other causes reduced the numbers to a reasonable size. The old rivalries took some time to die down and many years passed before a single general manager with full authority could be appointed. Inevitably there were a number of such role duplications.

The Belfast Central Railway

In Dublin, where the company headquarters were located, the North Wall branch was in the course of construction when the GNR came into existence. This was speedily completed and gave valuable access to the docks and to the lines of other companies. Another useful connection was being planned at the same time in Belfast. This was the Belfast Central Railway which had been incorporated on 25 July 1864 with a proposal for a branch just south of Great Victoria Street Station, up to the Belfast and Northern Counties station at York Road and across the Lagan to the Belfast and County Down at Queen's Quay. With a new central station between these three the plan had obvious merits in that it linked all three railways which up to then had no interchange within the city. However the financial support was slow in coming, the contractor was owed a large sum, the land had not been paid for, the secretary sued the company for his salary and the board resigned en masse.

A new board of directors was persuaded to take up where the old one had left off and proceeded to cut the plans drastically. The link up with York Road Station was dropped as was the proposed new central station. (The latter was finally built by Northern Ireland Railways a century later and today its remaining services operate out of it.) The original BCR was not a great success; reversals were necessary between Great Victoria Street and Queen's Quay, reducing the line's usefulness. The GNR agreed to take over in 1885 and ceased passenger operations on it immediately, the advent of trams having had serious effect on urban traffic, and the line was used solely as a goods transfer facility. Only in recent years has the line proved its value with the opening of Belfast Central Station.

Nearby was the Dublin and Antrim Junction Railway, a 20 mile branch running from Lisburn north to Antrim Junction where it met the B & NCR's line out of York Road. This provided a useful through connection from Dublin towards Derry without going through Belfast and is today used by CIE goods trains operating to Derry as well as the rerouted Belfast–Derry passenger service. The line was originally worked by the UR and was in time absorbed by the GNR.

The port of Greenore had quite a busy steamer service to Britain during the last century and thus was quite well served with railways. The Dundalk Newry and Greenore Railway (see Chapter 7) opened in 1876 but some years prior to that the Newry and Enniskillen Railway was incorporated (31 July 1845) to build a line from the harbour inland to Fermanagh. The company only managed to get as far as Armagh and changed its name accordingly. The first section to Goraghwood opened in 1854 while construction pushed ahead into the undulating country of Armagh. This section required two tunnels, one of them a mile long which made it the longest in Ireland. The Newry and Armagh, as it had become, joined the GNR in 1879. Similarly truncated was the ambition of the Newry Warrenpoint and Rostrevor which reached Warrenpoint on 28 May 1849 but got no further towards Rostrevor. It too became part of the GNR in 1886.

County Down was the next target of the expansionist Great Northern. The two lines to Banbridge from Scarva and Lisburn had been leased to the original companies which formed the GNR in 1876 and these provided a useful foothold for an advance on the seaside town of Newcastle, then the preserve of the Belfast and County Down. Ballyroney had been reached from Banbridge on 14 December 1880 and the B & CDR, anxious to preserve its lucrative traffic from its larger neighbour, drove the best bargain it could whereby the two companies met at Castlewellan. However the GNR had a distinct advantage in that it could run trains into Newcastle while the B & CDR had to be satisfied with having fairly worthless access to Ballyroney.

One other branch which should be mentioned was the 4½ mile line off the Clones to Cavan route which served the pleasant little town of Belturbet on the River Erne. This left the main line at Ballyhaise and opened on 29 June 1885. A few years later the Cavan and Leitrim narrow gauge line reached Belturbet where it shared the GNR's station and other facilities such as a windmill for pumping water. The Belturbet branch was for most its life worked by a little 2–4–2T engine which has been preserved in the Belfast Transport Museum.

Hill of Howth tram

In the Dublin suburbs the GNR's Howth branch was generating good revenue so that the company decided to expand the service it was operating. The Hill of Howth has always been a popular spot for day trippers and picnickers, giving a lovely walk to the top with outstanding views of Dublin Bay in either direction. The company thought that one way to tap this potential would be to build a tramway from Sutton to the summit and down to Howth village. It was a 5 ft 3 in. gauge electric tramway, 5¼ miles long and the first section opened to the Summit on 17 June 1901 with the remainder a few months later. The gradients were steep as might be expected and with open top vehicles the trip was popular with Dubliners and visitors. There were ten cars in all, four of which were preserved when the line closed on 31 May 1959: two are in Ireland, one in Britain and another in the USA. The Howth tram features dramatically and sadly at the end of David Thomson's *Woodbrook*. He gives a moving description of the last time he saw Phoebe near the Summit just before he boarded the tram on his way back to England.

First in its class

With its route mileage almost complete what sort of company was the Great Northern as it entered the twentieth century? It was without doubt the supreme Irish railway. It served the two principal cities, its trains were faster and more

Map of the GNR network from the 1913 annual report

punctual than any others, its rolling stock the most modern and the best maintained, staff morale and pride were high and last but not least it was the most profitable Irish railway. When most were happy enough to be paying a 3 per cent dividend it managed 6 per cent with ease. The *Enterprise*, the aptly named crack express of the GNR, covered the distance between Dublin and Belfast in a time that is quite respectable today. The GNR was the first to use electric lighting throughout its coaches and provided an excellent restaurant service on the principal routes. Its locomotives were regularly painted in a distinctive blue shade with deep red edging and showed up well against the carriages of varnished teak with gold letters and numbers turned out from the company's Dundalk works. The Great Northern was, quite simply, the best.

Part of its success was surely its policy of constantly assessing and adapting services to the needs of the general public. An example of this was the introduction of sleeping cars in 1908 which were heralded thus:

> The public are respectfully informed that sleeping accommodation is now provided for First Class Passengers on the night mail trains, leaving Dublin for Londonderry and Belfast at 8.20 pm and Londonderry and Belfast for Dublin at 9.30 and 10.00 pm

The GNR/GSR Belfast to Cork Enterprise *about to depart from Amiens Street station*

respectively. The charge for this convenience is 5/- per passenger (25p), irrespective of distance, in addition to the ordinary First Class fare. The carriage will be placed in a convenient place after arrival at the destination so that passengers can leave it at any time up to 8.00 am.

The fact that the service was not a great success does not detract from the worthwhile motives in trying to provide it. Sleeping cars were no longer provided after 1918.

Also commendable was the decision made in 1950 to extend the *Enterprise* run as far as Cork. It may be wondered why this was not tried previously, but before nationalisation it may well have been that inter-company rivalry would not allow such an experiment. From 2 October the train left Belfast at 10.30 am and reached Cork at 5.15 pm with three-quarters of an hour stop at Amiens Street. The through service ended in 1953 though for a time it was run by no. 800 *Maeve* and her sisters on the Dublin–Cork stretch. These engines were the most powerful ever built in Ireland and had no trouble handling the heaviest trains on the GSR and CIE. The *Bundoran Express* was another regular feature of GNR services. Its purpose was to attract visitors from Dublin to Bundoran where the company had its own hotel, the Great Northern. It was a summer only train and also carried many pilgrims to Lough Derg. The timing from Dundalk westwards hardly merited the title 'express' but the train did run non-stop between Pettigo and Clones as the line crossed the border at several points and any stop would have required a customs examination.

County Donegal Railways

By the turn of the century most of the GNR lines had been either built or acquired by takeover. One notable exception was the large narrow gauge network of railways in Donegal. For such a sparsely populated county, Donegal was very well supplied with railways, the first being the Finn Valley which opened in 1863 as a standard gauge line worked by the INWR and maintained its independence when the GNR was formed in 1876. Further on was the West Donegal Railway which merged with the FVR to form the Donegal Railway in 1892. The following year the sensible course of changing the Finn Valley line to narrow gauge (three feet) was adopted. It was this joint network which attracted the attention of the GNR board and when the Midland Railway of England expressed an interest in the Donegal lines it was quick to say it wanted to be in on the deal. The result was the launching of the County Donegal Railways Joint Committee in 1906 (see Chapter 9). Predictably it became one of the best run narrow gauge systems in Ireland and lasted until 1960.

Dundalk engineering works

At the time of the 1876 amalgamation each company had its own engineering works. The D&BJR and INWR had their shops at Dundalk and this was chosen as the main centre, being the most convenient and well equipped. From 1881 all engineering work was carried out there, including locomotive manufacture and maintenance, the construction of railcars, railbuses, coaches, wagons, road buses, lorries, station, hotel and railway furniture, electrical work, carpentry and repairs of all kinds. The works covered a large area and turned out a great number of excellent locomotives, many of which survived long after the dissolution of the GNR.

GNR no. 171 Slieve Gullion on a steam excursion at Dun Laoghaire

Characters

Being one of the largest networks the GNR had more than its share of 'characters' on the staff, not least because being an employee of the company was a matter of prestige even when jobs on the railways were easy to come by. One driver based at Derry took such pride in maintaining his engine in top condition that he used to climb along the boiler while the train was running to oil the inaccessible parts. His fireman, one Frank Donohoe, decided to cure him of this dangerous habit and have a bit of fun as well. One day while the driver was out with his oil can he put on a horrific carnival mask and went down the far side of the engine. Suddenly he stuck his head round the corner and peered at the driver. The poor man got such a fright that he screamed and clambered back to the footplate as fast as he could, saying that he had just seen the devil.

Donohoe was a bit of a practical joker and on another occasion he was transferred to Belfast on a temporary assignment. He was a great one for carving his initials on every available piece of wood until one day the foreman tackled him about the ubiquitous 'F.D.'. Quick as a flash came the reply: 'It's those Belfast men, sir. It means Fuck Derry!' It may well have been Frank Donohoe who christened a popular pub near Great Victoria Street Station 'the Glue Pot' because it was so hard to get out of.

Naturally among railwaymen there were popular stations and others which were viewed as a place of exile. For many, Omagh fell in the latter category, especially for Derry men who were transferred there and were more or less forced to set up a home in the town. One fearless character refused to accept such banishment and if he could not get back to Derry after the day's work in Omagh would bed down for the night in the station hut. This so annoyed one senior driver that he used to write unprintable comments on the wall above the sleeping man and even concealed rotten fish under the floorboards to discourage him.

Others were more than happy with being posted to a quiet country station such as Alec Lindsay the signalman at Lisbellaw. He took great pride in keeping his station neat and tidy, growing flowers on the platform and personally cleaning the lavatories each day. One day an American visitor was waiting for a train and complaining loudly about the weather, the lack of stimulation in the town, the state of the world and sundry other matters. Finally he asked for directions to the 'washroom'. Lindsay indicated the large Gentlemen sign further up the platform saying: 'Pay no attention to that, just go on in.'

At Monaghan the station master, J. H. Doogan, was known as 'The Count' from his aristocratic appearance. One day he received a query from head office at Amiens Street about the non-return of receipts from the public convenience slot machines at the station. Without hesitation he wrote back: 'A wave of constipation has hit the area!'

The same station was the scene of an adventure which seems to be out of a Laurel and Hardy film. Just before the First World War an unusual passenger used the station. It was a lion in transit to a circus. Naturally Leo aroused great interest among the staff and of course the inevitable happened: the lion escaped. It appears that one inquisitive person did not secure the cage door and so off he went seeking whom he might devour. In fact he was fairly harmless and despite the universal terror the beast was easily cornered and captured without loss of life or limb.

Nearby at Clones a dreaded passenger was Lieutenant Colonel J. C. W. Madden, a director of the railway who claimed all the deference and respect due his exalted position. One morning he stormed into the stationmaster's office demanding that a chimney sweep occupying his usual first class compartment be removed instantly. Anxious for peace the stationmaster set off along the train to eject the unfortunate sweep. But in the meantime one of the staff had got there ahead and slipped him a first class ticket which he produced for inspection. There was nothing Madden could do but stomp off and find another compartment.

This same Madden got his come-uppance at Amiens Street Station when he demanded the dismissial of a driver who had ordered him off the footplate of his engine which he was trying to prepare for departure. Madden was considered to be interfering in the operation of the railway and the driver's action was upheld.

The advent of diesels

The CDRJC was the first company in Ireland to experiment with diesel as an alternative to steam locomotives. Most of the early railbuses were built at the Dundalk works of the GNR which observed this development with close interest. The great potential of these was clearly in operating services on branch lines where low traffic density did not justify running a steam locomotive. Thus they were ideally suited to the Donegal lines, of which the GNR was part owner. By the 1930s the design had been almost perfected, using standard road vehicles converted for rail operation. Two Dundalk engineers patented a system of pneumatic tyres within a steel rim known as the Howden–Meredith wheel. Six railbuses were built in this way, one of which came to grief on the Dundalk Square Crossing, luckily not on its maiden voyage. These ugly little vehicles worked all over the system and were extremely useful in maintaining services on uneconomic branches.

At the same time railcars were in the process of making an appearance. In 1931 the first two petrol driven railcars emerged from Dundalk to work on the CDRJC and the following year the GNR began producing railcars for its own use, this time diesel engined, with the classification A and B. By the time C was built great improvements had been made. It worked the service between Enniskillen and Bundoran, carried more passengers than its predecessors, had a cab at either end and ran nearly 190,000 miles before needing an overhaul. It was also much cheaper to run. With the formula nearly right the company went into production and came up with several more vehicles right up to the outbreak of war. Then someone came up with the brilliant idea of running the cars in multiples with a driving railcar and one or more trailers. Thus was born the multiple unit railcar set. The power unit which keeps almost every branch line in Britain in business first saw the light of day on the GNR working suburban trains in the Dublin area.

For many years such units formed the backbone of CIE services as well, but have now been replaced by locomotive hauled trains. The system is still used on NIR and of course the new electrification scheme will involve the use of multiple unit vehicles. The chief advantage of this kind of train was first of all its low cost of operation and secondly its flexibility in being able to stop and start anywhere along the line. This made it particularly attractive on local branches where there was stiff competition from road vehicles. The principal architect of all this was G. B. Howden who came to Dundalk from the English LNER in 1929. As chief mechanical engineer he was also responsible for the rebuilding of the troublesome Boyne viaduct and became general manager in 1939. Later he held the same job with CIE and UTA successively and headed the board which administered the GNR before its dissolution.

The First World War and after

The opening of hostilities in 1914 saw the GNR in a very healthy state. Second in size only to the GS & WR it was by far the most prosperous of the Irish companies with a good deal of its business coming from the industrial north and the quite densely populated east coast. Its trains were at their busiest with six running on the *Enterprise* route each day. The company had a confident, successful air which was noticeable to anyone associated with it. Track and rolling stock were in excellent condition and profits were good. Like the rest of mankind the last thing it needed was a world war.

Some of the immediate effects were beneficial: increased industrial production carried by rail, movement of troops and equipment, a strong sense of contributing to the war effort by greater efficiency. Then the negative aspects began to be felt. Costs rose dramatically as fuel and materials became scarce. Energy resources were diverted away from civilian needs to the war effort with a resulting curtailment in services and most of all wages began to rise to keep up with inflation. Half way through the war the government took over the railways but before that there was the rising in Dublin. The 1916 rebels tried to gain control of the termini but in fact only Westland Row and Harcourt Street were taken. But the GNR line was blown up at Fairview as was one of the viaducts north of Malahide. With the city more or less under siege and the area round O'Connell Street gradually being devastated there was a growing food shortage. At the end of the week a special bread train was run from Belfast to Clontarf with 10,000 loaves aboard, which greatly relieved matters.

In the same year the railwaymen threatened strike action if a pay increase was not met and they even had the support of that pillar of the establishment *The Irish Times*, which saw state control as the only solution. A number of wage increases followed the government takeover but these were well short of the rise in the cost of living. Fares and rates were at the same time tightly controlled so that almost every company found itself returning a large deficit. Even with the substantial hike conceded in 1920 revenue stayed far short of expenditure.

The European war ended just as the Anglo–Irish war was getting under way and with talk of home rule some of the Ulster counties demanded to keep the link with Britain. A boycott of goods from Belfast was introduced by Sinn Fein which of course struck at the heart of the GNR's trade. The compromise treaty signed in 1921 accepted the establishment of a Dublin parliament but with a separate governing body for the six counties which were to remain part of Britain. Partition was a disaster for the Great Northern for even with the £670,000 compensation paid under the 1921 settlement it had suffered appalling damage. Then to add salt to the wound the Civil War aggravated the disruption although the North was not as badly affected as areas like Wexford and Limerick. On one occasion John Bagwell, the company manager, was kidnapped, chiefly because he was a senator in the Free State government although he was later released unharmed.

The international railway

When peace finally came in 1923 the GNR had to come to terms with operating an international railway. Its lines crossed the newly established border in seventeen places, six of them between Clones and Cavan where the boundary is particularly circuitous. Facilities for customs examination had to be provided at the company's expense, timings eased to allow for the delay and two sets of tariff duties applied. At one point there were two different timetables in operation as the two states were on different time scales. Other oddities included the use of two locked liquor cabinets for use on either side of the border on account of the different excise rates.

Of course the whole affair was a golden opportunity for smugglers as it is virtually impossible to seal such an impractical division. It must be said that the men of the GNR were never ones to let such a chance slip. There were not many trains which crossed the border that did not have some item of contraband aboard. Newry was, and is a prime spot and one signalman there between the wars knew most of the tricks played by train crews. Worse, he did not hesitate to tell them he knew until one day the fireman on a train passing through the station had his revenge by heating the staff in the firebox for a few minutes just before passing it to him.

The difficult years

When the fully expected amalgamation of railways came in 1925 the GNR was excluded as it operated in both states. Almost simultaneously the impact of road operators began to be felt. True to form the GNR confronted the competition head on, running bus and lorry services of its own and buying out as many of its rivals as possible. These were a serious threat, for anyone with the price of a vehicle could set up a haulage business while the restrictions imposed on a railway providing the same service were enormous. Finally the Irish Government got round to doing something and in 1932 passed the Road Transport Act which required anyone operating a road transport business to have a licence and comply with numerous regulations on safety and standards. No such help came from the Northern government. In fact the Road and Rail Traffic Act of 1935 removed control of all road vehicles from the GNR and, despite assurances to the contrary, they were run in competition with the railways. For the GNR, as for most rail companies in Northern Ireland, this was the beginning of the end.

The fact that the Great Northern was rapidly developing a new form of transport which was nothing short of revolutionary (diesels) shows that it was never willing to passively accept setbacks and misfortunes. The picture in the 1930s while all this was going on was extremely gloomy. The world was just starting to recover from the great depression which followed the Wall Street crash but for most people life was still hard. It is as if another war was needed to stimulate the world economy, even if it was to armaments production.

The GNR was badly hit and receipts dropped like a lead balloon. In an attempt to balance its books the company made a number of economy drives until finally resorting to the drastic step of cutting wages. This was naturally rejected by the men and resulted in the 1933 strike.

The events leading up to the strike were outlined in the company's AGM which *The Irish Times* reported in detail on 1 March 1933. The report has numerous references to items such as 'abnormal fall in receipts' and attempts at 'a big economy drive'. Despite the fact that the company had carried over 73,000 people to the Eucharistic Congress in Dublin the previous year it had to admit that for the current year it had 'disappointing results'. In fact 1933 was the first year the company recorded a loss. The causes were said to be trade difficulties, tariff restrictions, economic depression, necessary fares increases, poor worldwide economic conditions. Today we sum up all that with the word 'recession'.

The meeting went on to describe the measures adopted to remedy the problem: economies which saved £60,000, faster trains to win back passengers, diesel experiments, coordinated road and rail services, some lower fares and most controversial of all the wage reduction all round. One shareholder complained of the unfairness of the imposed wage reduction while the directors and senior officials suffered no such cut. In fact the chairman claimed that he and his colleagues had reduced their own fees by a larger percentage than that forced on the railwaymen. In due course the Free State government acted to make up the shortfall for employees based south of the border but by the time Belfast had stepped in early in the new year the strike was on.

As ever the Great Northern kept an eye out for an opportunity and when the ailing Dundalk Newry and Greenore Railway came on the market it acquired it on 1 July 1933. Its own railbuses were perfectly suited to the undemanding passenger numbers on this line and there was still a reasonable traffic in cattle through the port of Greenore (see Chapter 7).

The 1930s continued to be difficult years for the GNR as for most Irish companies so that the boost given by the outbreak of the Second World War was all the more welcome. To add to the complications of its international status there was the additional hazard of operating in one country which was at war and another which remained neutral. There were some benefits from this however as large numbers of people travelled from the North to escape the rigours of harsh rationing and to relax in the southern capital which was then without a blackout. Most of the GN's system being in Northern Ireland it was of course subject to attack in air raids and numerous precautions were taken to alert staff on what to do in such event. One document issued in 1942 is humorously over-enthusiastic. It called for the obliteration of all station names except those 'whose lettering does not exceed three inches and cannot be seen or understood from a highway, other than the station approach'. Obviously the company believed that no German agent would have the audacity to trespass on its property in order to discover his whereabouts. Similarly the only other signs permitted were those 'situated under the station roof so that they cannot be seen or understood from a highway or low flying aircraft'. The company also issued dark warnings of the perils of leaving railway uniforms unattended where they could be picked up by saboteurs, spies and agents provocateurs.

Restrictions on private travel and strict petrol rationing added to the GNR's business and with military transport much in demand the lines were at their busiest for years. Fuel shortage being a severe problem in the south it was not unknown for GN engines to find themselves with a good deal less coal on leaving Dublin than they had when they arrived, sometimes in exchange for an item which was particularly scarce north of the border. Tea and sugar were in that category and the customs men were kept frantically busy searching passengers and crew alike. Although the company had no fierce objection to smuggling it did not like the delays it caused to its services, nor the bad publicity when its staff appeared in court over it. Wire was placed under the carriage seats—a favourite spot for concealment—and at one time wooden seats were introduced to foil the smuggler.

The end of the road

The coming of peace was greeted universally and restaurant cars were seen once again on the GNR as if to indicate the end of the hard times. In the same year CIE had replaced the GSR, without substantially affecting the GNR. But with the coming of the Ulster Transport Authority in 1948 things began to change. The new authority took over the NCC, the B&CDR and was given limited powers over the GNR. By now the latter company was in its most serious financial crisis yet with expenditure way ahead of receipts and the gap widening daily. In February 1949 the chairman sounded an ominous warning about the future of the company and on 6 December 1950 the board announced its intention to close the entire system. Meanwhile second class was abolished from 1 January 1951 and first class fares reduced to a little more than the old second. This was five years ahead of most other major companies.

The closure was diverted by immediate government action on both sides of the border which promised to make good any operating losses. This was only a temporary measure and in due course the two governments revealed that they planned to restructure the company and run it as a joint concern with a state-appointed Great Northern Railway Board which unfortunately rarely acted with unanimity. This came into effect on 1 September 1953 and brought to a close the independent life of that fine old lady, the Great Northern.

The policy of the UTA and the Northern government was decidedly in favour of road transport over rail and no time was lost in beginning the closures which in time have stripped the province (and parts of the Republic) of almost all its rail services. Three years later Stormont announced that unilaterally it planned to close the greater part of the GNR system north of the border. Dublin protested as did the GNRB itself, saying that if this happened many lines would run to nowhere if they stopped at the border. Belfast was adamant, saying that a saving of £14,000 would be made and that what CIE chose to do with its share of the GNR was none of its affair. In addition it had decided on the abolition of the GNRB.

At the subsequent inquiry the GNRB general manager J. F. McCormick said that the savings would be minimal and that no lines should close before diesels were tried on them. The NI government rejected the findings and announced a date for the closures. The government in Dublin had no alternative but to close the remaining stump lines which would be hopelessly uneconomic to work on their own. The final act was the dissolution of the GNRB on 1 October 1958 when staff and assets were divided between CIE and UTA—a sad end to a fine railway.

Among the first lines to go on 30 September 1957 were Clones–Omagh, Glaslough–Portadown, Bundoran Junction–Bundoran and the Fintona branch. Other lines followed in the years after with the road development plan in full swing. One of the last to go was the Belfast–Derry line via Omagh which saw its last trains on 15 February 1965, followed by the Belfast Central line the same year.

So intent was the Stormont government on the destruction of the remaining railways that it quickly sold off the fine old Great Northern hotels which had once done a first class trade at Bundoran, Warrenpoint and Rostrevor. Hundreds of GN men lost their jobs and the savings made on the closures sounded hollow against the millions being poured into a motorway network which looks very impressive but can hardly be the province's most urgent requirement.

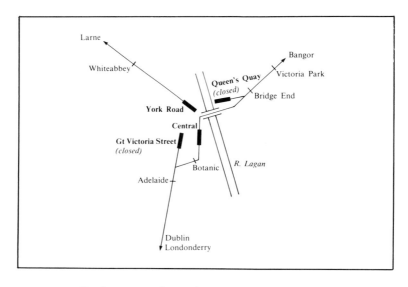

Railways in the Belfast area as at 1983

Today all that remains of the GN system is the Belfast–Dublin route, the Howth and Drogheda–Navan branches and the Lisburn–Antrim spur, now used by Derry trains. Railway policy in the North has now thankfully changed; the link line in Belfast has been revived and the city now has its long planned Central Station. CIE and NIR operate the fine *Enterprise* jointly and while the timings may be faster with powerful modern diesels the magic of the Great Northern is gone forever.

6 The Belfast and Northern Counties Railway

THE first section of what later became the Belfast and Northern Counties Railway (and later still the Northern Counties Committee) began life as the Belfast and Ballymena Railway and was launched on the general public as early as 26 April 1836. The shares advertised were quickly taken up but the proposers had put the cart before the horse in issuing a detailed plan of the route to Belfast with a line out to Carrickfergus. The chief difficulty facing the engineers was the steep plateau running north–west from Belfast and how it should be avoided. Opinions differed and by the time the controversy was settled many of the original promoters had fallen away. It was 1844 before a new scheme was launched with a revised path and this got parliamentary approval the following year. Viscount Massereene broke the earth near Whitehead on 6 November 1845 and not content with turning a single sod the noble gent filled a barrowload, ran it along a plank and tipped the soil out, all to the music of the 26th Cameronians who happened to be on the spot. With difficulty the viscount was restrained from further bursts of industry to attend the opening festivities consisting of an 'elegant collation' and a 'sumptuous banquet'.

But the way ahead was still not clear for there were many delays over land purchase. Most owners refused the offers made which must have been rather ungenerous and one in particular, Patrick McQuillan, had grievances on several grounds. Not only was the price less than he expected but he also ran coaches between Antrim and Belfast which would be put out of business when the railway came. As a final insult the company wanted to acquire his inn in order to demolish it to make way for the trackbed. Eventually these and other problems were sorted out and the line was ready for inspection early in 1848. The Board of Trade's report was not favourable, noting the omission of such necessary items as signalling, mileposts, ballast and solid station buildings. Obviously the line was quite unsafe and far from ready for public use. This appears to have been one of Dargan's few failures and he hurried to make the necessary improvements. These were finally passed by the same inspector and the line opened to Ballymena, Carrickfergus and Randalstown on 11 April 1848.

The Belfast terminus at York Road was two miles from the centre, a cost saving exercise, and was designed by Lanyon. It was a large, delightful, classical building with a central portico, two stories and two pavilions. The passenger facilities were at this stage less impressive, consisting of one platform which handled all the traffic and held the company offices. A minor accident in later years provided the incentive to add a second platform with siding accommodation and to move the goods area to a separate part of the station.

Fares on the new line were quite expensive: Belfast–Ballymena was 7/- (35p) return first class although there were cheap day returns and reduced subscription and family tickets. Even so receipts were lower than expected and in the 1850s dividends were on average a modest 1½ per cent. Dargan completed the extension to Cookstown in November 1856 which left the main line at what became Cookstown Junction. When the GNR reached the town in 1879 each company maintained its own station and even ran competitive services to and from Belfast on a fairly amicable basis.

The Londonderry and Coleraine Railway

The Londonderry and Coleraine Railway was authorised on 4 August 1845. It had an ambitious plan to link those two places involving the reclamation of large areas of coastline on the shores of Lough Foyle in order to save on construction costs and land purchase. Not surprisingly progress was slow, not least because the directors were based in London and all major decisions had to be referred there. It was not until the end of 1852 that trains began running as far as Limavady with the line to Coleraine opening the following year. It is a very picturesque route, most of it following the shoreline and dipping through the cliffs by means of a number of tunnels. The Derry terminus was at Waterside, the present NIR site, on the east of the Foyle. Once again traffic was slow in picking up and a number of government loans were sought to tide the company over its initial difficulties. These included the short-lived Magilligan branch which opened in July 1855 in the hope of feeding passengers to a ferry service across the lough to Donegal but closed three months later, a record for an Irish railway.

Not disheartened by this setback the company announced plans for other extensions, such as between Coleraine and Castledawson. Apart from the inevitable

The imposing exterior of York Road station Belfast (NCC)

The Belfast and Northern Counties Railway 107

first-sod-turning nothing came of this. One or two accidents occurred around this time which indicate that operations were less than 100 per cent safe—not calculated to win public confidence. By 1855 the company's finances were in a critical state and the line was leased to the contractor. Peter Roe was brought in from the MGWR as manager and this capable man who started his career as a ticket collector managed to reverse the decline with new measures to attract passengers.

The BBC & PJR

With rails to Coleraine from Derry and to Ballymena from Belfast a 30 mile gap remained between the two cities of Ulster. This was filled by the Ballymena, Ballymoney, Coleraine and Portrush Junction Railway which was called forth to its high destiny by the incorporation of 8 July 1853. One of the forces behind the project was the Earl of Antrim who accurately foresaw the potential of Portrush as a seaside resort if it were accessible by rail from Belfast and Derry. Dargan won the contract and received a large holding in the company in payment; in return the directors received a free pass for life. Just prior to the opening on 4 December 1855 a special train ran from York Road to Portrush carrying the 'wealth, intelligence and beauty of the North' to the seaside.

The river Bann at Coleraine was still uncrossed by rails, through passengers having to change trains and stations here for several years as at Drogheda. Meanwhile sale of the line to the Belfast and Ballymena was approved in 1858 and a year later a new railway bridge was opened across the Bann. It was built of iron and wood, with sixteen fixed spans, and two which opened for shipping thus allowing through running of trains between Belfast and Derry for the first time. This bridge was replaced by an entirely new one in 1924 further downstream.

At Portstewart a local noteworthy objected loudly to the detrimental effects of the iron horse on his locality and managed to prevent the railway getting nearer the town than two miles! A steam tram later provided a service to Portstewart from the station which was in due course renamed, more accurately, Cromore. Antipathy was also in evidence from the local clergy who fought against Sunday trains. The directors politely but firmly regretted they were unable to suspend such services.

The Northern Counties

With its additional mileage and expansionism the B & BR decided that a change of name was due and so settled on the Belfast and Northern Counties Railway. In the same year, 1860, the company had taken over the running of the Londonderry and Coleraine which it bought outright eleven years later, thus bringing to an end this 'most unfortunate railway' as it was described in Parliament at the time. With control of the entire Belfast–Derry line things were looking up for the Northern Counties as it was known. The new company had a much more professional approach to running a railway than its predecessors. A novel element was the introduction of villa tickets. This gave anyone building a 'villa' of a minimum value within a mile of certain stations a free first class ticket to Belfast valid for *ten years*. Second class tickets on a similar basis were later introduced for lower priced dwellings. This scheme played a large part in developing many Belfast suburbs by encouraging families to move from the smoke and dirt of the inner city to the clean air of what was then open countryside.

Traffic and receipts on the company's lines were good and every effort was made to attract passengers, especially third class; the line was one of the very first in these islands to carry third class on all trains (October 1862). The local wit quickly renamed the B&NCR, 'Big Nancy Coming Running', reflecting the smart, efficient image the new company had. (This is very different from the SL&NCR which was similarly nicknamed 'Slow, late and never comes'.)

The B&NCR was known for the very active participation of its shareholders in all matters relating to the railway. Apart from Sunday trains, a highly contentious issue was the sale of alcohol in station refreshment rooms. This was so strongly opposed by the temperance lobby that before long they all became 'dry'. Time-keeping was the overriding concern of one proprietor who went to the length of keeping meticulous records over his stretch of line. Another complained volubly about the arrangements at Whiteabbey station where the ladies' first class waiting room was placed near the third class 'shed' so that lady travellers had to pick their way through the assembled artisans in order to await their train in comfort.

Larne Harbour

The shortest sea route between Ireland and Britain is the stretch of water between Antrim and Scotland, the ports of Donaghadee and Portpatrick being the favoured points for many hundreds of years. However both of these harbours are exposed on what is often a choppy crossing and in time were replaced by Larne and Stranraer. The B&NCR was not slow to see the benefits from this traffic and did not delay in extending the Carrickfergus line to Larne Harbour in 1862. The first passenger steamer ran a few days later with connecting trains at both ends. So rough was the sea that the boat took 4 hours, instead of 3, for the 39 mile trip. Returns were poor for the Carrickfergus and Larne Railway (worked by the B&NCR) and no-one was surprised when the steamer service was withdrawn at the end of 1863.

Magheramorne loop, near Larne

Plans for a revival were announced in 1871 using a better boat more able to withstand the ravages of a stormy crossing. The following year the *Princess Louise* entered service, a luxurious though rather underpowered steamer with good train connections for Glasgow and London from Stranraer. Storms and erosion were a constant problem on the Irish side, particularly around Whitehead, and great efforts were made to protect the track from landslides on the one hand and the ravages of the sea on the other. This time the Larne service took off and thankfully both train and steamer are still with us.

The men at the top

Part of the success of the B & NCR lay in its personnel, a number of whom stand out. An almost revolutionary appointment was made in 1870 when the highly talented Bowman Malcolm was taken on as locomotive superintendent at the age of 22, a position he held for 46 years. Malcolm brought in a number of new ideas in locomotive design, particularly in the area of compounds. He was one of the key personalities in the B & NCR, a strict disciplinarian and strong on temperance. His staff notices contained regular warnings on the dangers of drink to morals, health, happiness, family life and safety. He was not keen on smoking either and once sent out a memo saying: 'Enginemen must not smoke when, at, or, passing stations: it looks slovenly.'

Another first class manager was the benevolent Edward John Cotton, one of the patriarchs of Irish railways who came over from the Great Western and the Railway Clearing House in England. He was manager of the Waterford and Limerick at the age of 24 and while with the B & NCR was responsible for most of the improvements made in running the company. Joseph Tatlow remembers him with great affection.

> One thing especially gave me pleasure; my monthly visits to the Managers' Conference at the Irish Railway Clearing House in Dublin... The leading men at the Conference were Ilbery of the GS & WR, Cotton of the B & NCR, Plews and Shaw of the GNR, Ward of the MGWR and Skipworth, manager in Ireland of the LNWR... Pax vobiscum, kind, warm-hearted Edward John! You were an ornament to the railway world and always my friend.

The Derry Road

Soon after the B & NCR opened the through route to Derry the GN made its presence felt by running competing services through Omagh. This route was $100\frac{1}{2}$ miles long, as opposed to 95 via Coleraine, but smart timing and comparable fares made the competition real enough. Both companies then realised the bad effects of unrestrained competition and as often happens fares were fixed over the two routes and a price war averted. An early handicap for the B & NCR was the condition of the track owned by the late unlamented Londonderry and Coleraine. The permanent way and station buildings were in a very poor state causing great discomfort and regular delays to services. A great deal of money was needed to put them right, including a fine new station building at Waterside in Derry which was opened in 1875, the present terminus for Belfast trains. On the other side of the Foyle there was a goods store, later to become the GNR station.

The company was well satisfied with itself as the 1870s drew to a close with the number of passengers carried and revenue taken at their highest. In February 1880 the Derry Central Railway opened being a revival of an earlier scheme which failed. The line ran from Magherafelt northwards to Macfin near Ballymoney and was worked by the B&NCR from the start. The company's prospects were bright for the route was through good farmland and prosperous market towns such as Garvagh. Notwithstanding this potential, response to the prospectus was slow and at one stage landowners on the route were asked to accept payment in shares or (most unlikely) to give their land free of charge for the good of the community! So poor was the company that when one of its bridges collapsed killing two men it offered its profound sympathy to the relatives but claimed it had no cash to compensate them—a statement which was unacceptable even a hundred years ago.

The usual celebrations accompanied the opening, denying the previous claims of penury. The god of railways must have disapproved of such callousness for takings were extremely poor and in 1888 the line was the only one in Ireland to show a fall in receipts. The company's final years of independence were marked by disputes with other railway companies, banks and local authorities, all of which it blamed for its poor performance. Absorption by the B&NCR was only a matter of time and took place in September 1901 on the instructions of the Board of Works.

Also diverging at Magherafelt was the 8 mile Draperstown Railway which from its opening in July 1883 was worked by the B&NCR. It too was absorbed in July 1895.

The Hopkirk fraud

Despite the depression caused by the Land War and agrarian agitation in the 1880s the B&NCR more than kept its head above water. Then, at a shareholders' meeting in 1885, news of a gigantic fraud leaked out. Up to then meetings had been stormy with the unusually active participation customary with the B&NCR, when new blood was drafted onto the board in the person of John Young; he was a successful chairman of the company for many years. Just at this time the Hopkirk affair burst into public view. Hopkirk was the company accountant, with Lilley his assistant acting as bookkeeper. Between them they embezzled the railway of well over £16,000 during the years they were employed at York Road. They were so ingenious that even during the trial no-one was able to discover exactly how they had done it. Hopkirk was sentenced to five years for his offence and the judge added that if proof were available of his almost certain other offences the sentence would have been much heavier. Lilley died opportunely before the case came to trial. The amount of money involved was obviously considerable but even more harmful was the damage to the company's name.

Immediately after the case one religious shareholder stood up at a meeting and delivered himself of the opinion that the fraud was an indication of divine displeasure at the continued running of trains on Sundays! The fundamentalist school must have been soothed when coincidentally special Sunday excursions were suspended after a train full of Home Rule supporters was nearly sabotaged on an excursion from Belfast to Portrush. The ban meant the loss of very valuable revenue from the Loyalist outings on 12 July (Battle of the Boyne) and 12 August (Relief of Derry) and it was not long before they were restored.

Tourism

The development of tourism and holiday travel was not neglected by the B&NCR. The Giant's Causeway, Portrush, the Glens of Antrim and Whitehead were among the popular tourist spots served by the company's trains. The *North Atlantic Express* was run every summer to and from Portrush, with a time of 80 minutes for the 67½ miles; a respectable achievement. In keeping with this policy the company set out to acquire a number of hotels in key holiday resorts on the lines of those run by the GS&WR in the South. The first of these was the Northern Counties Hotel at Portrush. It was aimed at the de luxe tourist class with over 100 bedrooms in a fine location near the sea. Like many hotels then and since it was faced with a slack off season. The management countered this with an inspired campaign of 3 day packages during the winter. In Belfast the Station Hotel (later the Midland) was opened at York Road in 1898. Another novel venture was the so-called 'Holden Train'. This was a special excursion which ran week-long walking tours throughout the North. The trains covered 400 miles with luxury accommodation and all meals for only £2.7.6 (£2.37½). A Larne hotelier, Mr Holden, was the organiser and used a special train of first class saloon carriages for his trips, each with its own wagon-lit type dining car. The carriages were specially built at York Road and after a time the scheme was taken over by the company and ran successfully right up to the First World War.

Narrow gauge

No account of the B&NCR would be complete without mention of its involvement with a number of narrow gauge railways in north–east Ulster. The first of these was the Ballymena, Cushendall and Red Bay Railway which formally began life on 18 July 1872. It purpose was to convey the rich mineral deposits (mainly iron ore) in that part of Antrim to the sea. The 16½ mile line was unique in that it reached a height of 1,043 feet above sea level. The line was 3ft gauge and opened as far as Retreat on 8 October 1876. It was intended that the ore would be shipped to England from Red Bay but Larne became the port of departure and the line never got any further, making the Cushendall and Red Bay part of its name superfluous. Given its height above sea level it is no wonder that the gradients on the line were excessive: it was an almost unbroken ascent for almost 15 miles with three miles at a punishing 1 in 39. Originally planned as a freight only line the B&NCR on its takeover of the railway in 1884 began a limited passenger service over part of the route which lasted until 1930, ten years before the total closure of the line.

Similar to it was the Ballymena and Larne Railway, another three foot gauge line which was incorporated on 7 July 1874 for a useful branch between the harbour at Larne and the busy Co. Antrim town, with a branch to Doagh. Passenger services began on the 'main line' on 24 April 1878 and six years later there was a connection with the BCRBR at Ballymena. In July 1889 the line was taken over by the B&NCR and most of it was closed between 1930 and 1950. Trains met the boat at Larne and there was even an express to Ballymena which did the 25 mile journey in an hour. The coaches used were comfortable by narrow gauge standards and at the closure worked for many years on the County Donegal railways.

It is generally accepted that County Antrim produces the best Irish whiskey, the famous and venerable distillery at Bushmills being located within its boundaries.

A certain amount of that precious liquid was on occasions entrusted to the Bally-mena and Larne Railway, especially when it was controlled by the B&NCR. And it was not unknown for a wagon or its contents to go astray on its journey between the two places, especially at an enchanted spot known as Baile na Si where mortal man ventured at his peril...

The third line in this grouping, the Ballycastle Railway, survived as an independent concern as late as 1924 and is therefore treated separately in Chapter 9.

Takeover by the Midland Railway

With the new century beginning the B&CDR found itself in a very healthy state with a modern, efficient railway and good returns. Like most Irish companies its network was mainly complete and at its most profitable. It was not to be wondered that an outside interest should cast an acquisitive eye on it. That concern was the Midland Railway of England which for some years had been anxious to diversify and broaden its interest by acquiring a medium sized railway in Ireland. To this end it had built a brand new harbour at Heysham with a view to running a new, more direct steamer service direct to Belfast. A takeover of the B&NCR seemed to be exactly what the Midland was looking for and early in 1903 the first moves in the courtship were made. An attractive offer was put to the board which it in turn recommended for acceptance at the AGM. The motion was passed unanimously and control of the company passed to the Midland Railway.

The new regime did not bring about any startling or sudden changes. Liveries stayed the same, the original staff were kept on and there was no sudden shift in policy. The name of the company did change: it became known as the Midland Railway, Northern Counties Committee whereby the network was controlled by a committee sitting in Belfast, three from York Road and three from Derby. It was a good time for a takeover and the NCC continued on its prosperous way right up to the First World War.

Adding to that prosperity were a number of road vehicles, which, being quick to see their potential, the B&NCR introduced as early as 1902. A feature of the road services was steam goods wagons plying to and from the rail depots with a bus service around Whiteabbey and Greenisland. Open-top touring buses followed soon after and wherever possible the company bought out rival bus and lorry operators in its area thus managing to contain the growing competition from road vehicles. So intense was this policy that before the Second World War the NCC had a fleet of 130 buses and 60 lorries.

The period after the end of government control up to the outbreak of the Second World War was a difficult one for the NCC. Road competition continued to grow and while receipts also grew steadily expenditure shot far ahead of it. The Midland was happy enough to leave matters in the capable hands of Bowman Malcolm until he retired. In 1925 the company was pleased to report that it had carried nearly 3¼ million passengers, not counting 2,600 season ticket holders, a healthy state of affairs which was the envy of many other Irish companies. However, the good times were not to last much longer. The depression which followed in the late 20s and 30s was a severe blow. As the NCC took over and ran competing bus services it cut back on its rail services throwing many men out of work. Even worse, cuts in wages were demanded by the board as the only alternative to total closure. Naturally the men refused to accept any cuts and a strike was called in 1933, beginning on January 31. Malcolm Speir, the NCC manager, appealed for restraint, but to no effect. The strike lasted until April and caused great bitterness. Some services ran with non-union men and the company even brought in workers from England to break it. The strike was a lost cause, times were very hard even if you had a job and by the spring the men had been beaten. The NCC then proceeded to make an example of the strike leaders and sacked them, an unpleasant side of industrial relations of the time. The strike was not the complete disaster predicted by the management and only one or two minor lines, shaky enough anyway, closed as a direct result.

Greenisland loop

A major problem facing the company in its attempts to improve its services was the necessity for all Derry bound trains to reverse at Greenisland. Authorisation for a loop line which would eliminate this had been obtained many years ago but had been postponed on the grounds of the cost involved. In an attempt to cope with the perennial unemployment figures the government had granted funds to the NCC for projects such as doubling track on the Larne line. With the crisis of those out of work as bad as ever approval was given for the building of the Greenisland loop with the aid of state funds. The plan consisted of a branch which left the main line at Whiteabbey and rejoined the original route $2\frac{1}{2}$ miles further on. The job was considerable, with major engineering works involving bridges, viaducts and numerous cuttings. The diversion was complete on 17 January 1934 and the opening was accompanied by the usual festivities. The new line saved over 10 minutes on the journey and enabled the company to introduce the *North Atlantic Express* which ran from Portrush each morning and returned from Belfast that evening.

By now the NCC was strongly under the Midland influence with the same livery and the LMS emblem on the side of its coaches. Despite the uncertain financial position, new rolling stock continued to come out of York Road. In 1937 the railway took full advantage of the coronation celebrations when the new king and queen visited the North. Numerous specials were run from all over the province, in particular for a youth rally at Balmoral. Other excursions included seaside returns for a modest 6d ($2\frac{1}{2}$p) which were highly popular and touring tickets with accommodation at NCC hotels for £6 per week.

The Pole inquiry

Unfortunately such bonanzas were few and far between and in the light of the worsening conditions of many public transport concerns in Northern Ireland the government called in Sir Felix Pole, the ex-general manager of the Great Western Railway to report on how best services might be improved. Pole came up with the idea of a transport board which would coordinate all public transport and run it as a joint operation instead of in competition. The plan was formally implemented the following year and looked on paper as if it would be the saving of the railways, with pooled resources and fully complementary road and rail services. In fact the opposite happened: the road competition was united in its assault on the railways and allowed to provide duplicating services all over the North; the scheduled pooling of receipts never really happened. Instead of being the saviour of the railways the Northern Ireland Road Transport Board (NIRTB) seemed hell bent on their total destruction. They might well have succeeded then were it not for the outbreak of the Second World War. Two further public inquiries were held in 1938 and 1939 (even today Irish railways are never short of an inquiry or two) but their findings had little impact.

War conditions

September 1939 gave the railways a transfusion they badly needed as there was more than enough business for both road and rail interests. In fact with the strict rationing of petrol the advantage swung back to the railways. Increased industrial output, the evacuation of children, troop and munitions movement, greater agricultural production, all brought huge demands on the rail system for fast transport. The Larne–Stranraer route was especially busy as most military traffic passed through those ports and on to the NCC being unable to pass through the Free State which remained neutral during the war. A regular feature of the system was the leave train from Larne which set out every morning from the harbour and often consisted of as many as 16 or 17 coaches. It covered almost the entire six counties, dropping carriages at various points with the majority travelling to the military bases around Belfast and the aerodromes at Limavady, Ballykelly, Eglinton, and Maydown as well as the naval base at Derry. The same train repeated the performance in reverse each evening.

Large numbers of British and American troops were drafted to Northern Ireland during the war and always seemed to be going somewhere by train. For the first eighteen months or so the war was not taken too seriously by the home population; blackout enforcement and rationing were treated as a bit of a tiresome joke. With the build up of land and seaborne forces in the six counties in preparation for the Battle of the Atlantic, the city of Belfast experienced its first air raids in April 1941. This new and terrifying form of warfare took its toll on the railways. York Road station was heavily damaged and a number of railwaymen killed. Offices, workshops, the hotel and about twenty coaches were all destroyed. A month later another raid completed the destruction including all the company records which were lost in the blaze. The damage was made good in time but the disruption caused took many weeks to make good.

Further north at Ballykelly, about 15 miles from Derry, there was an air base which was being rapidly developed in the struggle against U-boats far out in the Atlantic. At the outbreak of the war the main runway stopped just short of the Belfast–Derry railway line by about 80 yards. With the arrival of heavy bombers it became necessary to extend the runway to accommodate them. The RAF approached the NCC and told them of the proposal to extend the runway half a mile over the line. Naturally the NCC were most unenthusiastic about sharing their main line with fighters and bombers and suggested that as they were there first the air force should make alternate arrangements. As might be expected the military got their way.

The result was a most extraordinary rail/air crossing point like nothing else in these islands. A miniature signal box was built on the Belfast side of the base and elaborate safety precautions introduced. Aircraft normally had right of way and there was a direct link between the signalman and the control tower. The staff of the latter, with their highly sophisticated ATC equipment, regarded the railway block instruments as a hazardous relic of the dark ages and American flight crews in particular were fascinated by the whole arrangement. During the war there were of course some hair-raising escapes and near misses as aircraft, many of them damaged, made an emergency landing. On several occasions both during and after the war, an aeroplane and a train decided to use the runway at the same time, luckily without serious accident. Signals, telegraph poles, speed notices etc. were all at miniature height and more than once there was blue language heard from irate pilots about how much it cost the taxpayer to keep an aircraft circling while a train made its leisurely way across the airfield.

Amalgamation

When the war ended most of the troops had been moved to the continent bringing to an end the boom which had lasted for six years. Road competition started up with renewed vigour and once again the question of the future of the rail system was aired. Clearly a merger of the NIRTB and the railways was the only solution. Nationalisation came into force in Britain on 1 January 1948 and under the Transport Act (NI) in the same year the Ulster Transport Authority was formed on 1 October to run all public transport in the six counties. Being owned by the LMS (successor to the MR) the NCC became for a short time the Railway Executive, Northern Counties Committee. It managed to stay clear of the UTA umbrella until April 1949 when it was bought for £2,668,000. The story of that unhappy organisation is told in Chapter 10.

The dissolution of such a progressive company as the NCC was a gloomy sight. After a shaky start it had consolidated its constituent railways to provide an excellent service right up to and after the last war. It had been a pioneer in many fields of railway activity such as railcars, electric signals, diesel locomotives and had even for a time run its own air service from Belfast to Glasgow, Liverpool and London. This was known as Railway Air Services and lasted until 1947. Much of the system has of course been ruthlessly chopped since the formation of the UTA but it is fair to say that the pride of the old NCC men has survived in the first rate service given by Northern Ireland Railways. Today all that survives is the commuter line out to Larne, the Derry route and the Portrush branch—it could be worse.

The Belfast and County Down Railway

The first meeting of this fairly inconspicuous railway was held in the Donegall Arms Hotel, Belfast on 23 February 1845. The initial proposals were quite modest and having succeeded in stalling a number of rival plans the promoters received permission for a line from Belfast to Downpatrick on 20 January 1846. In fact the first section to be built by Dargan was that to Holywood which opened on 2 August 1848. In the meantime a separate company, the Belfast Holywood and Bangor Railway, managed to get permission to build the line between the latter two towns. The B & CDR directors felt this was a situation up with which they would not put but there was little they could do about it for the moment. This stretch included Helen's Bay, a delightful station built in Scottish baronial style with a rampart facade of gables and cloisters. The local magnate, Lord Dufferin, had his own waiting room at Helen's Bay which opened on to a long flight of steps and a tree-lined avenue running the four miles from his house to the shore. The railway crossed this avenue by a magnificent decorative arch, ablaze with coats of arms, devices and heraldic insignia.

Holywood did not produce the expected returns and before long the B & CDR was forced to sell the line to the Bangor company in order to build its extensions into south Co. Down. The BH & BR was thus able to run its trains into Belfast and shared the Queen's Quay terminus although a strict demarcation was enforced. In fact when the intruder fell on hard times some years later the B & CDR bought the entire Bangor line for a modest sum.

Newtownards was reached on 6 May 1850 but it was to be another eleven years before the expected extension to Donaghadee opened. At that time the town had a sporadic mailboat service to Portpatrick in Scotland and in order to encourage this the harbour was developed at great expense. As in many such projects the mail service went elsewhere—to Larne in this case. Donaghadee was also blessed with a most incongruous station, a stark warehouse of a place which bore a large notice board proclaiming 'Railway Station' to the sceptical.

South from Comber ran the main line originally authorised towards Downpatrick. Ballynahinch was reached in September 1858 and Downpatrick itself in March the following year. The obvious extension to the popular seaside resort of Newcastle was promoted by the Downpatrick Dundrum and Newcastle Railway. This line opened in March 1869, was worked by the B & CDR and bought out entirely by it twelve years later. The railway brought quite a deal of prosperity to Newcastle. The company built a golf course and even its own hotel the Slieve Donard, a large edifice with 120 bedrooms. The hotel is built of solid red brick, although Mourne granite might have been preferable. While still involved in construction the railway decided to redesign Newcastle station, by then shared grudgingly with the GNR (see Chapter 5). The new building was also of red brick with a rather strong resemblance to a cathedral. It featured a squat nave, huge glass transepts and an enormous clock tower quite out of proportion with the rest. There was nothing if not variety in B & CDR buildings.

The Belfast terminus at Queen's Quay was quite a magnificent specimen of railway architecture. Prior to the 1911–2 alterations, the interior was rather crude with heavy wooden girders much in evidence. The revamp produced a bright, airy building with a certain resemblance to an elongated Kingsbridge. For some years before the Belfast Central Railway was built it remained in splendid isolation from all other railways but with the opening of Ballymacarrett Junction all this changed. When the UTA closure policy was at its height the old isolation was restored when the line was broken in 1965 and dmu railcars had to be transferred by road for service on the Bangor branch. Queen's Quay has now sadly been closed with the transfer of all services to Belfast Central; it had in recent years been badly damaged by bombs both in the last war and the more recent troubles.

Early in this century there was a philosophical attendant at the gents' lavatory in the station who was heard to say: 'I am the master of my fate; I am the captain of my soul.' It is good that what appears to be a lowly occupation should induce such peace of mind.

Many of the B & CDR's lines had been promoted during the 'Railway mania' of the mid 1840s: 'Railways through hills, across arms of the sea, over or under great rivers, spanning valleys at great heights or boring their way under ground, across barren moors, along precipices, over bogs... No scheme was so mad it did not find an engineer.' The method of working was also quite haphazard, although apparently accepted at the time. The *Belfast Newsletter* of 4 August 1848 has the following, rather worrying description of a train's arrival at Queen's Quay.

On the Newtownards line, which descends a long hill into the Belfast terminus, in order to save shunting, the engine was uncoupled when descending the hill, and steamed in front into a siding, the train following to the platform by its own momentum. Men working near the terminus assisted the brakesman, who stood on the top of the carriage, to check any superfluous speed, by throwing stones and pieces of timber on the rails in front of the vehicles.

It is a miracle that this did not cause repeated derailments. By 1877 things did not look well for the B & CDR. Its shares were worth a fifth of the original value and there had been no dividend paid for many years. Many expected the whole railway to fold and they were hardly inspired with confidence when the board of the company resigned en masse, swiftly followed by its solicitors. It seemed that everyone who could was getting out while there was time. The arrival of Joseph Tatlow as general manager helped to reverse the decline. His salary was £500 p.a. and he enjoyed the change from smokey Glasgow. While with the B & CDR he lived 'near the city, with open country and sea views around me, occupied a neat little detached house, with a bit of garden... where the air was pure and clean'.

Things did improve for the company and dividends were paid from the 1890s onwards. The Bangor line showed itself to be quite prosperous and many people travelled on it to and from Belfast. As the *Newsletter* said soon after the opening: 'being a perfect level, the movement is very easy. The carriages are fitted up very elegantly, and with every regard to comfort. The arrangements for the transfer of traffic are carried out with the utmost satisfaction and punctuality'. Robert Lloyd Praeger wrote a *Guide to the B & CDR* which was published in 1898 just after its finances began to improve. It is a good write-up for the company and for the county: 'With a capital of close on a million and a quarter, running annually about 600,000 train-miles on a line 76 miles in length, and carrying annually over four million passengers', the railway sounded very impressive to potential passengers and investors alike.

With a good steady traffic on the Bangor line the company decided to diversify into operating steamers from there to Belfast in a strange competition with its own rail services. There were at one time as many as six sailings daily taking 55 minutes for the trip. Occasionally boats ran to Larne which made more commercial sense and challenged the NCC for Belfast passengers.

Carriages and engines

The rolling stock of the B & CDR was a curious mixture of ancient and modern. At the end of the last century six comfortable bogies were introduced followed by as many again the next year. Then, abashed by its own extravagance, the company suddenly went back to using uncomfortable little six-wheelers again. It even entered the market for second hand vehicles of this kind and purchased a number from other companies who were discarding them. As a result, in 1925 only one in 16 was a bogie; a ratio which cannot have endeared the railway to the travelling public which now demanded greater comfort than ever, even in third class.

Happily the locomotive stock was more contemporary. After the First World War, Beyer Peacock delivered a number of powerful engines which worked mainly on the heavy trains of the Bangor line. Thirty locomotives were enough to run all its services which apart from the Bangor line were light enough. There was a certain flirtation with diesels, the first such locomotive being ordered from Harland and Wolff in 1933. It had an odd appearance, like an adapted steam engine, with a cab at the rear and a large chimney at the front. A second followed four years later and survived well into UTA and NIR days. Locomotives generally were well maintained largely on account of the fact that each engine had its individual crew who were solely responsible for its upkeep along with a relief. Also tried for a time was the GS&WR experiment of railmotors—a 56 seat coach attached to a locomotive giving it a quaint articulated appearance. These lasted from 1902 to 1918.

Ballymacarrett

The last war had a limited effect on the company's lines, less than on the GNR or the NCC. Many Belfast people moved out of the city when the air raids started and with troop movements from the various camps in Co. Down the railway was kept busy. Such were the demands at these times that rolling stock was frequently borrowed from other lines, even from as far away as the GSR.

However, a hard blow fell on the B&CDR with the Ballymacarrett accident in 1945. It happened on the morning of 10 January when a train from Holywood ploughed into the back of a stationary train from Bangor which was waiting for signal clearance before entering the terminus. Wartime working conditions were in force with the complication of a dark foggy morning. Twenty-three passengers were killed and 41 injured. The B&CDR had up to then operated the very dicey system of allowing trains to proceed after halting for two minutes at a stop signal and repeating the procedure at the next signal. Under bad weather conditions the driver was supposed to extend the time to four minutes but in both cases he could proceed without telephoning the signal man. (The reason for this was a shortage of signal boxes and personnel, a dangerous cost-cutting exercise.)

The auto-coach in the lead demolished the ancient six-wheeler at the rear of the Bangor train and ended up embedded in the next coach. This train was packed with shipyard workers and suffered almost all the casualties—hardly anyone in the auto-coach was injured. The speed of the Holywood train was disputed, as was the fog level, but the auto-coach must have been doing at least 20 mph to cause that amount of damage.

The causes of the accident were found to be faulty train equipment, excessive speed, bad weather conditions, and the presence of illicit passengers in the driver's cab, but most of all the highly dangerous two minute rule which allowed drivers to pass danger signals without adequate precautions. The rule was of course immediately changed, along with much stricter section controls. Liability for the accident was found to lie with the company and compensation of £75,000 was awarded, a heavy financial burden for the ailing railway. Even with the subsequent takeover by the UTA it was clear that drastic measures were needed if the company was to survive.

No one expected that the measures introduced would be quite so drastic. Nor indeed that the B&CDR would disappear almost entirely. The UTA had received authority to take over all the railways in Northern Ireland as from 1 October 1948. The price paid for the B&CDR was nearly half a million pounds, a generous offer by any standard given the condition of rolling stock, track and buildings. However, it caused great argument, some shareholders saying the line was worth much more while members of the government said the price was quite inflated. The sale agreement contained such optimistic phrases as 'complete coordination between the Board and the County Down Railway... detailed plans... the greatest possible use shall be made of the combined staffs and assets... so that better and more economical services may be made available'.

The delightful interior of a GNR A2 first class saloon
(Welch Collection, Ulster Museum)

The coordination policy was largely one of closures. In March 1949 the UTA announced that all the old County Down lines would close with the exception of that to Bangor. There was a huge outcry and a long fought legal battle but the verdict went against the railway and the closures followed. This set the pattern for the UTA while it lasted. The Comber line was a particular bone of contention: it was double track, in good condition and well placed to serve the growing urban population of Belfast. William Robb suggests in his *History of NIR* that the Comber line was included so that in the negotiations the UTA could be seen to compromise by allowing it to continue and thus have an easy passage for the ending of services on the other lines. To its surprise the Board allowed the closure of all the lines submitted and rather than retract the Authority let matters stand.

Thus, by the end of 1950, all that remained was the Bangor branch as it is today with regular services into Belfast Central, many running through to the former GNR and on to Lisburn and Portadown.

7 Standard Gauge Lines

The Sligo and Northern Counties Railway

THE SL & NCR was a standard gauge railway operating in a quiet part of north-west Ireland. Its line was 48 miles long in total including a 5¼ mile stretch shared with the MGWR and ran from the latter's terminus at Sligo to the Great Northern at Enniskillen. The route was through sparsely populated, poor country and its life was marked by great difficulties, even more so than most Irish lines. The passenger demands were never great and when the Ulster Railway was operating its four-horse coach on the same route in 1862 it must have been sufficient for the number of people travelling. The coach however took 5½ hours for the journey.

The first part of the route to open was that from Enniskillen to Belcoo in 1879 and here progress halted as shortage of capital delayed the opening of the remainder until 1882. Wages for the construction workers were 7/6 to 10/- (37½–50p) a week for a ten hour week, payable in gold half-sovereigns. There was no shortage of labour, as might be expected. The promoters were a group of prominent Sligo businessmen who saw great potential in the cattle shipments from the area and the mineral deposits around Lough Allen. Parliamentary approval had been granted in 1875 and construction was carried out with the utmost economy, hence the severe gradients, sharp curves and no less than 28 level crossings. At Collooney the SL & NCR joined the MGWR line from Dublin and had running powers over it to Sligo.

A selection of SL & NCR tickets

120

The line ran through some rather bleak but quite beautiful parts of Fermanagh and Leitrim. After leaving Enniskillen it crossed the Erne by a fine girder bridge which caused some maintenance headaches after it was built and required a speed restriction. Ten miles per hour was also enforced on the numerous bends and curves. Each of the 28 level crossings had a cottage attached which the occupier held rent free with a salary of 2/4 (11½p) a week for opening the gates as required. Florencecourt was the first station on the run west and is unusual in that there is no town or village nearby, it being the name of the Earl of Enniskillen's mansion three miles away. As if to compensate, it was advertised as the station for Swanlinbar ('Swad' in the local dialect), 6 miles away and even Bawnboy, a forbidding 10 miles distant. After the small halt at Abohill the line ran along the shores of Lough Macmean, a pretty stretch as far as Belcoo. This was the site of a stone quarry which was busy up to the First World War and there was for a time an engine shed and a turntable provided to transport the stone.

Belcoo was offered as the alighting point for Blacklion, a mere half mile away (on the doorstep by SL&NCR standards) and more imaginatively for Dowra, a brisk 9 mile walk. So happy were the directors with the propinquity of their station to both towns that in 1908 they renamed it 'Belcoo *and* Black Lion'. This was unusual in that Blacklion, being in Cavan, is in the Republic while Belcoo found itself in Northern Ireland. Belcoo later became the British customs post and Glenfarne, a few miles further on, that for the Irish customs. One traveller on the route, towards the end of its life, describes the customs examination at Glenfarne thus: 'A Customs man climbed into the railbus, took a good look at all three of us, then climbed out again.'

Manorhamilton, 24¾ miles from Enniskillen, was the operational headquarters of the railway. The offices and repair shops were here although the registered office was at Lurganboy, nearby. The station house was a fine sturdy building of cut stone and most repairs to wagons and carriages were carried out here, major jobs going to Dundalk. The company offered Manorhamilton as the station for Glencar waterfall. In fact Glencar is nearer Sligo but there was no point mentioning that if you wanted people to use the SL&NCR.

At Dromahaire tourists were enticed to alight for 'Lough Gill, O'Rourke's Castle, and Banqueting Hall, Creevelea Abbey and other historic places'; Drumkeeran, a mere 7 miles away, was also mentioned. Collooney was the last station owned by the company and was the source of a good deal of cattle traffic which was shipped onwards through Enniskillen to Belfast and Larne.

In Sligo the railway was called 'the Northern line', in Fermanagh 'the Sligo line' and between the two it was known as 'the Sligo–Leitrim'. The seal of the company showed two locomotives facing each other head on, one of them being derailed. This symbolised the defeat of an earlier routing scheme via Bundoran but was open to other interpretations as well.

Although receipts met running costs from the beginning they were not enough to cover interest repayments or the hire of locomotives and rolling stock. As early as 1894 the Treasury announced plans for the forcible sale of the line. Both the Great Northern and the MGWR expressed interest and even got as far as preparing to divide the railway at Manorhamilton and run it jointly. However the plan fell through and the company remained independent right up to its closure. It is interesting to speculate how different matters would have been if the takeover had happened. Other schemes which would have affected it almost as much met equal local opposition. One of these was the Ulster and Connacht Light Railway which, if it had materialised, would have consisted of a single narrow gauge line from Greenore as far as the west coast of Galway!

For most of its existence the SL&NCR relied on cattle for its survival. The projected mineral traffic never materialised to any great extent and the number of passengers was limited to say the least. Nonetheless the company made valiant efforts to attract excursion business. One trip from Sligo was optimistically advertised to Bundoran via Enniskillen; this was 91 miles by rail but only 20 by road. You can't blame them for trying. Regulations on the carriage of animals were numerous. One working timetable notes that 'live stock must not be taken over from Foreign Companies unless in good order'—it was more often the case that cattle arriving at Enniskillen were in a dreadful state after their journey on the SL&NCR and had to be revived by pouring water into their ears.

When partition came in the 1920s the company was operating in two states with all the complications therefrom. When the 1925 amalgamation took place to form the GSR the SL&NCR was excluded because it crossed the border. In addition to providing all the paraphenalia of customs, excise, bonding and tariffs there was the added complication of trade boycotts between the two states. Much of Sligo's former considerable trade with Belfast was diverted to Dublin and thus away from the SL&NCR, with the fortunate exception of cattle, which remained largely untouched.

Even more disruptive was the Civil War period with the usual pattern of burnings and derailments. Sligo station was destroyed by Anti-treaty forces and the company lost one of its engines, *Glencar*, when it was sent off driverless down the incline to Sligo quay. Another incident was more light-hearted. A cattle train was running from Collooney fair to Enniskillen and as it came down the hill into Dromahaire the driver saw that the level crossing gates were closed and someone was waving a red light in front of them. Not being well up on these matters the light-waver had not allowed enough stopping distance for the train and although the driver applied his brakes hard the engine smashed through the gates and screeched on for some distance before coming to a halt. The ambushers collected their wits and raced after the train. They climbed aboard and explained they wanted to prevent the advance of General Sean McEoin. The driver conceded the point but to minimise the destruction asked to be allowed to proceed to Dromahaire. The Irregulars agreed. On arrival the driver asked what was going to happen to the cattle which would suffer greatly in the derailment. The men were adamant and the argument went forward and back until a compromise was reached: the line behind the train was torn up, a few empty wagons derailed and the train proceeded unharmed to Enniskillen. This was one of the more humane incidents of the war in what was called by one of the participants 'a dark and sordid era'.

From 1925 the SL&NCR continued on its merry and impecunious way. The Free State government awarded compensation for the disruption suffered in the previous years but the company remained completely if perilously independent. Whether this was good or bad is debatable. On the one hand, the line kept its unique character (but so did the C&LR which was merged). On the other, control from Dublin might have smoothed its somewhat rocky path in later years, even if it was unlikely to prolong its existence.

As road competition for the meagre passenger traffic on the route grew, the company quickly got involved in diesel traction. The first railbus arrived from the

GNR works at Dundalk in 1935. It was a standard road vehicle (without the steering wheel) fitted with Howden–Meredith steel tyres around the rubber ones. These railbuses were highly successful being able to stop anywhere and could negotiate the most difficult bends without any problem. Most important of all they cost 3d a mile to run against a shilling a mile for a steam locomotive. At around this time the Stormont administration awarded a 'grant in aid for any losses... attributed to the economic difficulties' between North and South. The terms allowed for an amount to be paid equal to any operating profit in order to encourage the line to strive for liquidity. This seems to have had a beneficial effect for the working timetable of June 1936 gives five trains in each direction: two railcars, two mixed and the other railcar or goods. The fastest was the railcar which took two hours for the journey.

The Second World War brought the expected boost in business as fuel shortages caused a lot of traffic to be diverted to the SL&NCR from the GSR. Operating partially in a state which was at war the company removed all station nameboards along the length of the line. A former engineer of the company, G. F. Egan, described the period succinctly: 'In the war years 1942–5 receipts were satisfactory, but rising costs of materials and increases in wages absorbed most of them, and a gentleman called the Income Tax Inspector absconded with the balance.'

There was a remarkable expansion in the later war years and after. The company took delivery of a new railcar and two new locomotives were ordered to replace the old stock. These were named *Lough Erne* and *Lough Melvin* and as the company could not afford the full purchase price they bore plates on the cab side saying they were the property of Beyer Peacock, the manufacturer. They were later sold to the UTA and ended their days on the Belfast dock lines. These purchases, although necessary, added to the financial difficulties, especially as the Northern Ireland government reduced its grant to a fixed £1,500 a year. There was a strike in 1951 and before long the shareholders were calling for the company to be wound up. Fortunately the Irish government chipped in with £3,500 p.a. and the North followed with £3,000 which kept the wheels turning, but still did not cover the entire costs of the system. The management was forced to ask for more and more subsidies to prop up the ailing system.

G. F. Egan gave an articulate description of the problems of the railway in an article in the IRRS Journal in 1951. There were about 130 people employed and maintenance of the line was a great problem. The angle of the banks on the route was much too severe so that in heavy rain, slips occurred frequently, blocking the line. The yards at Manorhamilton were much too cramped as were the railway cottages, some of which had only two rooms but extensions were added later. In building the line, he said, timber and iron were often used where bricks and mortar were needed. Sleepers were used sparely, being eleven to the rail length instead of twelve. The many curves and bends combined with steep gradients to wreak havoc on locomotives while at Dromohaire the railway ran on the site of the original road which was diverted alongside for three-quarters of a mile. Among the items in use on the line were 35 underbridges, 3 overbridges, 230 pairs of gates at field crossings, 193 culverts and pipes, 28 public road crossings, 24 gatekeepers' cottages, 6 station premises (5 with dwelling house), 8 goods stores, 6 signal cabins, 2 attended and 2 unattended halts, offices in Enniskillen (at the GNR station), a house in Collooney with workshops, stores and offices in Manorhamilton. Mister Egan concluded his summary with the comment: 'If anyone can tell me what is in store for the Sligo Leitrim I shall be glad to hear of it.'

Under such rather stressful and uncertain conditions morale was never very high. What was the point in trying to promote efficiency if the end was expected daily if not hourly? Many of the signals were quite ambiguous with arms drooping from the horizontal. Some had a slot in which the arm was meant to disappear when off but seldom did. Others were attached to telegraph poles when the original post had rotted away. Various accounts of trips made in the 1950s convey the air of despondency, such as Rolt and Whitehouse in 1952 (*Lines of Character*): 'The driver sat motionless with shoulders hunched gazing with an abstracted and somewhat melancholy expression at the road ahead.' Another traveller, Denis Ireland, describes a halt at Belcoo as 'one of those long, silent, contemplative pauses during which without the sound of steam escaping from the engine, you feel you ought to be saying your prayers'. Similarly, 'no-one got in or out at Collooney and a philosophical taxi driver drove philosophically away from the station as if he never expected that anyone would'.

Sligo, Leitrim & Northern Counties Railway Company.

NOTICE

Of closing down of Rail and Road Services.

Consequent on the decision to close down the Great Northern Railway lines through Enniskillen as on and from 1st October, 1957, this Company will be unable to operate its services after 30th. September, 1957, and Notice is hereby given of the closing down of all Rail and Road services operated by this Company after that date.

No Passengers, Merchandise or Live Stock traffic will be accepted at any of the Company's Stations, including Sligo, Ballysodare and Enniskillen, which cannot reach its destination before midnight on Monday, 30th September.

All Merchandise on hands at Stations must be taken delivery of by consignees not later than Wednesday evening, 2nd October, 1957, and clearance of goods under Custom detention effected not later than same date.

By order of the Board,

Enniskillen,
20th. September, 1957.

E. W. MONAHAN,
Secretary & Gen. Manager.

Notice of the SL&NCR's closure

The working timetable contained such pious exhortations as: 'Platforms must be regularly swept by Traffic Staff; sweepings to be removed and not deposited on the rails'. A somewhat more alarming instruction was to the effect that 'the automatic brake must not be depended on for holding the vehicles as after a lapse of time the brakes leak off'!

The ever-present threat of closure became a reality in 1957 when the UTA announced that it planned to end all services through Enniskillen as part of its run-down of railways in the North. Without a rail connection in Fermanagh the SL&NCR had no future and in the autumn all employees received the following letter from the company's general manager:

> I have been instructed by the Directors to give you notice terminating your employment with the Company after the completion of your registered term of duty on Saturday October 5.
>
> The necessity of doing so is very much regretted but it will be recognised that the Directors have no alternative, and I have been asked to convey their appreciation of your loyal and faithful service to the company.

The last train ran on 30 October and as it wound its way through the mountains lights were flashed or a blazing turf was waved in the dark as a final salute.

After the closure most of the rolling stock was auctioned off, a good deal going to the UTA. One vehicle, railcar B, was kept in service by CIE and renumbered 2509. It has been used for various light passenger duties. In 1970 I joined an IRRS excursion in this squat 59 seat railcar from Waterford along the partially reopened Dungarvan line to Ballinacourty. It was very pleasant rattling along, feet dangling from the open doors on a no liability ticket, and thinking of the days when it trundled between Sligo and Enniskillen. Up to quite recently 2509 languished neglected at Limerick Junction but there are plans to preserve her and hopefully this will happen before it is too late. Happily one locomotive, *Lough Erne*, has been preserved by the RPSI.

The Waterford and Tramore Railway

There were not many Irish railways totally isolated from the main network, but this was one. Running for 7¼ miles from the city of Waterford to the popular coastal resort of Tramore (*Trá Mor*, the great strand) it was remarkably busy and prosperous throughout its life. The line had its own station in Waterford at Manor Street near the centre; it was in fact nearer the city than Waterford North although there was no physical connection. The line was built by William Dargan, single throughout and had no unusual engineering features apart from the odd level crossing. Dargan received a number of shares in the enterprise as part of his contract.

The first trial run was on 2 September 1853. Prior to that rolling stock had been delivered to the railway by sea as Waterford had not yet been reached by the W&LR. So enthusiastic were the dignitaries on the first train that a second return trip was made before retiring for the *de rigeur* banquet. There were only two stations on the line, the termini, which were almost identical in appearance, rare enough for the time. Since strict economy was the keynote of the line no doubt the directors saw little point in preparing two sets of station plans when one would do. Both buildings had a rather spectral, gothic appearance; with their lean angular lines, slender gables and high chimney stacks they could well be imagined in a

Hammer horror film. A full moon and a few bats would seal the impression. In fact the interiors were quite different. They were warm and tidy, well looked after by an attentive staff. Right up to the closure there was a fine grandfather clock in the Manor Station, made in Waterford, whose pleasant chimes were a feature of the railway.

Unlike so many Irish railways the W&TR was prosperous and successful right from the start and throughout its life. An extension to Dunmore East was soon considered but the inhabitants of that pleasant fishing village vigorously opposed the idea for fear it would become as vulgarly popular as Tramore. Not put out at being spurned the company did everything it could to promote Tramore, even carrying building materials free of charge for new residents.

Starting from Waterford was quite an occasion and was marked with great ceremony. Five minutes beforehand a bell sounded, tickets were thoroughly examined and the carriage doors locked. Once again the bell rang and, all those not having business with the Waterford and Tramore Railway having withdrawn, the platform gates closed. The guard then blew his whistle, the driver replied with a hoot and the train moved with decorum out of the station. Despite this elaborate procedure safety standards were dubious. There was no signalling, as in theory only one train was allowed on the line at a time. Formerly there was a passing loop, the train having to wait there until the one arrived from the other direction. On at least one occasion the driver grew tired waiting and pulled out on to the line. Luckily a railwayman spotted the two trains heading for each other and was able to stop them in time.

Among the special excursions was one in the 1930s for poor Waterford children. No less than two thousand were carried to the seaside, led by the mayor and aldermen. During the day, which went like clockwork, the children demolished 7,000 packets of sandwiches, 600 lbs of sweets, 400 lbs of cooked meats, 350 four pound loaves, 1,440 pints of milk, 10 cases of apples, 19 cases of oranges and 4,800 minerals! How many got sick is not recorded.

Traffic reached a peak during the summer months when it seems the whole city of Waterford struck camp and headed for the sea. In the 1950s diesel railcars were introduced to replace the stock supplied at the GSR amalgamation. By this time the railway was busier than ever. In 1953 there were 14 trains daily in each direction, the first at 0825 and the last at 2330. The 0910 train from Tramore at one time had one first class compartment which was by hallowed tradition reserved for a number of prominent railway and business magnates. It was generally known as the House of Lords. Lesser mortals such as dogs travelled in special dog compartments set into the side of a number of coaches. These were not divided into three classes.

Despite the fact that the branch was as busy and efficient as ever CIE seemed determined to close it, ignoring the fact that regularly there were more passengers wanting to travel than could be carried. So 106 years after the opening, on 31 December 1960, the last train ran. A few years later a new station building was opened at Waterford North. At the opening the Lord Mayor praised CIE for investing in a bright, new if rather soulless building. But he couldn't help adding: 'We'll never forgive you for closing the Tramore railway'!

Cork lines

Not so long ago Cork was very well served by railways as would be expected for the third largest city in Ireland. Along with the GS&WR services to Dublin, Limerick, Waterford etc., trains left from four other terminals for all parts of the county. Most remarkable of all was their relative affluence. Narrow gauge lines have never been a licence to print money, here as elsewhere, but these little railways were quite well off.

Thus it seems all the more surprising, considering the growth of Cork city and county, that they should have disappeared so completely and so soon. Standard gauge trains continued to run on the CB&SCR up to 1961 and Glanmire Road is still open for the Cobh line as well as main line services northwards, but all the others have gone, many as early as the 1930s. No-one could accuse the GSR/CIE of adopting the wholesale policy of closures that happened elsewhere. Many lines of social value were kept on long after harsh economic reality should have condemned them, such as the West Clare and the Cavan and Leitrim. Yet Cork seems to be the exception. One cannot escape the uncomfortable feeling that here the executions were carried out just a little too swiftly.

The Cork Macroom Direct Railway

Several lines were promoted between Cork and Macroom in the 1850s and 1860s. The one to succeed was that which left the C&BR's line at Ballyphehane to run west as far as Macroom. This was the Cork and Macroom Direct Railway (as opposed to any other more circuitous proposition). Incorporation took place on 1 August 1861 and work began a year later at a cost of £5,500–£6,000 per mile—a modest outlay. By 1866 the line was nearly ready and the first train ran on 12 May. The official opening took place twelve days later and followed the usual pattern. One item of interest referred to that day was that the stagecoach operator had sold off his vehicles the day before and gone out of business.

In Cork the company shared the C&BR's terminus at Albert Quay, a convenient arrangement but rather expensive at approximately £1,500 per year depending on the number of trains. Over 80,000 passengers travelled in the first six months, a promising start that continued for several years. However, relations with the Bandon company began to go downhill, chiefly over the rent and the priority given by the host to its own services. The Direct decided that it was time to move out and looked around for a suitable site for its own terminus. Capwell was the spot chosen in 1877 and the new station opened on 27 September 1879. It was a pity that the two companies could not reach agreement on the question of rent and related matters as the new company could have done without the expense of building its own terminus.

Nonetheless the line prospered and in 1878 a very handsome dividend of $7\frac{1}{2}$ per cent was paid, much higher than most other lines; those that paid any dividend at all that is. It emerges that the directors drew on the reserve funds to do so, this being justified by the chairman who said it was unlikely there would be a heavy demand on such reserves barring a fatal accident, an extremely remote possibility. Scarcely a month later that is exactly what happened.

On 8 September the 7.15 pm train from Macroom left the rails near Ballincollig at some speed, killing five people and seriously injuring thirteen. Apart from the deaths and injuries the line suffered a great deal in loss of reputation as well as having to pay out £15,000 in compensation. General Hutchinson carried out the subsequent Board of Trade inquiry and found over 3,000 sleepers and 100 rails in a dangerous condition. The cause of the accident was therefore poor maintenance of the line. Warrants for the arrest of the directors and superintendent were then issued; a rather extreme measure as they were unlikely to flee the country. As well as the compensation paid out train speeds were reduced on certain sections and one train daily was cancelled in each direction.

Capwell was rather remote from the city centre but the Direct was glad of the independence it gave. When the link with the GS&WR from Albert Quay opened in 1912 the board resisted pressure to restore its connection with the Bandon line at Ballyphehane. Of course this meant the loss of useful through traffic but two years later the matter was taken out of the company's hands when the government ordered a link up between the two systems. Grudgingly the Macroom built a sort of a connection. It was a siding which ran obliquely between the two railways and allowed some transhipment but only by means of reversals. Through running was impossible, thus obeying the letter if not the spirit of the order.

The second half of the year 1912 was the best yet with a revenue peak of £11,200. Passenger and tourist traffic was particularly heavy, aided by the movements of military from Ballincollig barracks on the outbreak of war. A regular sight was the daily consignment of laundry which was sent all the way to Clonmel to be washed and back again! The disturbances following the Treaty brought trains to a halt in September 1922. When the GSR amalgamation took place the Macroom was in a healthy state and the line joined the new system with its head high unlike some which staggered into the fold gratefully. The Macroom was busy, prosperous and well run.

Among the changes made under the new regime was the closure of Capwell and the transfer of services to Albert Quay. But the days of plenty were numbered with a certain indifference from Kingsbridge and the ever growing menace of competing road services. The decline was speedy and the last passenger train ran on 29 June 1935. A daily goods continued for some years with the odd passenger excursion. The final blow fell in 1950. Oddly enough the circumstances were similar to those which ended the Cavan and Leitrim nine years later. In both, it was the decision of the Electricity Supply Board to build a power station which brought the trains to a stop. In the case of the Macroom a hydro-electric plant was about to be built which would, before long, cause severe flooding along parts of the track. CIE was not at all reluctant to end services and the closure took place on 10 November 1953, the day of the monthly fair at Macroom.

The Cork Bandon and South Coast Railway

The CB&SCR consisted of a number of independent companies which formed the total route mileage of 94 miles. They were the Cork and Bandon (the principal constituent), the Cork and Kinsale Junction and the West Cork Railway. Between them they served a large part of south–west Cork, operating out of Albert Quay station, south of the Lee. The Cork and Bandon Railway was incorporated in July 1845 with a proposal for a line 20 miles in length between Cork and the busy town of Bandon. Its early days were beset by administrative and financial squabbles. Because of the poor response of shareholders and others to the company's attempts to raise extra capital, at one stage the Public Works Loan Commissioners, who were one of the chief backers, issued a warrant for the sale of the entire railway. Further delay was caused by what would nowadays be called a power struggle at board level. The company's offices were initially located in London but a large group of directors and shareholders felt quite rightly that it would make more sense if they were in Ireland. The battle went on for some time with eventual success for the Irish party.

No sooner was that settled than the contractor who was building the line, Fox, Henderson & Co., downed tools because he had not been paid. As there was no sign of his bills being settled he took further action and soon the sheriff of Cork arrived to take possession of all the company's property. While all this was going on great effort was being made to win the contract for carrying mail between Cork and Bandon. Understandably the post office was not impressed with the reputation of the C&BR and declined to entrust her majesty's mails to its care. This minefield of obstacles was finally overcome and construction went ahead. Beyond Ballinhassig, the engineer decided that a tunnel was needed and with some difficulty a 900 yard hole was cut through Goggins Hill. The Cork–Bandon section opened at last in 1851.

Leaving the Cork and Bandon line near Upton ran the Cork and Kinsale Junction Railway, a branch to the pleasant harbour of Kinsale. The incorporation took place in April 1859 and the railway opened four years later on 27 June 1863. The branch was quite short, 11 miles, and was worked by the C&BR until being taken over entirely in 1879. Kinsale has always been a sizeable fishing port as well as a very popular resort so it is all the more surprising that this line should have been one of the first to be closed in the 1930s.

Bantry station and town

Further west a company was formed in 1860 to extend the C&BR as far as Dunmanway, a little under 18 miles. This was the West Cork Railway which opened in 1866, and yet another company took the railway as far as Skibbereen in 1877. Both of these were in theory quite independent but were worked by the C&BR and subsequently absorbed by it. Further extensions followed a similar pattern: Drimoleague to Bantry (July 1881), Skibbereen to Baltimore (1893), Clonakilty Junction to Clonakilty (August 1886). All of these merged in time to become part of the Cork Bandon and South Coast Railway, which was born in 1888.

With its route mileage stabilised and the odd branch joining from time to time the CB&SCR became quite a respectable outfit with a steady if unspectacular traffic throughout West Cork. The C&MDR for a time shared its terminus at Albert Quay which, although central enough, was rather isolated from the main rail network. There were a number of proposals over the years to build a line across the river to join the GS&WR at Glanmire Road but it was not until immediately before the First World War that this became a reality. The agricultural and fishery produce of Cork needed the direct outlet that such a line would give, its sale depending on how quickly it could be moved from the producer to the markets of Dublin and Britain. In the year that the CB&SCR was formed, a railway commission had recommended the link up and in 1906 a government grant of £25,000 was awarded for the project. With the sea route from Rosslare to South Wales open, the English GWR offered £75,000, the Harbour Board gave £10,000 and the Bandon railway chipped in with £15,000.

The three-quarter mile line ran between the two termini and crossed the Lee twice by means of bridges which were raised or lowered as required. A separate company was formed to run the line, three board members being from the GWR and one from the CB&SCR. The offices were at Paddington Station, London. The line was a great benefit to the CB&SCR and there were regular goods trains over it. At one time it was planned to provide through passenger services for the many visitors on their way to West Cork, but apart from a short period in 1914 passenger trains were a rare sight.

The CB&SCR was quite a profitable concern for many years but after the 1914–18 war the all too familiar pattern of growing losses emerged. Thus it was one of the first to come to terms with the need for amalgamation and willingly joined forces with the GS&WR which had for some time worked the Cork City line. Unlike a number of other Cork railways the main part of the CB&SCR was given a new lease of life with the introduction of diesels to Clonakilty, Bantry and Baltimore. Multiple units and locomotive-hauled trains were used for many years and provided a useful service to that area until the inevitable closure overtook the railway, but not until 31 March 1961. Passenger traffic had been dwindling for some time but goods had remained steady.

The Dundalk, Newry and Greenore Railway

Another quite unique railway was the DN&GR. It was, as they say, 'a wholly owned subsidiary' of the English LNWR. Its 26½ mile V-shaped line ran from the port of Greenore on the Carlingford peninsula to join the GNR at two points, Dundalk and Newry. The main reason for the railway's existence was the hope of the LNWR for extending its Irish business by developing Greenore as a cross-channel port. The English company was not new to the field since it was already involved in the Holyhead–Kingstown and Stranraer–Larne routes and saw great potential in a third route from Greenore to Holyhead. Local support was not lacking, chiefly from the INWR (later to become the GNR), but dwindled after the incorporation of 1870. The line was thus built entirely by the LNWR and opened in 1873. There is an inscribed stone on the quay at Greenore which reads: 'This port and railway were opened for public traffic by His Excellency Earl Spencer KG, Lord Lieutenant of Ireland, April 30, 1873.' The next day a regular boat service began to Holyhead and, in 1877, to the Isle of Man. The station at Greenore was quite small but there was an impressive hotel built nearby, by the railway, which also spent quite a lot of money developing the town as a seaside resort. The line forked just outside Greenore, the Dundalk route running due west along Dundalk Bay. The terminus there was at Quay Street with a connection to the GNR main line via the famous Square Crossing.

A year and a half later there was a fatal crash at this crossing when the 5 pm train from Dublin to Belfast ploughed into a train from Greenore. Twenty-seven people were injured and two others died. The cause was lax signalling, as the Dublin train clearly had an open signal.

The northern route from Greenore to Newry was spectacularly beautiful, running as it did along the shores of Carlingford Lough and giving fine views of the Mourne Mountains. This section opened on 1 August 1876. The Newry terminus was at Bridge Street and again there was a through route to the GNR at Edward Street. In later years an express service ran from Belfast by this route connecting with the boats at Greenore.

It was very quickly realised that the majority of the DN&GR's passengers would be four-legged rather than two. The expected rush of cross channel trippers never really appeared but there was a constant stream of cattle using the route. This was in part due to unsuitable boats which made heavy going in bad weather. The problem was that most bipeds preferred to go via Kingstown if they were heading south and through Larne if going north—in both cases the crossing was shorter and the connections more suitable. Undoubtedly this was partly the fault of the LNWR which failed to make the option sufficiently attractive to entice more people to use it. There is no reason for instance why, with modern boats and fast connections, the Greenore route could not have been a serious rival of the Belfast–Liverpool steamer. Another option would have been to transfer from Holyhead to Liverpool.

In 1916 the company lost one of its vessels, the TSS *Connemara*, when it collided with a collier off Greenore. It was on 3 November and there was a gale blowing at the time. The collier was without lights and both ships sank immediately. Every single person on the *Connemara* died: 51 passengers, 31 crew members and 4 railwaymen. Only one man on the collier out of nine survived. Oddly enough some of the animals on the company's ship managed to swim ashore and were picked up near Greenore.

Like a number of other lines partition meant that the DN&GR was owned by an English company but operating in two separate parts of Ireland, as if it had not enough troubles already. Fortunately the cattle trade remained steady and in 1928 over 100,000 passed through Greenore. However the LMSR (successor to the LNWR) decided that it really could not cope with such a drain on its resources and approached the GNR with an offer it could easily refuse. After some lengthy negotiations the GNR agreed to take over the running of the line from July 1933, employing railbuses for the dwindling passengers using the railway. Under the new operators, losses were greatly reduced but as the cattle traffic was drawn away to other routes the deficit began to mount once more. From 1948 ownership passed to the newly formed British Transport Commission which ran British Railways. Faced with the problems of a moribund rail system in the UK the BTC decided it could no longer prop up the Greenore railway and asked both Dublin and Belfast if they would take over the system as part of the re-formed GNR. Both administrations decided against this (the BTC can hardly have been surprised) and the closure was announced from 31 December 1951. One very comfortable carriage has been preserved and now resides in the Belfast Transport Museum.

---

*Berry's Irish Railway, Steam Packet, Mail and Stage Coach
Time Table and General Advertiser*

A number of these commercial timetables were issued in the mid-nineteenth century under various titles: Morgan's, Wyers', Walsh's etc. They are very informative in that they give the services month by month as the lines were built.

Even more interesting are the advertisements they carried. Most were aimed at the more affluent traveller offering exclusive accommodation, products and services but occasionally the mask of respectability slipped and the reader comes across an item promoting a Doctor Morton of 93 Lower Gardiner Street, Dublin, which appeared in the October 1850 edition of Berry's Guide. Doctor Morton offers 'Confidential Medical Attendance in all Cases of Syphilis' and declares that he has 'devoted many years to the study and treatment of the Clap' with 'opportunities which occur to few, of seeing every stage and symptom of those dreadful maladies in their various forms'. Furthermore his Celebrated Purifying Pills were 'an effectual remedy in all cases of Gonorrhoea, gleet, stricture and diseases of the urinary organs'. The anxious passenger was no doubt relieved to know that Doctor Morton was 'the safest person to whom the unfortunate can apply for relief' and that 'in all cases the most inviolable secrecy may be relied on'. We may be sure that many of his clients were in transit between Amiens Street Station and Monto, both of which were near to hand.

A clairvoyant neighbour of Doctor Morton's was 'Madam Lorenzo, the Mysterious Lady' who features in the same issue. She charged '2s 6d for Each Private Interview, from Two to Four O'Clock P.M.' but lets the side down by adding: 'The Working Classes from Ten to Twelve O'Clock Noon, One shilling each.'

Further on the innocent traveller who wants to check his connection will find him or herself enjoined to purchase a copy of a book in a sealed envelope entitled 'MANHOOD—The Causes of its Premature Decline, with Plain Directions for its Perfect Restoration'. This little almanac covers such topics as 'diseases of the generative organs, emanating from Solitary and Sedentary Habits, indiscriminate Excesses, the effects of Climate, Infection etc.'. There must have been a demand for it: the author claims to have sold 49,000 copies.

8 The Listowel and Ballybunion Railway

BALLYBUNION is a sleepy little seaside resort in Kerry whose main claim to fame today is the annual batchelor festival, when hordes of unattached persons descend on the town in search of a mate. But in the last century it was even more noteworthy for being the terminus of the most extraordinary railway ever to operate in Ireland: the Listowel and Ballybunion Railway.

This was a 9¼ mile monorail based on the system of a French engineer, François Marie-Thérèse Lartigue. M. Lartigue had high hopes for his invention and took out patents in a number of countries. The advantages claimed for the Lartigue monorail were ease and economy of construction and operation, making it ideal for remote rural areas where traffic demands were not high. The monorail was slightly misnamed, having in fact three rails resting on an A-shaped trestle. The top rail carried the rolling stock and the two side rails balanced the whole.

Plans for a railway between Listowel and Ballybunion were first raised in 1883 when a group of residents petitioned the local authority for a tramway. The idea

Lartigue and main line stations, Listowel

133

Liselton station, the only intermediate stop

was well received and the promoters began looking for a builder. Not to be out-done a rival group proposed a standard gauge (5 ft 3 in.) line on the same route while both groups were opposed by a third who foresaw only losses and rising debts from either scheme. While the various projects were sorting themselves out M. Lartique arrived in Co. Kerry and surprised all and sundry by announcing that this was where he intended to construct his revolutionary monorail. The citizens were delighted that theirs was the spot chosen and differences dissolved overnight, except among those who considered all railways to be gall and wormwood. In April 1886 the Westminster House of Commons solemnly passed the second reading of the Listowel and Ballybunion Railway Bill and in due course Her Majesty gave her gracious consent. A prospectus was published the following year and the company was in business.

The projected traffic was seen to be livestock, children travelling to and from Listowel College, tourists and (unusually) sea sand. A local landowner, George Hewson, agreed to allow the company to draw as much sand as it required from the seashore at the edge of his estate on payment of 1d per ton of sand. Meanwhile Ballybunion was developing as a sea resort and a number of houses and holiday villas were under construction. With these activities in mind the promoters painted a rosy if rather insubstantial picture of the railway's future.

Work began in earnest late in 1887 and in keeping with the claims of its inventor the railway was completed in a matter of only five months at the remarkably low cost of £30,000. So far the promise of the line held good even if, as a contemporary

The terminus at Ballybunion; note the points

account notes, 'many difficulties naturally arose during the construction in matters of detail'. This bland statement conceals difficulties of a more fundamental nature. The system required that all rolling stock be balanced equally on either side of the trestle. The 'coffee pot' locomotives had to be built in the same way by Hunslet. There were great savings in the track laying and sharp curves were

Ballybunion, with possibly Mr Behr on the left

possible but orthodox level crossings and points were out of the question. Instead, where the line crossed a public road the track could be unhinged and moved aside to allow traffic to pass through. This action automatically put the signals at danger. Other crossing points had a curious drawbridge affair which was lowered to rest on the top rail by a system of pulleys. A third means of crossing the line was by way of a special set of steps attached to each train. Turntables, which were essential, were much in evidence on the line and described by the company itself as 'eccentric'.

Ballybunion station

Fritz Behr was appointed managing director and by February 1888 the line was complete and ready for inspection by the Board of Trade. In preparation for the opening the company prepared a booklet to publicise the railway. It has a rather whining tone and anticipates many of the criticisms made later: 'The position of the line is not well chosen for the purpose of displaying the particular advantages of the Lartigue system'. Other problems mentioned in it are bogs and drainage, nearness to roads and route limitations:

> These difficulties could easily have been avoided by removing the Railway to a certain distance from the public road... It must, therefore, be kept in view in inspecting this Railway, that it does not in any way represent a model for laying out a Lartigue Railway under ordinary circumstances.

The booklet goes on to describe the operation of the railway.

> The rolling stock consists of three engines with two horizontal boilers, each provided with tenders of a novel construction. These tenders are fitted with cylinders and a special gear, which allows the surplus steam of the engines to be used on steep inclines in order to give additional power and adhesion to the engines... Trains can be run with

The turntable at Ballybunion

even greater safety than on ordinary lines at a speed up to 20 miles per hour without any difficulty.

The opening took place, suitably enough, on Leap Year Day, 29 February 1888. A large party of local and national dignitaries was invited to attend and a number of continental visitors came to see the monorail in operation. A special train left Killarney at 0930 bringing the guests to Listowel. At noon the first train with over a hundred passengers left for Ballybunion. Mr Behr acted as host, guide and master of ceremonies, welcoming the guests and answering queries about the railway. Some of these commented, rather ungraciously, on the amount of noise in the carriages—not surprising given how near the running rail was to the passenger seats. Mr Behr dismissed these gripes as teething troubles, but unfortunately it became a permanent feature of the system.

At Ballybunion all descended for a (necessarily) brief tour of the town and retired to the station for lunch. There was much speechmaking and toasts as was the norm on these occasions and plans for an extension to Tarbert were mentioned, according to newspaper accounts of the day. That night there was a banquet in the Railway Hotel, Killarney (now the Great Southern) at which M. Lartigue said he was delighted to see the system in operation and hoped it would be the first of many such monorails in Ireland and Britain. The first regular passenger train ran a week later.

There was one intermediate station at Liselton and in summer four trains ran each weekday with half that number in winter, indicating the reliance on seasonal business. Ten years later the W&LR published a Programme of Tourist, Seaside and Excursion Arrangements in which it described Ballybunion as 'one of the most popular and health restoring places in the Kingdom. The railway connection with

Listowel is by the Lartigue single rail railway, one of the novelties of the age'. The journey took 40–45 minutes for the 9¼ miles. Even with a leisurely average of 15 mph there was an uncomfortable pitching motion, especially on the curves and the seats being back to back you were liable to crack your skull against your companion's on the sharper bends. Gradients were steep in places and on some occasions the passengers had to alight for the train to make it up a sharp incline. As if it did not have enough to contend with there were a number of sabotage attempts in the early days, mainly by disaffected landowners and ratepayers. However no serious injuries resulted from these.

It was soon clear that traffic expectations were overestimated as returns were much lower than expected. By the turn of the century the company was in receivership. However the trains kept running and for a brief period a small profit was made. State control during the First World War and the years after kept the company going although it suffered many attacks during the Civil War. Mail robberies and disruptions became so bad at one point that services were suspended for a period.

In 1924 plans for the amalgamation of all railways in the state were announced. A notable exclusion was the L&BR on the grounds that it was hopelessly un-economic and that extensive renewal was needed throughout. An appeal was inevitably launched noting that over 200,000 passengers were carried between 1913 and 1915 and stressing 'the national importance and necessity of maintaining and improving the existing railway service between Listowel and Ballybunion'. Just as inevitably the appeal was turned down and the company announced it could no longer continue services. In August an excursion from Limerick carried 860 passengers to Ballybunion. Two trains were needed to carry this number but one broke down, forcing the passengers to walk the remaining distance. Closure finally came on October 14 1924 when the last train ran and the line was as quickly taken up and dismantled as it had been laid down.

A lunar-type landscape behind the station at Ballybunion

Inevitably with such an unusual railway, there are numerous stories of its eccentricities. Many centre on the balancing problems of the rolling stock. One lady wanted a piano delivered to Ballybunion, causing consternation in that there was unlikely to be a second piano on the same train! The solution arrived at, was to place the piano on one side of the wagon with two calves on the other. For the return journey one calf was placed on either side. There is also a tale of a farmer who bought a cow at Listowel and borrowed another for the train trip to Ballybunion. A second animal was then needed to return the first one borrowed and so the business went on for most of that day until he had lost his own cow, acquired two he did not want and owed the company a small fortune in freight charges.

Today there is little to be seen of the L&BR. One survival is the bell which was once rung at Ballybunion station to announce departures. This now has a place of honour in Listowel national school. Apart from Lawrence's many pictures there is also a silent film of the railway in action which is still fondly regarded in the area. Bryan McMahon described it as 'the queerest railway in the world' but, he added, the local people loved every wheel of it.

9 Narrow Gauge Lines

The Ballycastle Railway

THE Ballycastle Railway was a 16¼ mile narrow gauge line in Co. Antrim which opened in October 1880. Leaving the B & NCR's main line at Ballymoney, with whom it shared a station, the line ran north to the seaside town of Ballycastle near Rathlin Island and the coast of Scotland. The Board of Trade had earlier reported that 'the Railway cannot be opened without danger to the public' and thus the company missed the tourist season on which it was greatly dependant. Ballycastle was then a popular seaside destination among the people of N. Belfast. The opening ceremony was as lavish as that of a major national railway with the *Coleraine Chronicle* giving full coverage of the events including the ritual smashing of a bottle of bubbly against the side of an engine. Luncheon was taken in the decorated goods shed with eleven champagne toasts to (as E. M. Patterson puts it) everyone 'ranging from the Queen to the carriage builders'.

Within a couple of years of opening the company adopted the free building tickets scheme whereby people building a house of a certain value in Ballycastle were entitled to a free first class ticket for seven years. The value limitations were intended to attract the right class of person. The system lasted for nearly twenty years and was highly successful. At the same time a canny gentleman of the cloth offered the railway £20 for a first class ticket for life. The company considered the offer carefully but as he was only 51 and disgustingly healthy decided against the offer.

In 1885 there was high drama in north Antrim when a liner the SS *Sarnia* went aground on Rathlin. The passengers were rescued and found that they and their luggage were unscheduled travellers on the BR going to Belfast by rail, instead of by ship. By the following year, Edward John Cotton of the B & NCR was managing the Ballycastle Railway. He was a heavyweight in every sense and quickly got the railway on its feet. Twelve years later the company was making a healthy profit under his management and Cotton was voted £500 by the board, it being discovered that he had worked without payment up to then. So the BR chugged quietly into the twentieth century, the routine being only occasionally disturbed by the odd lapse in discipline. One Sunday the driver and fireman on the afternoon train from Ballycastle were seen to be intoxicated. This did not stop them taking out the train, a bit later than usual, and they compounded their offence by the use of 'party expressions'. The event is all the more surprising given the difficulty in getting a drink on Sundays at the time.

The railway had quite an unusual coaling method. The fuel was carried in wicker baskets from the mines to the station. The bunkers were then filled and four baskets actually emptied on to the footplate. This made working conditions for the crew extremely difficult being up to their ankles in coal for half of each round trip. The line also had a very high percentage of third class passengers, 91–4%. The battle against insolvency raged on during the early years of the century, as with most small railways, but the BR seems to have given up the ghost sooner than the majority. In 1924 the Board announced that all services were to cease, the losses being unsupportable. However, negotiations began with the NCC, then owned by the LMSR in London, who made the miserly offer of £12,500 for the whole line. This was reluctantly accepted after some efforts to raise the price and trains began running again in August that year.

Headquarters were transferred to Belfast and operations greatly simplified in an effort to economise. Ballycastle station was demolished and a duller, more functional edifice replaced it. Most of the track was relaid (very necessary by then) and service trains were used to convey the ballast. Thus regular trains were seen to stop frequently at odd spots in the middle of nowhere as men began to unload sleepers or ballast to the amusement or annoyance of the onlooking passengers. Eventually the line was brought up to NCC standards.

The Second World War was less of a trial for the BR than the years after. In fact from 1939 onwards the line was exceptionally busy carrying food supplies to and from Ballycastle as part of the policy of food decentralisation to escape air raids. But the bitter winter of 1947 was a severe test. One train was caught in snow drifts for three days, although the passengers were rescued after one night in the brake van.

Rumours of closure were beginning to be heard at about this time. In 1948 there was some talk of conversion to standard gauge but this was never feasible given the highly distinctive, neat little bridges which would have to be replaced. There was also the tunnel at Capecastle which would have required major alteration. From April Fool's Day 1949, the BR became part of the UTA and the axe was not long in falling. The UTA announced that all services would end from 3 July 1950; hardly surprising even with the blinkered policy of that body. The coalfield which the line had drawn on during its early days were soon exhausted and only on fair days was the railway in any sense stretched. At all other times traffic was light. A number of coaches were sold to the County Donegal Railway and the engines were cut up at Ballycastle.

The Cavan and Leitrim Railway

The first proposals for a railway in this rather poor area were made in 1883. A meeting at Ballinamore on 14 September resolved to promote a light railway between Belturbet and Dromod via Ballinamore with a tramway to 'open up the coal and iron districts of Arigna and Lough Allen'. On 19 September *The Irish Times* described the project as 'the most important line which would be opened in Ireland under the Tramways Act'. The project was heavily publicised with lavish analysis of the expected returns from mineral, animal and passenger traffic.

There was no shortage of support for the new railway and work began in late 1885. The three foot gauge line eventually ran to 48½ miles (excluding the Arigna valley) and opened on 17 October 1887. The gentlemen of the press were taken for a preliminary run and expressed their enthusiasm for the 'armchairs, sofas and movable soft chairs' provided in the first class carriages. They also appreciated the 'nice paintings of Irish scenery' on display in each compartment. All the coaches were eight-wheelers with an attractive domed clerestory roof. Each had a railed veranda at either end and a footplate over the coupling. With the engine cowcatchers, the red–brown livery and the bell they had a curiously American appearance.

First returns were overwhelmingly good and it looked as if the railway would be a great success. Most services had to be extended and livestock traffic was particularly heavy. On 30 September 1889 over 80 wagons were carried from various fairs over the C&LR. Even with this high demand the first recorded surplus was not made until 1893 and that included the baronial guarantee. About this time W. H. McAdoo came on the scene as traffic manager. A former GNR stationmaster at Dundalk he forsook that busy junction for the relative backwater of Ballinamore. He was a rather stern, controversial figure but he worked hard and in the main had the company's interests at heart; he served the C&LR well.

Personnel

There were a number of level crossings on the line and these were worked from a cottage specially built for the purpose. The conditions of occupancy attached were very one-sided as we can see from an agreement between the railway and John Hanly of Dereen dated 26 January 1911. The cottage was rent free provided he or his family worked the gates for any train, day or night as required. The agreement also stated that he must 'give up same, peaceably and in good order to the Company at any time on receiving one week's previous notice'. No doubt these were standard terms at the time but they seem rather unfair.

Mr Hanly was a bit restless opening and closing the gates at all hours of the day and night for in 1914 he suddenly decided to give this up, as well as his other job as a ganger on the railway, to join the army. The company was taken by surprise at his sudden departure and apparently only learnt of it when he returned after being refused by the recruiting sergeant 'owing to him having bad teeth'. Two months later he tried again and this time was accepted at Longford and sent off to the front, bad teeth and all. His wife, according to the railway, was 'still living in no. 26 Gate-house (Dereen) and minds the gates for us, and certainly does it well'.

There were some staff difficulties in the early days. Dismissals seemed to occur quite regularly, often for being on duty under the influence. Such was the pool of labour available that few were given a second chance. The company records show numerous letters from ex-employees anxious to regain their job. Many included pledge cards, recently signed in an attempt to show the sincerity of their reformation.

One employee, Pat Prior, was more fortunate than most. He lost his job in March 1920 as a porter at Mohill station for being two hours late for work on Monaghan Fair Day. This was on 25 February and, one of the principal fairs in the county, was a particularly busy time for the railway. His explanation makes interesting reading.

> I was on duty the previous night until 11 o'clock and when I got to my boarding house found my bed occupied by a cattle dealer. The very same thing happened to me on the previous night. My bed was also occupied by a pig dealer and I had to remain by the fireside on both nights.

This was the reason for his sleeping in and being late for work. It appears that on this occasion clemency was shown and Porter Prior was reinstated. Some time later a carpenter who blamed 'bad whiskey' for his repeated unpunctuality was not so lucky.

As well as fair traffic the C&LR built and developed two slaughter houses at Dromod. One of these was in the news in 1893 when it was 'burglariously entered...

and the kidneys of six pigs packed in a hamper ready for transit were cut out and stolen'—possibly by a rural Mr Bloom. Tourist traffic on the Shannon was also growing steadily. The W&LR advertised through excursion tickets to the Shannon via the C&LR. These were very popular with people coming from the north and heading for Galway or Kerry. They involved taking the GNR to Ballyhaise, changing for the branch line and changing again to the C&LR at Belburbet for Dromod via Ballinamore. Steamers connected at Dromod harbour to take the weary traveller on a soothing cruise as far as Killaloe. From that point he was securely in W&LR territory, far from its dreaded rival the MGWR. The leisurely boat trip must have made up for the frequent changes en route, although the return journey was made through Dublin.

The Reverend Digges

Despite all this receipts stayed depressingly low, remaining only half the amount predicted, and the railway was a heavy burden on local ratepayers. The C&LR's chief troubleshooter of the time was the remarkable Rev. J. G. Digges MA who joined the board in 1892. He was for many years private chaplain at Lough Rynn House, Mohill and a passionate apiarist. His following was not universal however for he was described by the *Daily Mail* as 'the most bloated pluralist, controlling the destinies of six companies, of which five are closely connected with bee-keeping and agriculture and the other one a railway'. He was a fiery character and a formidable opponent.

In 1906 he wrote a pamphlet called 'Fighting Industry and Financing Emigration', a defence of the C&LR and related enterprises. It is witty, topical and at times a critical piece, giving a sharp picture of the railway and life in the country at the time. For example, writing of the beginnings of the C&LR he says: 'The running of trains in those early days was not as smooth and comfortable as passengers might desire and careful men took the precaution to put their teeth in their pockets before embarking.' He also parodies the fussiness of early regulations and red tape telling how leaflets were handed out to passengers and placards displayed explaining: 'how to enter and how to leave, what to do with their feet, their tickets and their heads, and exhorting them neither to stand up nor to lie down, and, above all things, not to lock out of the windows'.

In 1903 a local wit had a go at the C&LR management, in particular, McAdoo and Rev. Digges by inserting a spurious advertisement in the *Leitrim Advertiser* and the *Cavan Weekly News*.

> Station master wanted. Railway training unnecessary. Must be sound theologian, having Divinity Testimonium; certified strict attender at all religious observances. Applicants from back streets, slums or Ballybay not attended to. None but 'upper ten' need apply.

It indicates a certain stuffiness on the railway management's part that it was not content to laugh at such a clever piece of satire and let the latter drop. Instead Stewart, the company secretary, wrote to both papers demanding an apology and threatening legal action if they failed to do so. The *Leitrim Advertiser* obliged but the Cavan paper never replied. On taking legal advice Stewart was told that the chances of a successful prosecution were slight and there the matter ended. It would be interesting to know who inserted the advertisements.

Operating problems

Coal was an early problem, Welsh coal being imported at some cost. Eventually the Arigna Mining Co. was set up by the C&LR to explore the coal deposits within three miles of the terminus. Iron ore was also mined there in some quantities for in 1833 no less than 5,000 men had been employed at the iron works and the mines. The quality of the coal was not good for it had a high ash content. Such was its low combustion rate that the local Church of Ireland bishop is said to have kept ten tons handy in case a fire broke out in his house. Not surprisingly excessive speeds were rare with such low grade fuel. As the Rev. Digges put it: 'Sixty miles an hour is unusual. Accidents from fast running are few. The trains do the thirty-five miles from Belturbet to Dromod in 2½ hours. At Dromod there is a refreshment room.'

There was a series of sabotage attempts on the railway in the early part of this century. A midday train was struggling up a steep incline with a full load of passengers and cattle when suddenly, near the top, it came to a sudden stop. Nothing the crew did could get it moving. If the brakes had been faulty, the rails greasy or a coupling weak, nothing would have stopped it rolling back down the incline, at the bottom of which were an S-bend and a river bridge. The crew got out, rather shaken and found the vacuum brake on the last wagon had been deliberately released. This was quickly repaired and the train went on its way. Next day when the train reached the spot exactly the same thing happened and the next day and the next. Extra precautions were taken which must have frightened off the vandal as for two weeks nothing happened. Then, in a moment of recklessness he struck again and was caught by the vigilant railwaymen! The saboteur was a dog. Each day when he heard the train labouring up the hill he sneaked out of a nearby farmhouse, sped across the fields and hid in the bushes until the train appeared. He raced alongside and snapped at the vacuum pipe until it came away and then vanished.

In 1903 the C&LR began to reconsider an extension up the Arigna Valley for easier access to the coal mines and another from Dromod to Rooskey. At the same time the Ulster and Connaught Light Railway Bill was announced. This projected a narrow gauge link up of the Clogher Valley Railway at Maguiresbridge and the C&LR at Bawnboy, providing a continuous railway from Greenore to Galway and taking over various companies on the way. Clearly the promoters wanted the advantage of surprise for no mention of this plan was made to the C&LR beforehand. Naturally the C&LR board were not so keen on the project. Leitrim County Council approved the scheme wholeheartedly while at the same time rejecting a more viable plan for the extension to the Arigna mines. Accounts of the meeting which gave the thumbs down to the extension show it was stormy. One of the councillors whom Mr Digges described as 'a man of magnificent physique, with lungs like an Atlantic liner's siren' stood in front of the mining company's chairman and shouted 'BOSH!' repeatedly at him as he tried to address the meeting. The name of this proponent of free speech is unfortunately not recorded. Some time later the council agreed to the extension, being encouraged by a government grant of £24,000 but later still once more rejected the plan. Mr Digges was very indignant about the whole thing.

There was growing opposition to the railway from a number of quarters, in particular the ratepayers who continued to subsidise it. The announcement of a commission of inquiry into all Irish railways in 1906 gave the critics a chance to voice their grievances. But the results of the inquiry were not at all bad and the C&LR continued in business. Religious and political outings of various hues brought in a good deal of useful revenue. The board had the usual reservations about Sunday trains but commerce prevailed and the directors admitted rather sheepishly that 'although not desirous of encouraging Sunday traffic they think it right . . . to allow the above Sunday trains to operate on exceptional occasions'. By far the biggest were the Orange lodge demonstrations which at times brought as many as 1,200 passengers on to the railway. A new engine *King Edward* was bought at this time to cope with the extra traffic but unfortunately it was so heavy that it damaged the track and could only be used on rare occasions. An increasing number of wagons was also built at Ballinamore workshops.

Trains were frequently stabled overnight at Dromod and Drumshanbo to work an early morning service. However several passengers complained of finding oil on the first class seats when they took the first train of the day. It was discovered that the engine crew were using the carriages as a dormitory in preference to the company's more sparse accommodation. From then on carriages were locked at night.

The Troubles had their effect on the C&LR. Train staff refused to work trains carrying British soldiers, sometimes with a trace of humour. One Mohill driver explained his refusal thus: 'It's like this. There's only half an hour in the difference. If I don't drive the train I'll be shot here; if I do I'll be shot in Ballinamore as a traitor. So I think I'll stay here and if I'm to die it'll be as a patriot.' During the Civil War trains were commandeered by both sides including one used by republican forces from Arigna for an attack on the barracks at Ballinamore. This was met by an 'invasion' of their Arigna stronghold by 900 men of the national army who travelled by a double headed, nine coach train, with numerous wagons, from Belturbet.

At Dromod the C&LR met the MGWR but relations between the two were never more than lukewarm. At Belturbet the company shared the GNR station, connections being provided at both for onward travel. Even with these, extensions were frequently mooted to Boyle, Strokestown, Collooney and even Sligo. The only one that materialised was the tramway to the mines. In May 1910 Henry Plews, general manager of the GNR, wrote to McAdoo inquiring about the success of experiments with acetylene lighting in carriages which was being tried out on the C&LR. McAdoo replied rather briefly that it was too soon to judge their suitability.

Control from Dublin

The impersonal nature of control under the GSR was strongly resented by the independent minded C&LR men. Red tape was thwarted and many incidents such as wagon derailments were quickly remedied without an official report. Occasionally the influence of Dublin could not be resisted, such as the time that a small industrial dispute broke out and an official was sent down from Kingsbridge to settle it.

Johnny Gaffney was the men's leader and he strode into the Ballinamore office with his cap on his head to confront management. 'Do you know who I am?' said the man from head office. 'I do not' said Johnny, feigning ignorance. 'I am Superintendent F. of the Great Southern Railways.' Quick as lightning Johnny came back with 'And I am Driver Johnny Gaffney of the Cavan and Leitrim Railway.'

Unwittingly CIE got it right when it listed the C&LR in its working timetable as a 'self-contained line'.

Hints of closure by the GSR had come as early as 1939 and continued during the fuel crisis of the war years and after. In 1955 the Electricity Supply Board announced that it was building a coal-fired generating station at Lough Allen which would take the entire output of the Arigna mines. There would thus be no need to transport coal over the C&LR. However a new coal contract brought a reprieve and for a time mines and railway were busier than ever. Ironically the locomotive stock was added to by engines from other light railways which had already closed such as the Tralee and Dingle, Cork Blackrock and Passage, Ballymena Cushendall and Red Bay. As one of the last surviving narrow gauge lines the C&LR attracted visitors from all over the world particularly when rumours of closure hardened into fact. The end was announced in 1959, the main reasons being an annual loss of £40,000 and the cost of essential modernisation. The last train, which was packed, ran on 31 March and the following day road services replaced the trains.

The distinctive red brick station buildings can still be easily spotted. Ballinamore has been greatly altered for conversion to a school but Mohill and Dromod are virtually unchanged. Two engines have been preserved: *Lady Edith* with one or two coaches was shipped to America and *Kathleen* has been beautifully restored by the Belfast Transport Museum.

For the whole of its existence the C&LR was affectionately known to the locals as 'the narrow gauge'. Rev. Digges records the following exchange overheard at the turn of the century:

> *US Visitor:* 'Say, Boss, is this the Cavan and Leitrim Railroad?'
> *Native:* 'No, misthur; that's the narra' gauge!'

The Clogher Valley Railway

It is questionable whether the Clogher Valley was a railway or a tramway; indeed it seemed unable to make up its own mind for it changed from one to the other after many years in business. The truth is that it was both and therefore qualifies, if only marginally, for inclusion in this book.

The 37 mile line ran through counties Fermanagh and Tyrone connecting the small towns of Tynan and Maguiresbridge. At either end it joined with the GNR line from Armagh–Clones–Enniskillen. In fact a through passenger from Tynan to Maguiresbridge would get to his destination far quicker on the GNR than on the Clogher Valley; but then few made the complete journey from one terminus to the other. The chief population centre en route was the village of Fivemiletown where the line decided it was definitely a tramway. Here as in other towns the railway strode boldly down the centre of the main street instead of lurking shyly outside as with many Irish lines.

The Tramways Act was the origin of the line, a three foot gauge being chosen as most suitable for the terrain and traffic expected. The rosy prospectus which appeared in 1884 foresaw private sidings for traders, a bus-type service for passengers and a gross profit of at least 50 per cent of receipts. Local landowners were the main proponents and launched the scheme as the Clogher Valley Tramway. Some local residents expressed concern over the effects of the tramway sections on the public roads as well as the danger to other users. But such fears were either soothed or ignored and the legal formalities being complete work began in June 1885, hampered somewhat by bad weather for the rest of that year.

While the quality of the construction work seems to have been quite adequate there was an unseemly dispute between contractor, engineer and supplier over the rails, sleepers and stonework. A financial hiccough stopped all progress in 1886 which was only relieved by a further injection of public funds. A good deal of expense was saved through sharing the GNR's stations at Tynan and Maguires-bridge, a sensible compromise. The intermediate stations were quite lavish in design and construction, being of red brick with a flourish of gables, arches and mouldings.

The year following saw the company getting ready for the opening of the line. So anxious were the promoters to get the show on the road that an irregular goods service started in February to the great inconvenience of the contractors who were trying to finish the railway. Such was the nuisance that it actually delayed the opening some weeks. The formal opening occurred on 2 May with the usual festivities which were so boisterous that, as the local paper had it, 'even bankers were jolly at the happy results of the day'. The public was admitted the next day with the inducement of special excursion tickets at reduced rates but only 100 souls partook of the opportunity; this was a little disappointing to the directors but dismissed as an initial reticence which would soon be overcome. Alas, it was not to be.

The gradients and curves on the line were very stiff in parts and although most of the track followed the public road occasionally the line fled into the open country to become a railway before wandering back after a few miles to the Queen's highway. Windmills for pumping water to the storage tanks were an unusual feature of the CVR and rather attractive they were. Times were loosely linked to the GNR services at either end but if you were not careful you could find yourself kicking your heels for a couple of hours at Tynan on the way to or from Belfast. In later years the timings were better coordinated and a delay of more than five minutes was quite rare. Of course if the 'tram' was late you need not expect the Northern to wait for you!

Traffic on fair days was very heavy with cattle trains starting at the most ungodly hour of the morning. Another busy period was 12 July—Orangeman's Day—when many specials ran all over the province, the Clogher Valley not excepted. Such was the demand and so uneager the company to turn any revenue away—either papist or puritan—that cattle trucks and even open wagons were given a quick scrub down and used as passenger vehicles. Generally passengers were well looked after with comfortable waiting rooms at the main stations. Caledon was another town where the railway partitioned the main street and being for a time without a proper waiting room the company made an agreement with a local townsman for the use of his front room to that end as well as for handling parcels. But the gent in question seems to have got tired of having strangers wandering in and out of his sitting room and leaving their goods and chattels all over the place for within a year the agreement had been ended.

Speed restrictions of 4 mph (not always observed) were in force at several points on the line. Some of the inclines were so heavy that the engines had to struggle hard to get over them with a heavy train. So many sparks were thrown out at these times that the engine exhaust quite regularly set fire to houses and cottages near the line. The occupants were not amused to find their *pied à terre* converted into a pyre and pressed for heavy compensation.

Everyone knows that a tramway is an inferior being to a railway so in 1894 the CVR decided to alert the world to its change in nomenclature, being henceforth and for all time the Clogher Valley *Railway*. The benefits were that it could take part in the Railway Clearing House System and issue through tickets to destinations all over the country and to Britain. At about this time a survey of the receipts showed that losses on the line were steady if not spectacular, the deficit being of course made good by the baronial guarantee.

Extensions were very much in the air at this time if not actually on the ground. One proposal was for a line from Newry to Tynan. Another advocated a link up with the Cavan and Leitrim at Bawnboy Road, south of Maguiresbridge. Altogether more ambitious was the Ulster and Connaught Light Railway which planned to build a line from Newry as far west as Clifden, taking in the CVR on the way. Needless to say none of these got further than the drawing board which is probably just as well as the business that could be squeezed out of that part of the country was limited to say the least.

When partition came the Clogher Valley found itself wholly in the North although it came very near the border at Tynan and Ballygawley. Tynan became the customs post for GNR travellers going south. A merger with the GNR was suggested at this time but Amiens Street declined the offer then and on a number of other occasions. Closure was hinted at and an inquiry opened in 1927 which found the track and rolling stock in poor condition. Being rather indirect and slow the railway was particularly vulnerable to road competition and the ratepayers of the area who had kept the trains running over the years were not anxious to prolong the life of the line.

A new committee of management came on the scene in 1928 with members appointed by the local authority and the Minister of Commerce in Belfast. A promising notion was the introduction of diesel railcars which cut operating costs greatly. This was no doubt at the suggestion of Henry Forbes of the Donegal Railway who was a member of the committee and a pioneer of this form of transport. They were highly successful. Sunday workings, long opposed, were soon after introduced but only grudgingly.

The economic depression of the 1930s and the Road Transport Act of 1932 sealed the fate of the railway which finally surrendered the unequal struggle in the early hours of New Year's Day 1942.

The Cork Blackrock and Passage Railway

This was the first railway to open in Cork city and received parliamentary approval on 16 July 1846, some years before the GS&WR reached the Munster capital. It was also unusual in that after it had been operating quite well for about fifty years the directors decided not only to double its length but to change from standard to narrow gauge. The engineer on the line was Sir John MacNeil and the customary initial ceremony involved Lady Deane's making what A. T. Newham delicately calls 'an incision in the ground' at the appropriate spot on 15 June 1847. A year later work was well in hand; the line was single but there was enough ground to double it if necessary. As a result of this the cost at £21,000 per mile was rather on the high side. Dargan was called in to finish the last stretch as far as Passage and the running was leased to a Dublin firm who also supplied the rolling stock.

The line opened on 8 June 1850 with the first train from City Park Station, a good ten minute walk from the centre. An enormous number of passengers travelled right from the start with as many as ten fully laden trains in each direction at weekends. The fares were 6d first and 4d second class ($2\frac{1}{2}$, $1\frac{1}{2}$p). At Passage the line terminated on the pier alongside the steamer berth. The company became involved in running these boats with excursions around Cork harbour and the islands which ran in conjunction with the trains. The ferry service between Passage and Queenstown began much to the annoyance of other shipowners. Competition was fierce and led to a fare war which was nothing like that felt when the Cork and Youghal Railway opened its line to Queenstown in March 1862. Finally a workable arrangement was agreed between the various shipping concerns and the C&YR fell on hard times until taken over by the GS&WR.

A compulsory but beneficial change of terminus in Cork was forced on the company in 1873. The Corporation decided it wanted to develop the quays near the original site and therefore subsidised the move to a much more convenient spot at Albert Street, near the CB&SCR's premises. (It would have been much more sensible to move into Albert Quay Station but the competitive spirit was too strong at the time.) The $1\frac{1}{2}$ mile diversion opened on 6 February 1873 at about the time that the railway's chief shipping rival folded and it acquired four vessels at excellent prices. Tourist development in the area around Cork harbour kept the trains and the boats busy even though the latter were scarcely used in winter. Goods were carried on most shipping services from the goods store and passenger berth near Patrick's Bridge.

With things going so well the directors were soon in the mood for extending their railway and Crosshaven—rapidly becoming a suburb of Cork—was the obvious place to aim for. It was decided that the line should be built to a narrow gauge at an estimated saving of about £30,000. Such was the delight of the board at the new gauge that it decided to change the existing route to narrow gauge as well and here the extensive land purchases of the builders paid off. Traffic was to become so heavy that it was necessary to double part of the line out of Cork as far as Blackrock, the only such narrow gauge line in Ireland. The necessary acts were passed and work began in 1897. Although fairly short there was a major obstacle to be overcome in the tunnel (1500 feet) which had to be dug between Passage and Glenbrook. Regauging continued at the same time between Cork and Blackrock. The capital needed for these three fairly large items was found to be lacking and work on the extension halted. Regauging did not stop and regular passenger services on the narrow gauge line began, after only a day's interruption, on 30 October 1900. Meanwhile the newly formed city tram company began to offer steady competition.

The numerous engineering problems were finally overcome, the tunnel completed and the line opened to Monkstown in August 1902, in which year a profit of £3,000 was recorded. Crosshaven finally got its trains on 1 June 1904 with services on a half-hourly basis in summer and hourly at less busy times. Boat trips continued to run, calling in at the various stations en route so that a pleasant day out could be made taking the boat out from Cork and the train home. The returns from the steamers were unpredictable, depending greatly on the weather. Most passengers for Crosshaven went the whole way by train so that all in all the shipping services were not a great success.

When war broke out in 1914 Crosshaven was closed to passengers by the military and all rail and boat services there ended. This was a substantial loss to the company and it found itself unable to meet its larger creditors. An inquiry into the railway found it was well and efficiently run although the recent extension and gauge conversion works had cost nearly three times the estimated £9,000 per mile. Even so, 1918 was the best year to date with gross profits of £45,000 and over the next few years the number of people wanting to travel often exceeded the capacity of the trains, especially on Sunday excursions. It must have been very annoying for the railway to have to turn away intending passengers and to remedy it several pieces of rolling stock were borrowed from the Swilly and the Donegal Railway.

The boom ended in 1922 with the Civil War. Carrigaline bridge and part of the Douglas viaduct were destroyed. Later Passage was the spot chosen by Free State troops for the advance on Cork from the sea, most having been brought from Dublin by ship. Douglas viaduct was repaired by the Railway Corps of the Free State army at the end of 1923 as well as a number of signal cabins and railway buildings. But independent days were nearly over and the CB&PR found itself part of the newly formed GSR, along with its rather troublesome steamer services. Some of the boats were disposed of immediately and a skeleton service maintained. In 1927 the double line section was singled and a few years later with the bus competition growing rumours of closure were first heard. Monkstown–Crosshaven closed, despite some protest, on 31 May 1932 and on the 10 September the final train left Albert Street for Monkstown. The four locomotives went to the Cavan and Leitrim where they were numbered 10L–13L and gave many years hard work. A number of relics survive of this prosperous little line, notably among the station buildings and the Glenbrook tunnel which for some time was used for storing oil drums and was lit by electricity at one end. It is unlikely that the Passage Railway could have survived into the 1980s although not impossible. But it seems obvious that its closure was to say the least, a little premature.

The Cork and Muskerry Light Railway

Much of the impetus for the 'Muskerry tram', as this little railway was known, came from the potential tourist traffic to the famous Blarney Castle with its eloquent stone. The Tramways Act gave the promoters the boost they required and the first meeting of backers heard of a plan to build a line from Western Road on the outskirts of Cork to Coachford, with a branch to Blarney. Interest was at first keen but suffered a decline when the ratepayers saw the extent of their liability if the line failed. Further opposition came from the Macroom Railway which although some way south saw a threat in the almost parallel route to Coachford.

After a number of such setbacks had been surmounted, Parliament gave its approval on 26 June 1886 and some time later the company issued its prospectus. Apart from the route described the plan contained a proposal for a tramway from Western Road to the station at Penrose Quay (GS&WR) and direct access at half-price from Blarney station into the castle grounds. Work began on the section to Blarney in February 1887 and General Hutchinson of the Board of Trade inspected it the following July. He praised it highly saying it was the 'best eight and a half miles' of track that he had seen on any tramway.

The line opened in August in time for the tourist season with six trains in each direction daily. There was a great demand for seats and in 5–6 weeks over 53,000 passengers were carried. Western Road was a rather simple building with fairly minimal facilities. Soon after leaving it the line crossed the river Lee and, becoming a tramway, ran along Western Road for some distance. Further on it abandoned the road and became a proper railway, winding its way through the fields of West Cork.

In 1888 a group from Donoughmore petitioned for a line off the Blarney route to their town. This was to be controlled by a separate company but worked by the C&MLR. The line was approved and opened on 6 May 1893, leaving the branch at St Annes. With its three trains daily this was the least prosperous of the three routes and became a drain on the larger company's finances. Relative prosperity followed with large numbers travelling to Blarney and Coachford and a healthy dividend was paid for many years. It is not surprising that the amalgamation plans first mooted in 1907–8 were distinctly unwelcome to the Muskerry proprietors and 1917 was the best year recorded. However a number of minor accidents suggest that maintenance of track and locomotives was not of the best.

When amalgamation did come it was accepted with mixed feelings. Shares in the railway were still highly priced but 1924 had shown a loss of almost £3,000, a disappointment to the proprietors who viewed their railway as a viable concern with a bright future. This was recognised by the GSR officials who considered it anything but a lame duck. The year 1927 saw the famous collision between the train and the steamroller outside Cork near Victoria Cross. The steamroller was working on road improvements at the time and no doubt each driver believed he had right of way and blamed the other as is customary on these occasions. No-one was seriously hurt although there was some damage to a number of carriages and the steamroller was out of action for several weeks!

The inevitable assault of buses and lorries reached a climax in the 1930s and for a time services were cut back in an effort to reduce the losses. On some Sundays there were no trains at all. Temporary relief came in 1932 when the Cork Exhibition was held near the terminus and a special halt opened to accommodate visitors. However it was only for a time and the GSR announced the closure of the railway in 1934, the final trains running on 29 December.

The County Donegal Railway

The County Donegal Railway was the largest narrow gauge system in Ireland with 124½ miles at its peak. The line consisted of several small concerns which merged to serve the sparsely populated districts of southern Donegal. It was a remarkably well run system which survived longer than most others.

Strabane got its first railway as early as 1847 and before long there was a group of local landowners who promoted a line westward from the town into Donegal. This was the Finn Valley Railway which first met in London on 22 May 1860, the principal directors being Lord Lifford and Samuel Hayes. Great economies in construction were promised and the route planned was from the L&ER station at Strabane to Stranorlar. The 5ft 3in. line was begun on 9 September 1861 when Lord Abercorn turned the first sod announcing ambitiously that the railway would be built in only nine months. In fact it was two years before services began on 7 September 1863. The line was operated by the Irish North Western (predecessor of the GNR) and being under-capitalised the receipts for the first few months were disappointing. Relations with the INWR were poor; the new company shared a small portion of its larger neighbour's tracks into Strabane in order to avoid building a bridge over the river but it was paying dearly for the privilege.

The first steps towards severing the link were made when the FVR decided it was time to run its own coaching stock, maintain the permanent way and employ station staff. The five new carriages were particularly welcome. One shareholder, a Mr Kerrigan from Stranorlar, remarked: 'Our comfortable, handsome carriages are a great boon, especially when one remembers the rickety, leaky old things that were supplied by the Irish North Western Company'. This man was the chief proponent of an extension from Stranorlar to Donegal although the line was in fact built by a separate concern, the West Donegal Railway and some of the personnel were common to both. Four months after the customary sod-turning, work began on 1 August 1880. Again the contractor made the mistake of starting late in the year so that the work was greatly held up by the harsh Donegal winter and a lack of enthusiasm from the people of Donegal town for the advancing railway! Four miles from the town cash ran out and there the line ended for a time with a temporary terminus.

Although built to a gauge of three feet the WDR was worked by the FVR which found it a drain on its slender resources. Trains began running on 25 April 1882 with horse drawn cars ferrying passengers the last four miles of their journey to Donegal town. Stranorlar thus became a busy mixed gauge junction from where trains departed to climb the Barnesmore Gap through the Blue Stack Mountains, a place notorious for hurricane force winds. Work on the final stretch into Donegal began in 1886 and the line opened on 16 September 1889; hardly a record breaking achievement. It had been clear for some time that the WDR would be behind schedule for in November 1888 the company sent a memorial to the Lord Lieutenant asking for an extended completion date, saying three years was insufficient. The capital for the project was lacking and the Commissioners of Public Works had to make up the shortfall. A few months later the Lord Lieutenant 'by and with the advice of Her Majesty's Privy Council in Ireland' gave them another eighteen months.

The exterior of the station at Killybegs

At about this time the government was busy encouraging the development of railways in remote areas of the country, among them extensions to the fishing port of Killybegs and to Glenties to be financed with public money. It was obvious that the time had come for the Finn Valley and the West Donegal to formalise their union and this was accomplished on 27 June 1892 when the Donegal Railway Company came into being. An equally logical step was the conversion of the whole line to the three foot gauge, this being much more suitable for the traffic and terrain in which the line operated. This broke the final link with the Great Northern, as the INWR had become. The Donegal Railway built a new station at Strabane, something it had been itching to do for years with a new bridge and approach to it. With regauging complete mileage stood at a healthy 75 and receipts were good. Still in the mood for extensions the company had its eye on Derry, the source of much of its traffic. The GNR already had a line from Strabane to the maiden city and was horrified to discover its insolent neighbour planned a duplicate link. Despite its loud protests the extension was approved and the parallel route opened in August 1900. The narrow gauge approached Derry east of the Foyle which was thus served by four railways: the Great Northern, the Northern Counties, the Londonderry and Lough Swilly and the County Donegal, each with its own terminus in the city, a pair on either side of the river. Victoria Road was the CDR's station a rather splendid edifice which was linked to the others by mixed gauge tracks over Carlisle Bridge. The Ballyshannon branch took longer, opening on 21 September 1905, another direct assault on the mighty Great Northern and its monopoly in the area.

The English Midland Railway which had acquired the B & NCR in 1903 was still keen to expand its business in Ireland and had looked at a number of potential lines to take over. Its eye fell on the CDR and it opened negotiations with the latter company for a merger. The GNR meanwhile was extremely anxious about the growing Midland influence in its half of the country and opposed the sale of the line unless it could join as an equal partner, seeing this as a golden opportunity to gain control of this annoying little railway which was thriving despite every expectation to the contrary. In due course an agreement was signed whereby the Midland and the GNR became joint owners of the line under the title of the County Donegal Railways Joint Committee. This came into force on 1 May 1906. The head offices stayed at Stranorlar while the Midland took over the Strabane to Derry section. The final addition to the network was the Strabane and Letterkenny Railway which ran its first train as late as January 1909 and was largely controlled by the CDRJC. Relations between these two companies had not always been so cordial. Four months earlier the S & LR had issued a half-yearly report which stated:

> The entire railway, with the exception of the Junction at Strabane, is now complete, and a portion has been passed by the Board of Trade Inspector, who would have passed the entire Line had the Junction been completed. The responsibility for the delay in executing the works at the Junction rests with the CDRJC.

Thus the CDRJC found itself with 124½ miles of worked track through some of the most beautiful countryside in Ireland. Tourism was strongly promoted using attractive illustrated booklets issued free with timetables, containing information on the attractions of the Donegal highlands. Henry Forbes, the dynamic secretary and general manager came to Stranorlar in 1910 and was largely responsible for the company's success. It was he who pioneered the use of diesel vehicles, making full use of the GNR's resources and facilities. The president of the LMSR said of him that he brought to the railway 'a remarkable degree of prosperity in the circumstances peculiar to Donegal, and turned an operating loss into a net receipt of £16,000, equal to 25% of the gross receipts'. A novel feature of the system were the special cinema trains which ran late on Saturday nights between Strabane and Stranorlar. A large number of request halts were opened and the administration of the railway brought up to date.

The First World War arrived with the usual mixture of benefits and problems. The company engineer, Livesey, produced a reinforced concrete sleeper which he said could replace the imported wooden ones. He also suggested manufacturing grenade cases at the Stranorlar workshops but nothing came of either project.

The minute books of the post-War years catalogue the disruption suffered by the railway which took the usual form. Forbes kept the system running almost singlehanded, often at some personal risk. On one occasion in September 1920 Forbes (a Unionist by persuasion) was on a train which was held up by armed men at Drumbar. The manager jumped from the carriage and ran along the track to the engine with a revolver in his hand. Then he leapt on to the footplate and shouted at the raiders that he would shoot them if they did not get off the train. Both parties opened fire, apparently without injury, the intrepid Forbes managing to drive them away. Not content with that he chased them across a field, captured one and brought him back to the station where he was arrested by the RIC. Forbes was not a man to be trifled with.

Despite their proximity and resemblance in territory there were great differences between the CDRJC and the Swilly. The latter cast envious eyes on the thriving Donegal railway disguising this with open hostility. Through bookings on either line were as scarce as hen's teeth and any connections made at Letterkenny between the two were purely accidental. When Henry Hunt came to the Swilly there was some attempt to normalise relations and a thaw set in. At one point Hunt wanted to order some long overdue locomotives for his railway and approached Forbes with a request for a loan of a CDRJC engine to try it out on the Burtonport branch. Knowing the Swilly's reputation for running its equipment into the ground Forbes refused, but politely.

The roads in Donegal have never been of the highest quality and for many years helped to limit the growth of serious road competition to rail services. In 1930 four road buses arrived from the GNR and later a number of lorries. Railcars had arrived as early as 1907 and by 1926 were a common sight. Further vehicles followed, some being capable of drawing a trailer. Their flexibility and low operating costs were a great boon. Perhaps this would have been the right time for Forbes to step down in favour of a younger man with more up to date ideas for maintenance of some sections was beginning to fall behind. Yet staff pride in the railway was high; Harold Fayle described them as 'exceptionally capable and obliging'. They worked quite hard too: a railcar driver had to issue tickets, check parcels, watch for passengers entering and leaving, observe signals and crossings as well as drive the train.

However, even though it gave a first class service, the days of the CDRJC were limited. The Glenties branch was the first to go; running through an area of low population density it lost its regular service in 1947 and closed finally on 10 March 1952. From 1948 British Railways assumed the MR/LMSR share of the railway and continued to appoint three people to the committee. With the demise of the Great Northern, the other partner, the two Irish governments took over its share, thus effectively nationalising the CDRJC. The working timetable of June 1950 has a number of interesting items on the operation of the line. The booklet is headed 'Constant Vigilance is the Price of Safety! Take nothing for granted! Make SURE!' It also has a paragraph on station slot machines: 'The Committee derive a revenue from the sale of sweetmeats, etc. drawn from these machines; station-masters must have them regularly refilled and see they are in working order'.

The next line to go was that between Strabane and Derry which the UTA closed finally on 23 September 1955. The Victoria Road terminus became a warehouse and the new owners kept a signal on display outside which was raised and lowered to indicate when the building was open or closed. Excursion traffic on the remaining lines was still heavy, especially in summer but regular trains were lightly patronised. Containers were carried from 1955, some running from Dublin to Letterkenny.

Two years later application was made to close the Ballyshannon branch. This was granted subject to the improvements being made in the roads. Then in May 1959 the Committee announced plans to close the remainder of the system. The last passenger train ran on 31 December 1959 although the occasional special continued to run for some months after this. The company did not, however, go out of business for the following day it began its bus services which replaced the trains. The vehicles were hired from CIE and the routes were almost identical to the trains. The closure of the railway through Strabane was a serious blow in 1966 but bus services continued under the joint control of CIE and BR. Then in 1971, despite making a modest profit British Rail decided to sell its share to CIE whose influence had become dominant and on 12 July the CDRJC was finally dissolved.

There was an auction of rolling stock when the line closed at which an American, Ralph Cox, bought a large number of items including four locomotives, three rail-cars, ten coaches, 54 wagons, several miles of track and sundry items such as signal cabins and station fittings. His intention was to ship these to the US and there more or less rebuild the railway. Unfortunately Mr Cox's plans didn't materialise and much of his purchases were left exposed at Strabane where the elements and vandals soon got to work. Since then one locomotive, a railcar, a box van and a carriage have been preserved at Shane's Castle. The Belfast Museum also has a locomotive and a railcar and the Isle of Man railway is at the time of writing still running yet another railcar. The Donegal railway is well remembered for its friend-liness. In a most unusual tribute at the end of Dr Patterson's excellent book on the system the publisher recalls the warmth of his reception when he visited Donegal some years before: 'Relations between staff and passengers, and among the staff themselves, were eminently human'. Not a bad epitaph for a public transport company.

The Londonderry and Lough Swilly Railway

There were a number of grandiose schemes for railways in the Donegal area during the 1840s and 1850s, the most celebrated being what later became the County Donegal Railways Joint Committee. Less revered was the L&LSR, known as the 'Swilly' which operated mainly in the northern half of the county. Its origins were quite complex.

Among the stillborn schemes were the Great County of Donegal Railway and the Great North Western Junction Railway which in turn yielded the ground to the L&LSR authorised in 1852. Eight years passed before work on the line from Derry to Farland Point began. The Board of Trade inspected the route in October 1863 and found many shortcomings, such as the need for a number of bridges which were in fact never built. Haggling with the suppliers delayed the advent of rolling stock so that the first train did not run until 31 December that year. Permission for an extension to Buncrana having being obtained this line was opened without delay and was almost unheralded, perhaps because no-one knew if the Board of Trade had sanctioned it.

Realising that their line would never be a goldmine the directors imposed, right from the start, the most rigid economies in every aspect of the railway's operation down to discouraging the running of trains after dark so as to save on lamp oil! The locomotive suppliers decided that now was the time to take action to get their money but the company pleaded for more time. The request must have fallen on deaf ears for soon after the sheriff of Derry seized the locomotives in question and two carriages for good measure. By chance another pair of engines had just arrived from a different supplier (less well informed on the company's prospects) and the Swilly managed to keep the trains running. That year the company succeeded in recording an ominous deficit and already closure was mentioned as the only solution. The boat trips it ran from Farland were not a success.

Another wrangle broke out over the road crossing at Pennyburn near the Derry terminus. The Board of Trade mentioned the danger several times and that since 1859 the company had been required by law to make it safe. Despite numerous appeals and threats nothing was done and the Swilly went on its way regardless. The management of the line was very inadequate. Staff resignations were high, both voluntary and involuntary; most men worked a 14 hour day which rose at times to 21 hours. Wages were exceptionally low and strike action to increase them was met with dismissals and evictions from company houses. The exodus was apparent at management level as well. Locomotive inspectors barely had time to unpack their bags before they were gone, many finding the conditions intolerable and interference from the board a constant problem. Engineers were also a breed in transit for every minute expense had to be justified to the chairman in person. The penalty for misconduct, short of dismissal, was exile to Burtonport. Many a railway servant was sent to contemplate his misdeeds in that isolated spot.

Not all the staff were so inadequate. The stationmaster at Fahan bore the illustrious name of James Bond. Being of a scientific bent he decided to construct a windmill near the station and attached a generator to it. Fahan thus became the first station in Ireland to be lit by electricity.

The Letterkenny Railway

Most railways require one or at most two acts of incorporation but the Londonderry and Letterkenny Railway was so reluctant to come into existence that it took six, the first in July 1860 and the last in 1880. This nominally independent railway was built to the three foot gauge and was worked by the Swilly which saw the advantages of the narrow gauge and decided to convert its line at once from 5ft 3in. The Letterkenny line opened in June 1883 before regauging was complete, but four years later the Board of Works took it over for failure to pay the interest on its state loan and the company ceased to exist. From that time the Board of Works and the L&LSR operated the railway jointly. The L&LSR station in Derry was Graving Dock, a good mile from the centre. The reason for this was of course economy in that it avoided buying land in the city. However there were some tram-lines built by the harbour commissioners which ran along the quayside into Derry. An agreement of sorts was reached in 1869 whereby the L&LSR was allowed to use these and trains ran to a new terminus at Middle Quay near the Foyle Road station of the Londonderry and Enniskillen. As might be expected the Swilly managed to have a row with the harbour commissioners over the payment of rates. Negotiations broke down but trains continued to run as before until the commissioners blocked the line by removing a rail or two. The Swilly was forced to revert to Graving Dock, a barn of a place at the best of times. After eighteen months impasse a compromise was reached but further disputes broke out over land ownership and from 1887 once again all trains terminated at Graving Dock. It should be mentioned at the end of this seedy quarrel that running trains over the tramway was in fact illegal but such minor considerations never seemed to bother the Swilly. Finally, in April 1897, a tram service began from Graving Dock to the city centre over the disputed lines.

There was never any question of the pennyless Swilly extending its lines further than Buncrana and Letterkenny without considerable outside help. This came in the form of government grants to promote railways by an act of 1883.

Fahan Pier with a few marooned L&LSR wagons

Carndonagh was the first destination mentioned but a combination of bad planning and incompetence meant that several years passed before the scheme was approved. With most of Donegal classed as a 'congested district' (i.e. with a population greater than the land could support at a minimum level) the new line did not promise to be highly lucrative. The routes to Carndonagh and Burtonport were finally approved, all being paid for with public money.

The Burtonport line was a meandering branch through hard mountainous country, most of it extremely poor, alternating between diamond-hard granite which had to be blasted with dynamite and soft, spongy bogland which hardly gave any foundation to the track bed. The chief purpose of the line was to open up the fisheries of Burtonport harbour which it did quite successfully. The Board of Works was closely involved in the construction and imposed even greater economies than the company would have if it were spending its own money. These included cheaper window-sills, lighter glass and the elimination of such luxury items as door knockers.

The Carndonagh service began on 1 July 1901 and seems to have passed off without great ceremony. The Burtonport route took longer and finally opened on 9 March 1903. Meanwhile both track and rolling stock were by now very much the worse for wear, being scarcely maintained if at all. Services were usually late and from time to time cancelled. Such was the public anxiety over safety that soon after the Burtonport line was opened a question was asked in the Commons about the company's working methods. Complaints grew to a crescendo until in 1905 the Board of Trade opened an inquiry into the operation of this branch. Joseph

Carndonagh, the northern terminus of the L & LSR

Tatlow headed the inquiry, the first of two which he conducted. The initial report gained little attention; Tatlow notes that he 'had to report unfavourably'. The Derry Chamber of Commerce was more forthright and summed up the problem as 'defective construction and inadequate and unsuitable equipment'.

Then in 1909 came the great windfall of the Scotter award; a grant of £10,000 was paid to the company to improve the railway and acquire new rolling stock. The benefits of these were minimal for poor maintenance quickly wore them out. Meanwhile the Strabane and Letterkenny had reached the latter town in 1909, much to the annoyance of the Swilly's management. With the bad feeling between the two concerns there was no question of a shared station, a natural interchange, although there was a siding of sorts between the two. Only after several years did they get round to talking to each other.

Despite Tatlow's report and the large grant things did not improve and once again in 1917 he was despatched northwards to analyse the ills of this unhappy railway. He did not mince his words. 'The line was not in good condition; was not and had not been efficiently worked, maintained or developed. I will not harrow the reader with a description of its condition', but he does. Graving Dock was 'a rough, uncouth structure, not lighted from the roof and the interior is very dark. It is also partially used as a goods store, and is malodorous and unpleasant.' The carriage and engine sheds were 'in a broken-down state such as absolutely beggars description'.

He went on to tackle other stations, criticising their design, construction and maintenance. Gweedore was 'dirty, slovenly, untidy and very deficient of paint. The ladies' room is a disgrace.' The locomotives were 'in a deplorable condition' the result of 'the employment of an incompetent mechanical staff, and careless

Gweedore with the Burtonport train departing for Letterkenny

and inefficient drivers'. The train staff system, a basic safety precaution, was in many cases quite unworkable. Neglect and extreme parsimony were the key points of Tatlow's report: 'Everything has, for years past, been allowed to run down'. After such a scalding attack the Swilly might have been expected to shut up shop and call it a day, for anyone who read the report would not entrust his safety or that of anyone he knew to such a line. In due course the chairman (John McFarland) resigned, not before time, and Henry Hunt was appointed general manager by the Board of Trade under Tatlow's direction. The latter describes Hunt as 'a good railway man, capable and experienced'. He was not over-modest of their joint efforts: 'Trains are punctual now, engines do not break down, carriages are comfortable, goods traffic is well worked, and delays are exceptional.'

The First World War had the usual effect on the Swilly: costs rose greatly but there was a large increase in military traffic not least because of the naval base in Lough Swilly. The annual report for 1921 notes that the railway and rolling stock 'have been maintained in as good order as possible, having regard to the circumstances and conditions arising out of the War'. After the First World War and the Anglo–Irish conflict came partition and the L & LSR found itself operating chiefly in the Free State but with its headquarters in Northern Ireland. As early as 1924 the Irish government was asked for a grant in order to pay for services to Carndonagh and Burtonport. This was agreed and the Northern government followed suit the next year. That year there occurred the worst accident in the Swilly's history when a train was blown off the Owencarrow viaduct and four people were killed. The accident happened on the night of 30 January 1925 when a train of three coaches and a wagon was crossing the viaduct during a particularly fierce storm. The gust which blew the carriages off the bridge must have been around 100 mph. The engine stayed on the rails but as well as those killed five passengers were seriously injured. Clearly a wind gauge should have been in use as on the West Clare but the Swilly's finances did not stretch to such items up to then. From that time carriages on the line were ballasted and services cancelled

Owencarrow, the scene of a disaster on the L & LSR

when the wind reached a certain speed.

In 1927 the board made an approach to the CDRJC in the hope that this considerably more profitable enterprise would take over running the Swilly. After a close look they declined such a liability. So the line struggled on with road services a growing menace. The company decided to fight back by starting its own extensive road services, possibly the most enlightened decision in the whole of its history. Buses and lorries were soon a regular sight on the roads of Donegal with the distinctive L&LSR motif. There was one farcical incident when Donegal County Council sued the company for damage to the roads by its buses! The first stretch to succumb was that from Carndonagh to Buncrana which finally closed on 30 November 1935. The remaining stump into Tooban Junction saw trains on two days a week in summer with buses and lorries at other times. The Burtonport extension followed on 3 June 1940 although there was considerable opposition here. By the time all the formalities were cleared business had picked up on account of the petrol shortage and the line to Gweedore was reprieved. Buncrana also had a full service once more. The anticipated air raids on Derry brought a good deal of commuter traffic on to the railway as many people moved out of the city into Donegal, reaching a peak in 1945. But the railway had its own fuel problems and turf was used as an inadequate substitute for a while.

Closure of the Letterkenny–Gweedore line came on 6 January 1947 after a government inspector found it highly dangerous (of course the whole system had been like that, on and off, for years). Gradually road services replaced the remaining passenger trains although the odd excursion was packed. By the early 1950s lorries were more than capable of carrying all the goods traffic and the final trains ran on 8 August 1953. As early as 1945 Harold Fayle had predicted such a demise when he said rather wordily in his *Narrow Gauge Railways of Ireland:* 'It may be said that the railway enterprise of this company will soon cease to exist.'

For many years and up to quite recently the Swilly survived in the form of its road services which gave a valuable service to the people of north Donegal, perhaps a good deal better than the railway ever had.

The Tralee and Dingle Railway

This little narrow gauge railway was possibly the most spectacular in Ireland although it had quite a chequered history. From Tralee the county town of Kerry it ran across the mountains to the pleasant fishing port of Dingle in the heart of the Kerry gaeltacht. The railway was approved in 1888 under the Tramways Act and opened on 31 March 1891. The main line was $31\frac{1}{2}$ miles long with a 6 mile branch to Castlegregory. The first part of the route was a conventional tramway which followed the main road but from Castlegregory Junction the railway began its punishing climb with 4 miles at 1 in 30. This set the pattern for the remainder of the route with a descent for two miles at 1 in 29 followed by alternating and equally sharp rises and falls into Dingle. There were two mixed trains daily in each direction which took about $2\frac{1}{4}$ hours for the trip.

At Tralee there was a short walk between the GS&WR station and the T&DR, the 'little station' as it was called. The two did have a rail link but this was only used by goods trains and the local youth did a brisk trade in carrying the bags of intending passengers. (Ernest Blythe and J. M. Synge have mixed accounts of the

September 1906 and it was found that the train crew had been on duty for over 19 hours—this was hardly conducive to safe working or staff well-being.

The GSR takeover brought some relief to the line and averted for the moment the imminent closure. The railway continued to provide a valuable link for the people of the Dingle peninsula who had long been virtually ignored by both British and Irish governments. Emigration from the area was heavy and many travelled from the 'little station' on their way to America. But by the late 1930s the line was at a critical state: either there would have to be extensive and large scale modernisation or it would have to be abandoned. The GSR decided on the latter course and as soon as the road to Dingle was brought up to standard rail passenger services ceased. The last regular passenger train ran on 16 April 1939.

From then until 1947 there was a daily goods service with the odd passenger excursion, especially to Castlegregory and from then until the final closure a monthly cattle special for the Dingle fair on the last Saturday of the month. These attracted scores of railway enthusiasts from all over the world, many of whom wrote an account of their trip. GSR and CIE were quite liberal about issuing tickets for these trains which L. T. C. Rolt described as 'the last piece of adventurous railroading to be found in these islands'. Everyone who took the cattle special recalls some adventure on the way such as a brake failure, water shortage, the fire going out, cars parked across the track, hugely excessive speeds (on a descent!), broken couplings, animals on the line and so on.

Along with the exquisite scenery there was an air of great excitement, if not actual danger. P. B. Whitehouse described it as 'the most remote and spectacular railway byway in the British Islands... I experienced a feeling of excitement and suspense such as I had never known before on rails... the feeling that anything might happen'. P. C. Allen said of it: 'I cannot remember when I enjoyed a journey more.'

The passenger service was replaced by a bus which took half the time for the run to Castlegregory and cut an hour off the trip to Dingle. The monthly specials lasted until 1953 but with minimum maintenance their days were numbered and to avoid a disaster CIE announced that the last train would run on 22 July; it was well patronised. Three locomotives were shipped north to the Cavan and Leitrim on the closure of the line, nos 3, 4, 5 where they did sterling work for many years. Number 4 was very popular at Ballinamore although she had not been liked in Kerry. The reason may well have been that the brakes were less than 100% effective—a slight problem on the C&LR but a nightmare on the T&DR! After a stint on the West Clare no. 6 followed on with a number of coaches. Number 5T was shipped to the US for preservation. Also surviving for a time was a solid little petrol driven railcar which was built at Tralee works before they were closed by the GSR. This lasted for many years as a permanent way inspection vehicle on various narrow gauge lines. The rails were of course lifted after the closure but the route of the line can still be clearly seen across the mountains and down to the port of Dingle.

Only the T&DR could manage a collision with a circus. It happened in April 1940 at Glenmore crossing; two horses were killed and an acrobat broke his leg.

The West Clare Railway

There were nominally two companies running this 48 mile narrow gauge line, the West Clare and the South Clare Railways although they were operated in effect by the one company. The West Clare was incorporated on 15 December 1883 for a three foot line from Ennis to Miltown Malbay under the Tramways Act and the company managed to get hold of a very prominent figure of the day for the initial sod-turning as the *Leitrim Advertiser* of 26 January 1885 notes: 'Mr Parnell turned the first sod of a railway between Ennis, Miltown Malbay and Ennistymon and afterwards addressed a large meeting at Miltown Malbay.'

The chairman of the company, William Murphy, was also engaged to construct the line but we should not read anything into that. General Hutchinson who seemed to spend all his time inspecting new railways made the Board of Trade inspection, found almost everything up to scratch and the line opened for business on 2 July 1887. Now if there is one thing the West Clare never boasted about it was punctuality and it started as it meant to go on. It soon became clear that the track was quite deficient in parts and that the locomotives were underpowered for the job demanded of them. The result of this was regular delays and derailments. No-one but foreign visitors ever expected the trains to operate according to the timetable. The journey was notoriously slow but through rather magnificent scenery which made up for the frequent unexplained stops.

In the meantime work had begun on the South Clare line from Kilrush/Kilkee to Miltown Malbay on 1 November 1890 with Mr Murphy on the job again. It was planned to open the railway in October 1892 but this time General Hutchinson took no less than four widely spaced visits to satisfy himself that the whole system could be trusted to accept and deliver passengers in one piece. The South Clare therefore opened in bits with the first through passenger train from Ennis to Kilrush on 23 December 1892 when they finally managed to satisfy and get rid of the hawk-eyed general.

The journey time for the trip from Ennis was three hours but quite often took half as much again allowing for avoidable and unavoidable delays. (Limerick–Kilrush was 73 miles by rail and 51 by road!) The train crews didn't allow such inhibiting items as a schedule to interfere with their way of running the railway. One indignant passenger wrote to the *Dublin Figaro* in 1899:

> I paid a visit to Kilkee a year and a half ago. I left Dublin before 9 am and reached Ennis at 3 pm. From Ennis to Kilkee I took nearly eight hours. Sometimes the train crawled and the rest of the time stood still. Returning I started at 9 am and reached my home in Dublin at 12.30 am the next morning. At Ennis we had just time to scramble into seats in the train to Limerick, but none to have luggage transferred; hence I arrived in Dublin minus everything I possessed, including my temper, and did not recover the missing property for two days.

Thus the testimony of one disgruntled passenger. Percy French's wicked satire on the railway, 'Are ye right there, Michael', is very well known and seems to capture the spirit of the West Clare perfectly. Accurate though it may have been a number of Clare public figures took great exception to the ballad and a court case followed.

Outside the spring and summer the spectacular scenery of north Clare was subject to fierce Atlantic storms and the risk of one of the little trains being blown away was a constant worry. Heavy ballast was placed in most vehicles and when the wind reached 60 mph only those carriages and wagons could be used. At 80 mph all trains stopped running, an anemometer at Quilty being used to record wind speeds.

After this very shaky start the West Clare got down to business and managed to

A pleasant scene at the West Clare terminus with Walker railcar no. 8889 and trailer

provide quite a creditable service. Travellers to Kilrush and Kilkee were quite numerous as was the steady stream of visitors to Lahinch and the spa at Lisdoonvarna. Monthly cattle fairs also brought considerable business on to the railway.

Ennis station in the late 1950s with a mainline train from Limerick on the left and a WCR railcar set on the right

When Harold Fayle visited Clare in the mid 1940s he was quite complimentary about it but predicted that it would not last much longer. But he was wrong for as early as 1928 the GSR had begun experimenting with other forms of traction on the line. Two petrol driven railcars were bought and put into service connecting with the main line trains at Ennis. In fact they were not very satisfactory and performed badly on the steep gradients. After a number of years they were relegated to the Kilrush–Kilkee section and withdrawn totally in 1941.

Cheque issued by the West Clare to a shareholder, William Barrington in November 1921.

In the 1950s CIE was faced with the question of closing the line altogether or investing in new rolling stock. To its credit it was decided to acquire two sets of diesel railcars from Walkers of Wigan which entered service in 1952. These performed very well indeed. Timings were greatly improved, there were fewer delays and passengers came back to the railway again. This effort prolonged the life of the line nearly ten years, making it the last surviving narrow gauge line in Ireland. The final train ran on 31 January 1961.

However, the West Clare did not disappear off the face of the earth. Bord na Mona bought up the railcars and used them for many years on its extensive bog railway system. Most delightful of all, one of the steam locomotives was restored by CIE and placed in an honoured position beside Ennis station with a sparkling livery of green, red and white. Ennis no longer has any regular passenger trains going through but the route of the West Clare can still be picked out where it ran along the main line for a mile or so before swinging west towards the Atlantic and in the stately presence of no. 5 *Slieve Callan* on its pedestal at Ennis.

10 The Last Sixty Years

THE idea that the railway companies in Ireland should amalgamate was not a new one and the fact that eventual unity did not come about until 1925 was not for lack of effort in some quarters. Soon after construction many systems realised they could not survive without the support of other concerns and more progressive companies such as the GS&WR and the GNR absorbed the smaller lines in their areas as they developed their network. By the end of the nineteenth century it seemed that the railway map had stabilised: those companies destined to prosper were doing so, those who were to lose their independence had also done so and all was right with the world.

However there were dissenting voices. One of the most audible was William Field MP who in the course of the Queen's speech in 1899 launched a bitter attack on the monopoly status of Irish railways, accusing them of crippling economic development by exhorbitant charges and narrow self-interest. His solution was a radical one.

> And we humbly represent to your majesty that the present railway rates and charges in Ireland constitute an intolerable grievance to the Irish people, and that measures should be adopted for the remedy thereof, either by the amalgamation of the management under state control, or by the state purchase of Irish railways, so as to reduce the tariffs, and further to increase facility of transit.

As might be imagined this went down like a lead balloon at Kingsbridge, Amiens Street and the Broadstone. But the honourable member was only warming up and went on to enumerate the various abuses he had uncovered. There were, he said, 303 highly paid directors for about 3,000 miles of line (one for every ten miles), 97 secretaries and under-secretaries and 60 other officials who received handsome emoluments.

> The cost of construction of railways in England has been calculated from £47,000 to £50,000 per mile; in Scotland, £33,000 per mile, and in Ireland, £15,000 per mile. It is strange that... we have higher rates charged than obtain in both those countries. The railway administration in Ireland has been a powerful factor in producing those evil results by strangling the commerce of the country and preventing the development of industries... the Irish railway companies pay lower wages to their employees, and work them longer, than many railway companies in Great Britain.

Of course the railway companies would have liked to boil him in oil but there was nothing they could do against parliamentary privilege. In any case most of the charges were true. The press soon got on to the story. *The Times:*

> There is much to be said for the contention that the system of competitive and privately managed lines, though it produces on the whole most admirable results in a country like Great Britain, is unsuitable for the economic and social conditions of Ireland... We are

168

not opposed to any method of dealing with the Irish railways, whether involving State possession or State management if it can be proved to be practicable and advantageous.

The *Financial News* joined the fray by quoting Sir George Findlay's comment that working four days a week he could do the work of all these directors and secretaries 'and enjoy the other two days salmon fishing on the Shannon'. Railway fares were 'eighty per cent higher than in England' and the average number of journeys made by each person was 4 in Ireland, 23 in England and 14 in Scotland. *The Standard* spoke of the 'well-founded discontent at the management of the Irish railways... There are far too many independent companies for a country so limited in its economic capabilities'. Another paper described them as 'monuments of mismanagement', but added, 'it is much easier to indicate the evil than it is to prescribe the remedy'. Finally Omagh Town Commissioners added its halfpenny worth when it described the rates charged by the GNR as 'excessive and exhorbitant'.

To support his argument for state control Field noted that the Swiss government took over all its lines in 1898 as had happened in Rumania. Most lines in Australia and New Zealand were state-run as were two-thirds in Prussia, half in Austria and two-thirds in Russia. In other words, there was a precedent established all over the world. The arguments in favour of amalgamation were hard to refute but of course, entering on their most prosperous years, the railway proprietors were totally opposed to such a notion. Within a couple of decades the story would be quite different. The Great War, including a period of direct government control, set the pattern for the future. Wages rose sharply, as they needed to, but fares lagged far behind. The Anglo–Irish struggle followed by the disastrous Civil War were a catastrophe for the railways and before peace returned most realised they could not continue as before. Expenditure continued to rocket as services slowly got back to normal and the damage was repaired.

Great Southern Railways

In January 1923 the newly formed Free State government expressed its willingness to assume control of the GS&WR which had suffered more than most from the attentions of anti-Treaty forces. The government proposed that all lines in the country should merge and very quickly the GS&WR, the MGWR and the CB&SCR had agreed on this. The main stumbling block was the DSER which wanted to link with the GNR, an impracticable idea given that the GNR was now operating in two states. The three partners merged in November 1924 to form the Great Southern Railway. From the 1 January 1925 every line operating wholly in the Free State was required to join what became the Great Southern Railways, the only exception being the Listowel and Ballybunion which had expired in a fit of pique on learning it was not to be invited to the party.

The newly formed GSR was a mixed bag. Its headquarters were at Kingsbridge and in fact it was dominated by the GS&WR in almost every way. It had over 2,000 route miles, a bewildering mixture of locomotives, rolling stock and a number of narrow gauge systems which required immediate attention. Apart from the usual symbols of centralised control—standardised nameplate, livery, tickets, etc.—many lines continued much as before until the more uneconomic were pruned off. In his *History of Railways in Ireland* (1927) Conroy summed up the problems facing the GSR as: declining population; a dearth of mineral resources; poorly developed agriculture; coastal population centres; uncontrolled road competition; overstaffing and excessive route mileage. He suggested tight legal restraints on road vehicle operators, running these services in harmony with the railways rather than in competition; the closure of many uneconomic rural lines; fewer stations and more halts; and, most interesting of all, a comprehensive electrification programme. In many ways the difficulties and the solutions proposed have not changed much in sixty years. The latter would have caused great unemployment and required a massive capital investment of which the state, much less the railways themselves, was quite incapable. As Michael Baker says, the GSR was not exactly born with a silver spoon in its corporate mouth.

A symbol of the standardisation which followed from the amalgamation was the most comprehensive listing of merchandise and goods rates. Charged by the truck, according to a booklet issued in 1930, were jackals, monkeys, pumas, tiger cats, bears, deer, hyenas, lions, sea lions, wolves, camels, elephants, ostriches and zebras. All were carried at the owner's risk, not to mention other travellers and the train crew. Among the more inanimate items were: 'corpses, ashes of cremated bodies, aeroplane wings, bees (live), busts (ladies), corset stands, feathers and feather boas, foster mothers (chicken rearers), hats (bulk in proportion to weight), limbs (artificial), machines (bacon slicing, bone grinding), magic lanterns, meggers, periscopes, rocking horses, ship's compasses, stag's heads, stuffed birds, animals and fishes, wine in jars or bottles, wreaths (artificial), X-ray tubes', and many more.

Perhaps of more immediate importance than knowing the exact rate for periscopes or aeroplane wings was the condition of the rolling stock and permanent way. Both had suffered neglect for over ten years. A total of 623 locomotives were inherited from the various companies which merged in 1925. In fact the GSR had few resources to build new locomotives and the mixed fleet was kept going by the careful attentions of the men at Inchicore, the Broadstone, and Grand Canal Street works. Of course there was some attempt to reduce the great variety of classes and thus the maintenance costs but this could only be done by natural wastage. As the chief mechanical engineer put it: 'I like historic locomotives but I wish I had less of them!'

The variety was quite staggering and ranged from the tired old engines on the Tralee and Dingle to the 23 fine machines just being turned out by the MGWR at the Broadstone. These were the most promising of the GSR fleet and must have been a godsend when the engineer surveyed his array of engines. Those inherited from the DSER were all in a sorry state, and many had to be scrapped immediately.

Also requiring immediate attention was the track, both narrow and standard gauge. One of the first decisions was to single much of the double track in use. The main line to the west was singled in 1929 from Clonsilla out. In recent years this has proved a nuisance as with the build up of traffic many services to Galway and Mayo have had to be diverted via Kildare and now run from Heuston (Kingsbridge).

One problem not so easily dealt with was that of road competition. Coupled with the great depression of 1929 and the trade war with Britain the GSR found itself unable to pay even the 1 per cent dividend it had paid up to 1930. By this time there were innumerable private bus and lorry operators in Ireland who undercut rail fares and without standards of safety or service managed to cream off a great deal of the GSR's business. After numerous appeals the government stepped in with the Road Passenger Act of 1932 which enforced a licencing system on many of these fly-by-night operators and required a certain standard from those setting up in the transport business. More significantly, it also gave the GSR authority to run its own road services. Further legislation gave the company powers to discontinue services which were hopelessly uneconomic and so began the pattern of closures which continued up to recent times. Apart from the inevitable decline of the narrow gauge lines a number of standard ones also came under the hammer. One of the first was the line from Palace East to Bagenalstown, followed by the Edenderry, Killaloe and Castlecomer branches. Close on their heels were the lines to Killala (July 1934) and the branches to Clifden (April 1935) and Achill (September 1937). Other lines to lose their passenger services were the Patrickswell to Charleville route and of course the Tralee and Dingle which had been staggering towards oblivion for years.

At the same time the GSR began to operate its own bus and lorry services. These were not as coordinated as they might have been but, combined with the earlier limitations, managed to put some of the more disreputable 'cowboys' out of business. A major step was the takeover of the Irish Omnibus Company on 1 January 1934, thus absorbing a wide network of bus routes throughout the country. Along with a wide variety of economy measures the company resorted to the highly unpopular one of wage cuts. With hindsight these are hard to defend, given that wages were pretty low anyway. Dismissals were also used at all levels but while there was little you could do if you were sacked you could strike if the company reduced your wages. Those were the days when negotiations centred on whether a wage cut of $7\frac{1}{2}\%$ should be restored at $2\frac{1}{2}$ or $3\frac{1}{2}\%$!

By the end of the 1930s the carriage fleet was beginning to show signs of neglect. Hardly any new vehicles had been built since 1928 and while the existing ones were just about adequate for the slack season each summer put great strain on the fleet with the most decrepit vehicles being pressed into service. Inchicore began turning out new vehicles again in 1934 with a series of rather smart wooden-framed coaches in a bright maroon livery, a great relief after the initial battleship grey adopted for locomotives. Another innovation was the introduction of bi-lingual station name boards as part of the government's policy of promoting Irish.

An interesting development took place on the Amiens Street–Dun Laoghaire line in 1934 when a new system of electric colour light signals came into operation, replacing the usual mechanical lever frame. These were extremely efficient and used up to a short time ago but are being replaced as part of the electrification programme.

Coping with a large, varied collection of mainly obsolete locomotives led the GSR to look around at other means of hauling trains. Electrification of the entire system would clearly have been ideal but the amount of traffic would not justify the cost. However, the company came near to this with the excellent invention of Prof. James Drumm of UCD. He was responsible for a remarkable technique using rechargeable batteries for multiple unit trains which ran for over twenty years on the Bray line. A four wheeled Drewry railcar, no. 386, was the first to be converted and had extensive trials in 1930–1. The car was capable of developing 30 horsepower and running at 50 mph. The experiment was considered a success and a two coach train put into service in February 1932. The batteries were quite heavy, about 15 tons, and the following year a second set appeared on the Bray line followed by two more in 1939. They were seen frequently working out of Harcourt Street and Bray, where the recharging facilities were located.

A great deal of money was needed to carry out the research necessary to develop the technology of the Drumm battery and with the outbreak of the war those funds dried up. Nonetheless the trains kept many services going which would otherwise have had to stop, given the enormous fuel shortages of the period.

The Second World War was a watershed for the Great Southern Railways. From the start there were severe restrictions on private travel which brought passengers and goods flocking back to the railways. Foreign travel was strictly limited and this also helped as more people took their holidays at home. For the first two years the war was not taken very seriously on both sides of the border. Blackout restrictions and rationing were considered a nuisance and the thousands of Irishmen who volunteered to join the British forces went off to the war as if to a boy scouts camp. The GSR tried desperately to prepare for it knew not what. Southern Ireland of course remained neutral, which was not to say that it was totally out of the conflict. A circular of 4 July 1940 shows the state of mind at the time. It was issued by the GSR to all employees and concerns the possibility of invasion; whether from Britain or Germany is not stated. Some of the instructions seem quite naive, such as the order to keep signal boxes locked at all times and not to admit strangers without identification. This *might* just work at Kingsbridge but not at Inny Junction or Clonakilty. Delightfully vague is the instruction to gangers who come upon enemy forces sabotaging the track. They are told they must 'take such action as may be in their power to prevent damage'. How they

The interior of state coach no. 5406

were supposed to deal with a company of paratroopers intent on sabotage is not explained. It is also interesting to compare this with the admirably precise booklet prepared by the GNR two years later; of course by then it had had very direct experience of the war.

The coal shortages gradually became worse and more services were cancelled as the munitions industry in Britain consumed an increasing proportion of the output. Mid-1942 was the worst time of all. Most branches were without trains entirely and on the main lines there were services on only two days a week. In order to keep this skeleton service going anything combustible ended up in the firebox: low grade coal, slack, turf, wood, cardboard and the odd bunkerload 'acquired' from the GNR. Goods trains could take up to two weeks to get to Cork and passenger runs might well take a day and a half. It was ironic that this enormous crisis led to a temporary revival in canal transport, which a hundred years ago the railways had firmly destroyed.

Before the outbreak of war it was becoming clear that the GSR could not really continue without substantial aid from the government. Even though results during the war years were better than they had been for years it was felt that the good times would not last and that the problem could not be shelved any longer. A bill for the dissolution of the company and its merger with the Dublin United Transport Co. was prepared and finally passed in the Dail late in 1944. The name of the new body was to be Córas Iompair Éireann (Irish Transport Company) and from 1 January 1945 it was to have a virtual monopoly of all surface, water and air transport in the country. The board was made up of GSR and DUTC people and the company took the DUTC's wheel logo, quickly dubbed by disrespectful Dubliners as the flying snail.

The final days of the GSR were marred by a fatal accident near Portlaoise on 20 December 1944. It was not a major disaster but indicates the operational problems of the time and how, combined with human error, they could lead to such a mishap. The crash occurred at 2325 when the night mail from Dublin collided into the rear of a stationary cattle special. One person was killed and several injured. The cattle train had left Kingsbridge at 1530 and on reaching Sallins the fire had to be cleaned out and rekindled because of poor quality fuel. The same happened at Portarlington, just down the line. Three miles further on the driver had to stop for seven minutes to allow steam pressure to build up. This was repeated after another two miles and once more the driver decided to clean out the fire. (You can imagine the language!) While stopped for about half an hour the passenger train ploughed into the rear. The guard admitted that he failed to protect the train with detonators, which the rules state should be placed at quarter-mile intervals behind a stranded train but we can understand that he was otherwise occupied. (Detonators are laid on the rails and explode noisily but harmlessly when a train passes over.) The guard stayed in his van and was badly injured in the crash.

The night mail had arrived at Portarlington 25 minutes after the cattle train left. In order to attach a horse box the driver had to clear the siding where it stood and so moved his train forward past a signal. There is a conflict of evidence at this point, for the driver claimed he had a green light while the signalman stated he knew about the horse box but had kept the signal at danger until hearing from Portlaoise that the cattle special had arrived. Due to the complex track layout at Portarlington this highly illegal manoeuvre was common. Having attached the wagon, the guard maintained the advance signal was green, as did the driver and fireman, and the train moved out.

The signal man swore he kept the signals at danger the whole time and this was confirmed by several witnesses including his relief who came on duty at 2300. In addition the man on the early shift had telephoned Portlaoise three times in a quarter of an hour to ask if the goods train had arrived. It is unlikely he would have given the starting signal if he was that concerned about the train in front. In addition two witnesses on the bridge above the station were watching the train and both noted how odd it was that the train should leave against a danger signal. A further contributory factor was the lighting on the cattle train. The driver on the approaching train saw only one white light ahead which he took to be a train coming in the other direction. Normally the tail end would have three red lights but two were missing on account of the oil shortage and the third did not have the red filter glass, thus showing white.

Córas Iompair Éireann and the diesels

When the war ended travel restrictions were lifted and the fuel problems gradually declined. Simultaneously the CIE board expressed a preference for road over rail transport which, seeing that it was much more profitable, is not surprising. Even so the chairman announced that experiments with diesels were about to begin and if successful all trains would be diesel hauled in future. The winter of 1947 was particularly harsh and coincided with a revival of the old fuel shortages as stocks could not be moved from Britain. This gave the company the incentive to develop other forms of fuel. In fact the GSR/CIE had not been slow to experiment with a great variety of energy sources over the years including small shunters, petrol railcars, railmotors, steam railcars, Drumm battery trains and now the turf burner, the brain child of O. V. S. Bulleid who became chief mechanical engineer of CIE in 1949 and saw in turf the one natural resource with which Ireland was well endowed. The turf burner was tried out extensively especially on the Cork line

Possibly the finest locomotive ever built in Ireland, GSR no. 800 Maeve

but only ran on goods trains. When Bulleid left CIE in 1958 no further research was done on the project.

Following from the Milne report of 1948 the Irish government prepared a plan to nationalise CIE and this took place in 1950. Dieselisation was one of the first decisions of the new board and twenty diesel railcars similar to those working the GNR were ordered from England. Another forty were ordered shortly after and by the early 1950s they were a regular sight all over the system. The new railcars meant that a number of obsolete six-wheelers could be scrapped and the process was speeded up when new carriages began to emerge from Inchicore in 1951. So successful were the railcars that the company decided that future locomotives would be diesels. Up to then the heaviest Cork trains were hauled by the magnificent 4–6–0s turned out by the GSR works at Inchicore from 1939 onwards. These were the most powerful engines ever built in Ireland and among the largest in the world. Three such locomotives were built, *Maeve*, *Macha* and *Tailte*, legendary queens of pre-christian Ireland. They did superb work and could manage 100 mph with relative ease.

In 1950 CIE and the GNR agreed to extend the run of the latter's crack Belfast–Dublin express, the *Enterprise*, as far as Cork and for three years *Maeve* and her sisters were often seen hauling the express from Amiens Street through the Phoenix Park tunnel and on to the Munster capital. Happily, *Maeve* has been preserved in all her splendour and is the prize exhibit in the Belfast Transport Museum.

Meanwhile the dieselisation programme went ahead with three groups of locomotives planned to work all services in the Republic, along with the railcars which would then revert to branch line work. The first of what became the 1,200 hp A-class locomotives began to arrive in July 1955. These engines began working the Cork line and were then extended to the old MGWR section. Their daily runs were

CIE Radio Train approaching Killarney in the 1950s

GM loco no. 125; at 950 hp these are frequently worked in pairs on the lines to the west

far above those achieved by steam engines and they were numbered A1–A60. The second group B101–112 went into service in 1956 and were Sulzers, unlike the A-class which were Metro-Vickers. The latter began to deliver a lower power version of their first batch, the C-class, nos 201–234 with 550 hp. With the 19 shunters nos E401–419 built at Inchicore and three Deutz diesel-hydraulics G601-3, this was the foundation of the diesel fleet.

Of course as the diesels arrived more and more steam locomotives were scrapped, involving intensive retraining of crews and the adaptation of Inchicore works to cope with the new motive power. Despite the increase in train speeds and comfort which came with the new rolling stock losses on the railway continued to mount. CIE appealed for tighter controls on road operators to divert more traffic on to the railways but the fact remained that the public preferred the convenience of private cars except for a long journey. At the same time the rail network began to contract sharply as more and more branch lines and even main lines closed. Buses (owned by CIE) were taking a greater percentage of urban traffic. The Beddy report (1957) recommended drastic solutions: the closure of all but 56 stations, halving the route mileage and closer coordination of road and rail services.

While CIE was wondering if it was about to shuffle off this mortal coil the GNR did exactly that. No-one was very surprised when it happened. The network was divided at the border and rolling stock assigned equally to CIE and the UTA.

A fertiliser train passing Killiney

A train of modern CIE passenger stock hauled by 001

Kingsbridge was pleased to increase its railcar stock thus, but had little use for the steam locomotives, many of which were sold back to the UTA. Then in 1961 the first of a new group of engines from America began to arrive: the General Motors 950 hp B-class numbers 121–135. They are very American looking with a high cab at one end and arrived just in time, for the Metro-Vickers locomotives were causing endless problems and seemed to spend more time in the shops than out on the railway. Sharp words flew between Inchicore and Birmingham so it is not surprising that the next order went to the US. The GM diesels were excellent and before long a second order had been placed, nos B141–177, which arrived in 1962. These were built to a specific design for CIE and had a cab at both ends as had the third batch, B181–192, which came four years later and had a capacity of 1,100 hp. So pleased were the engineers with the GM locomotives that it was decided to re-engine the A- and C-class. The first transplant appeared in 1968 with a 1,325 hp GM engine and was renumbered A58r. Similar surgery was performed on the older railcars which had come to the end of their active life after being relegated to suburban services. These had their engines removed and were converted to work as loco- motive hauled stock. At present they are used between Bray and Drogheda but are very unpopular with commuters because of their uncomfortable sideways plastic seats. More attractive were the new Craven coaches which entered service in 1964 and have lasted very well indeed.

A train of new air-conditioned coaches hauled by GM loco no. 081

Steam officially came to an end on CIE in the mid 1960s although quite a few locomotives have been preserved, many of which run regular excursions around the country. The RPSI do sterling work in this area. Due to the fact that many railway stations have scarcely altered in over a century a large number of films are made in Ireland which require the running of steam trains with authentic stock. One of these was *Darling Lili* in 1968, when former GS&WR no. 184 was used. However, she was in such poor condition that she had to be assisted by a diesel locomotive disguised as a parcels van!

The first of the 071 class on arrival at Inchicore in 1976. At 2,250 hp these are the most powerful engines in Ireland

The most recent additions to the diesel fleet were the new 2,250 hp locomotives delivered by General Motors in 1976. They are numbered 071–088 and are seen on most of the heavier passenger and goods services. They are very handsome and can handle the heaviest loads with ease. At the time of writing CIE plans to augment its stock of carriages with a number of new vehicles, some of which will be built in Ireland and some abroad. With the rail network more or less stabilised it is hoped that the general trend towards increasing use of rail services will continue. Successive governments have realised the value of maintaining services on a radial basis from the capital with a coordinated suburban service. Imaginative advertising and an attractive package of special fares will hopefully continue the upwards trend in the number of passengers using the train. A very positive step was the recent reopening of the commuter service to Maynooth via

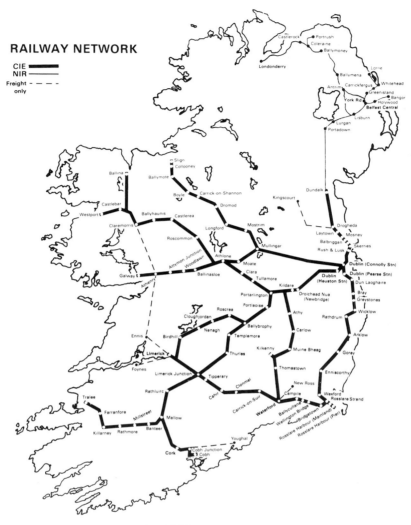

Map of passenger rail network, 1983

Clonsilla and Leixlip. Today mainline rail in Ireland offers a service which is the equal of most in Europe, with greater speed and comfort than ever before. Long may it continue.

Northern Ireland: the UTA and NIR

The story north of the border was for many years less happy, but today NIR seems to be strong and healthy. After the last war the Northern Ireland government set up the Ulster Transport Authority to take over rail and road services. The B&CDR was absorbed in 1948 with lavish promises of development and expansion. Unfortunately most of the development was to take place in the road sphere for the UTA quickly showed itself to be intent on closing down most if not all the railways it controlled. Most of the B&CDR was closed within months and various limbs of the NCC followed suit. Ironically the UTA continued with its plan to use diesel railcars and more units were introduced. For many people, especially railmen who lost their jobs, a most objectionable aspect of the authority's actions was the deception it used to veil the more controversial plans. There was talk of new invigorated services to the public which meant switching everything to the roads. Cries of the utmost penury were heard frequently while in the early 1970s, £120 million could be set aside for motorways. The government did little to restrain the authority apart from holding another inquiry which accepted the UTA policy and virtually gave it carte-blanche to close down the entire system when it chose to do so.

With the dissolution of the GNR the UTA applied the axe to most of the lines it inherited north of the border. The authority cut costs and services wherever it could so that passenger and goods traffic fell away adding to the mounting losses and the already low morale. Chunks of the main stations were taken over for road services—a clear enough policy indication if ever there was one. Clearly if things continued there would be no railways in the north at all, which would no doubt have pleased many. The 1963 Benson report recommended further closures and the ending of goods services. The final closure in this sorry tale was that between Portadown and Derry, the old GNR route. This caused more resentment than most; many felt that Derry had suffered enough neglect and indifference without having one of its two remaining rail routes axed. In fact, Benson had advised the closure of both lines to Derry but it was the line through Omagh which was chopped from 15 February 1965. By now it was no longer a question of which lines should close but which would remain open; from this point on, however, things began to look up.

By universal consent it was time to break up the UTA, and transport acts in 1966 and 1967 did just that. Ulsterbus took over its road passenger services and Northern Ireland Railways took over the remaining lines. As William Robb puts it: 'The UTA was dead and no-one mourned. It was formally buried on 5 April 1968.' It was a pity that one of the final casualties was the able managing director, John Coulthard, whose 18 month stint ended in May 1967. Coulthard was a popular and experienced railwayman who quickly learned that he had been hired to preside over the demise of all rail services. Naturally he opposed this policy and there were frequent clashes between himself and the board which led to his abrupt dismissal.

The new company lost no time in pressing the government to honour its commitment to develop the rail system even though many felt the patient was beyond recovery. One of the really daft ideas in the Benson report was that the Dublin line should be singled between Portadown and the border. CIE slyly responded with the suggestion that it would run the section if the UTA could not do so and, while the latter might have been tempted to agree, the political implications were too great. It did not, however, object to CIE running freight trains between Dublin and Derry.

In 1969 NIR was making valiant efforts to reverse the decline of the previous years and a number of stations became unstaffed halts, the guard issuing tickets on the train. A new set of BR carriages was bought the following year with three handsome diesel engines for the *Enterprise* service. These were named *Eagle*, *Falcon* and *Merlin* after the fine GNR locomotives of the 1930s. The commuter lines to Bangor, Larne and Portadown were developed and a number of new halts opened. Ironically the building of the M2 motorway brought a great deal of business on to the railways when over 4½ million tons of rock had to be shifted by steam traction from Magheramorne to Belfast. Road development caused new stations to be built at Larne and Portadown. All of this took place against the background of increasing disruption caused by the troubles. Bombs were regularly placed in stations and on trains, the line just north of the border being a favourite target. Both CIE and NIR have lost several items of rolling stock through trains being halted in that area. All three Belfast termini have also been attacked, as has the Europa Hotel alongside the former Great Victoria Street station.

Despite all this NIR received a terrific boost when the government approved plans for a revival of the Belfast Central Railway with a new central terminus to replace the other three. The Bangor line had of course been out on a limb for many years and with the running of through services one station could easily handle the traffic. Work began in 1973 on the new Central station at East Bridge Street. As Derry trains were now to run via Lisburn the line between that town and Antrim was relaid; trains for Derry thus head south–west for the first eight miles and then swing north again. Several features of the old Central Railway were incorporated but a new bridge was built over the Lagan. The new station is a tremendous boon and while it may not have the classic elegance of the old termini it saves that long and tedious trek across town to change trains. Queen's Quay closed in April 1976 and Bangor trains began using the new station. Great Victoria Street had to be demolished after frequent bomb attacks, Queen's Quay was also knocked down and a simpler structure replaced the NCC terminus at York Road, which is now used by Larne trains.

A new set of BR coaches was delivered for use on the *Enterprise* in 1981 and to go with them a pair of General Motors 2,250 hp locomotives. These are almost identical to the 071 class in use on CIE. They have been named *Great Northern* and *Northern Counties*. The suburban routes to Larne, Bangor, Portadown and Ballymena are now dubbed 'Citytrack' and many run through Belfast. Services to Derry and Dublin are 'Inter City'. Born out of adversary, NIR operate a fine service which will hopefully continue for many years to come.

Electrification

It is estimated that in ten years the population of the greater Dublin area will be 1,300,000, much of it in satellite towns. There have been various plans for an expanded urban railway dating back to the 1864 Metropolitan Railway scheme. A new version of this was the Rapid Transit System which was first mooted in the early 1970s. This was a revolutionary plan involving a fast rail system, partly underground and operating to and from a road/rail centre on the quays. The plan envisaged lines running out to Tallaght off the Cork line, to Ballymun leaving the Midland line near Phibsborough and to Blanchardstown centre along with an underground spur from Ballsbridge to the city centre serving Stephen's Green. The existing routes to Bray and Howth would also be part of the plan. A major feature of the scheme was the use of electricity in preference to diesel as the means of traction. The costs of the rapid transit plan would clearly be very high but the first phase received government approval in June 1979; this was the electrification of the Howth–Bray line and the building of a new fleet of commuter trains which would provide a frequent service from 0700 to midnight. Four car trains will run every five minutes during peak periods and every fifteen minutes at other times. The forty trains will be able to carry 25,000 people per hour, each two car unit having seats for 72 people and standing room for 170. The cars are being built in Germany and the first arrived in Dublin in February 1983, being tested on the

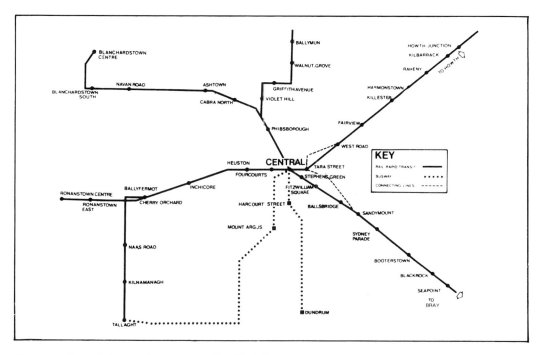

Proposed rapid transit system for Dublin

Howth–Howth Junction section. Each train costs approximately £1 million and features doors which are opened by the passenger from inside and closed by the driver. A most useful device is the 'chopper control' which reduces the current supplied at cruising speed and feeds it back into the network to power accelerating trains elsewhere. Automatic air suspension keeps the car at the correct platform level and will eliminate any step down or up.

About 1,500 people have been working directly or indirectly on the project with much of the technical equipment coming from Irish factories. The computer signalling is being made in Tralee, the overhead masts in Cork and the new track and concrete sleepers at the CIE works in Portlaoise. The most difficult area to negotiate was that between Dun Laoghaire and Sandycove, part of the old Atmospheric route. There the track bed had to be lowered to take the pantographs and there was some difficulty coping with the granite which had to be blasted in many places. There has inevitably been some disruption to train services while the electrification has been going on, particularly in off peak periods.

A central public address system will link all stations and trains to Connolly (Amiens Street) station. Among the safety features of the new trains is a system of pulse codes which are transmitted along the line and pick up signals from the track ahead: whether it is clear, there is a speed restriction or there is another train in front. If the driver does not respond to the signal the train is automatically slowed down and stopped if necessary. Undoubtedly the electrification programme is among the major advances in the history of Irish railways, much more so than the change from steam to diesel. The oil crisis has meant that it is no longer an attractive energy form whereas electricity can be generated from a number of sources. In Ireland it is produced from gas, oil, coal, turf and at a number of hydro-electric plants.

One of CIE's new electric trains on trial on the Howth branch

It is very gratifying that in a time of general recession such a worthwhile project has been given the go-ahead and that the system will come into operation so near to the one hundred and fiftieth anniversary of Ireland's first railway, the Dublin and Kingstown, which is part of the line being electrified. With the new carriages being constructed at Inchicore the future for railways in Ireland looks bright. It is hoped that there will be no more closures and that fast express trains using the most modern rolling stock and locomotives will attract more people and goods to the railways. There is no reason why CIE and NIR should not then begin discussions on the possible electrification of the Dublin–Belfast line. Cooperation between the two companies is good and this would be a useful venture of great benefit to both concerns and to Ireland, north and south.

Bibliography

Ahrons, E. L., *Locomotive Working in the 19th century,* Vol. 6, 1954
Arnold, R. M., *Golden Years of the GNR, Parts I & II.*
——, *NCC Saga.*
——, *Steam over Belfast Lough*, 1969.
Baddely and Ward, *Guide to Ireland*, 1895.
Baker, Michael, *Irish Railways since 1916*, 1972.
Barrie, D. S. M., *The Dundalk Newry & Greenore Railway*, 1857.
Bassett, G. H., *The Book of Wexford.*
Berry's *Irish Railways etc timetable*, 1850 onwards.
Boocock, C. P., *Irish Railway Album*, 1968.
Boyd, J. I. C., *The Londonderry and Lough Swilly Railway*, 1981.
Bulleid, H. A. V., *The Aspinall Era*, 1967.
Carr, Sir John, *The Stranger in Ireland*, 1806.
Casserley, H. C., *Outline of Irish Railway History*, 1974.
CIE/GSR Annual Reports.
CIE, *Railway Engineering Works Inchicore*, n.d.
Conroy, John, *History of Railways in Ireland*, 1927.
Creeder, C., *The Cork and Macroom Railway.*
Currie, J. R. L., *The Northern Counties Railway*, Vols 1, 2.
D'Alton, John, *Memoir of the Great Southern and Western Railway*, 1846.
Digges, J. G., *Fighting Industries and Financing Emigration*, 1906.
Dow, George, *Railway Heraldry.*
Dublin Metropolitan Railway, 1864.
Dublin Railway Travellers' Guide, 1850 onwards.
Dundalk and Western Railway Prospectus, 1837.
Fayle, Harold, *Narrow Gauge Railways of Ireland*, 1945.
Fayle, Harold, and Newham, A. T., *The Dublin and Blessington Tramway*, 1963.
Field, William, *Irish Railways compared with state-owned lines*, 1899.
Flanagan, Patrick J., *The Ballinamore and Ballyconnell Canal*, 1972.
——, *The Cavan and Leitrim Railway*, 1966.
——, *Transport in Ireland 1880–1910*, 1969.
Flewitt, H. C., *The Hill of Howth Tramway.*
Galt, William, *Railway Reform*, 1834.
Good, T. Morgan, *Irish Transport Chaos.*
GSR/Clements, R. N., *The Midland Great Western Railway 1847–1947*, 1947.
Hall, S. C., *Ireland, its scenery and character*, 1841–3.
Hajducki, S. Maxwell, *A Railway Atlas of Ireland*, 1974.
Head, Francis, *A Fortnight in Ireland*, 1852.
Herring, M., *The Young Traveller in Ireland*, 1951.

Illustrated Guide to the DW & WR, 1898.
The Irish Railway Problem, 1904.
Irish Railway Review, Vols III–IV.
IRRS London, *Irish Railways in Pictures (GNR)*, 1976.
Irwin, George O'Malley, *Handbook to the County of Wicklow*, 1844.
Ivatts, E. B., *Railway Management at MGWR stations*, 1885.
Journal of the IRRS, 1946 onwards.
Journal of the Kerry Archaeological & Historical Society (T & DR), no. 11.
Kidner, R. W., *Narrow Gauge Railways of Ireland*, 1965.
Lane, C. P., *Guidebook to County Kerry*, 1907.
Latimer, Isaac, *A Holiday Run by Rail and Road in Ireland*, 1871.
Lee, Joseph, *Formation of the Irish Economy*, 1969.
Leggatt, J. E., *Irish Commercial and Railway Gazetteer*, 1893.
Londonderry & LSR Tourist Guides.
McCutcheon, Alan, *Railway History in Pictures, Ireland*, 1969.
McGrath, Walter, *Some Industrial Railways of Ireland*.
McNeil, D. B., *Irish Passenger Steamship Services*, 1971.
Mallet, Robert, *Report on the Kingstown and Dalkey Railroad*, 1844.
Measom, G. S., *Guide to the MGWR*, 1866.
——, *Guide to the GS & WR*, 1866.
MGWR, *Ireland from Sea to Sea*.
——, *Through Connemara*.
——, *Tourist Guides*.
Middlemass, Tom, *Irish Standard Gauge Railways*, 1981.
Morrison, George, *The Irish Civil War*, 1981.
Morton, R. G., *Standard Gauge Railways in the North of Ireland*, 1962.
Murray, Kevin, *The Great Northern Railway*, 1944.
——, *Ireland's First Railway*, 1981.
Murray, Kevin and McNeil, D. B., *The Great Southern & Western Railway*, 1976.
Newham, A. T., *Cork, Blackrock & Passage Railway*.
——, *Cork & Muskerry Railway*.
——, *Listowel & Ballybunion Railway*.
——, *Schull & Skibereen Railway*.
——, *Waterford & Tramore Railway*.
Nowlan, Kevin B. (ed.), *Travel and Transport in Ireland*, 1973.
Ó Cuimin, P., *Baronial Lines of the MGWR*.
O'Mahony, John, *The Sunny Side of Ireland (GS & WR)*, 1901.
——, *Opening of the L & BR*, 1888.
Patterson, Edward, *Belfast & County Down Railway*, 1958, 1982.
——, *County Donegal Railways*.
——, *Clogher Valley Railway*.
——, *Great Northern Railway*.
——, *Londonderry & Lough Swilly Railway*.
Pender, B. and Richards, Herbert, *Irish Railways Today*, 1967.
Penny Journal, *Thirteen Views on the D & KR*, 1834.
Porter, John, *A Few Observations upon our Present Railway System*, 1847.
Praeger, Robert Lloyd, *The Way that I Went*, 1939.
——, *Official Guide to County Down*, 1898.
Prideaux, J., *Irish Narrow Gauge Railways*, 1981.
——, *Recollections of a Three Weeks Tour of Ireland*, 1970.

Report to the MGWR on the port of Galway.
Robb, William, *History of NIR*, 1982.
Rolt and Whitehouse, *Lines of Character*, 1952.
Roney, C., *How to spend a month in Ireland*, 1861.
Rowledge, J. P., *The Turf Burner.*
Shepherd, W. Ernest, *The Dublin & South Eastern Railway*, 1974.
Sprinks, N. W., *The Sligo Leitrim and Northern Counties Railway*, 1970.
SJW, *Locomotives of the GSR.*
Tatlow, Joseph, *Fifty Years of Railway Life,* 1920.
Tully, Brian, *Touring for Health and Pleasure (GSR)*, 1931.
Waterford & Limerick Railway, *Programme of Tourist, Seaside and Excursion Arrangements*, 1898.
Whishaw, Francis, *Railways of Great Britain and Ireland*, 1841.
Whitehouse, P. B., *Narrow Gauge Album.*
Whitehouse, P. B. and Powell, A. J., *Tralee and Dingle Railway.*
Younger, Calton, *Ireland's Civil War.*

The NIR Railbus, introduced 1982 for the service between Coleraine and Portrush

Index